Advance Praise for
Marketing as Strategy

"Professor Kumar has been an excellent coach and consultant for me and my colleagues at Akzo Nobel Decorative Coatings. His fine balance between academic theory and his many case studies from the practical world have been very inspiring. This book reflects that fine understanding. Very relevant and very interesting to read."

—*Leif B. Abildgaard*
President, Decorative Coatings Europe,
Akzo Nobel, The Netherlands

"A reader-friendly book on a subject that is usually difficult to write about in an interesting way. It combines a well-thought-out, structured approach with fascinating real business stories as practical examples to support the key concepts. A significant step forward compared to traditional books on marketing and retailing."

—*Thomas G. Bata*
Chairman, Bata International, Canada

"Dr. Kumar combines a sound, useful strategic framework with insightful examples from the real world of global business."

—*Dinesh Dhamija*
Chairman and CEO, ebookers plc, United Kingdom

"Far more than a marketing book, this is a strategy book that CEOs and line managers alike can use to help enterprises of all sizes drive growth and innovation. Readers will find the multitude of examples and case studies tremendously pragmatic and relevant."

—*Dan Ebbinghaus*
President, the Americas, SITA, United States

"Explaining the complete marketing life cycle with unprecedented clarity and drawing on an impressive array of recent corporate experience, this book will end the search for a true marketing treatise. It is fresh, steers clear of the esoteric, and has enough firepower to give marketers the momentum they deserve in driving innovation. *Marketing as Strategy* contains essential insights into the mind of the CEO and the practical applications of innovative concepts by large corporations across the globe."

—*Harsh V. Goenka*
Chairman, RPG Enterprises, India

"Outstanding! *Marketing as Strategy* is one of the most useful books I've ever read."

—*Johan Lundgren*
Managing Director, TUI Nordic, Sweden

"The marketing concepts discussed here go far beyond the corporate domain and can play a major transformational role leading to the eradication of global poverty and avoidable diseases."

—*Dr. G. Venkataswamy*
Chairman, Aravind Eye Care System, India

Marketing
as
Strategy

Marketing as Strategy

Understanding the CEO's Agenda
for Driving Growth and Innovation

Nirmalya Kumar

HARVARD BUSINESS SCHOOL PRESS

Boston, Massachusetts

To MK,
My transformational engine

To GB,
I am driven, she's driving.

Chapter 7 is adapted from Nirmalya Kumar, Lisa K. Sheer, and Philip Kotler, "From Market-driven to Market-driving," *European Management Journal* 18 (2000): 129–142. Copyright (2000) with permission from Elsevier Science.

Library of Congress Cataloging-in-Publication Data

Kumar, Nirmalya.
    Marketing as strategy : the CEO's agenda for driving growth and
innovation / Nirmalya Kumar.
        p.   cm.
    ISBN 1-59139-210-1 (alk. paper)
    1. Marketing. 2. Strategic planning.   I. Title.
HF5415.K83 2004
658.8'02—dc22

                                                                2003025721

CONTENTS

MANY STANDARD business functions have been undergoing radical transformations. Manufacturing no longer involves the mass production of standardized large lots, but the lean production of customized units of one. Purchasing has morphed into procurement, and finance now calculates the impact of diverse company activities on shareholder value.

Not surprisingly, new voices have been calling for the reinvention of marketing. CEOs cannot get clear, compelling answers about marketing's impact on the bottom line. The old adage of Sam Wanamaker—that he knows that 50 percent of his advertising works but he does not know which half—still haunts management. Consider the following:

Eighty percent of new fast-moving consumer products fail.

A thirty-second Super Bowl advertisement that few people can recall costs $2 million.

The average mass mailing produces a mere 1 to 2 percent response rate.

Salespeople expect eight of ten prospects to reject them.

Nirmalya Kumar offers not only a candid critique of the marketing profession but, more important, a clear agenda—indeed, the CEO's agenda—for meaningful change in the practice of marketing. He calls upon companies to deliver value and solutions, not products and promises. He believes that a company's marketers must understand their organization's culture and operations, from finance to supplier partnerships. They must collaborate on multidisciplinary teams, because marketing fails whenever any part of the company fails to focus on customers. Procter & Gamble is not great because of its marketing capability; it is great because all its functions are customer-focused.

Companies must more effectively manage their marketing assets, many of which are intangible, such as brand equity and relationships with customers, employees, vendors, distributors, and dealers. Marketers must protect and enhance the value of these intangible assets. Company boards must judge the company's performance not just on financial metrics but also on marketing metrics such as customer satisfaction, customer loyalty, number of lost customers, and perceived value of the company's offerings relative to competitors'. If marketing metrics start to dip, then the financials will likely deteriorate as well.

Today's marketers face new challenges. Consumers are time-poor and information-rich; they expect better quality, better service, lower prices, and more value for their effort and money. New channels are proliferating, traditional distribution channels are consolidating, and competitors now come from all over the world, increasingly with lower costs and sometimes higher quality.

Ironically, the marketing department is losing ground—and staff—to other units in the business just as marketing activities are gaining in importance to the company. Managers must see marketing strategy as the driver of corporate strategy. All value begins and ends with customers. As Peter Drucker said, "The purpose of a company is to create a customer. . . . The only profit center is the customer. . . . The business has two—and only two—basic functions: marketing and innovation. Marketing and innovation produce results: all the rest are costs."

Kumar introduces an intriguing framework for analyzing and planning marketing strategy in terms of the "three Vs": valued customer, value proposition, and value network. He applies this framework to several cases and shows how to distinguish competitors' strategies by mapping the relevant value curves and value networks.

Kumar proposes ways to deal with growing commoditization, price pressure, and the increasing market power of global mega-retailers. He argues that companies must manage their individual brands better and rationalize their whole brand portfolios. Each chapter concludes with a provocative set of questions that executives should answer frankly to move their company's marketing performance forward.

Professor Kumar strives to show how the marketing discipline could "become more strategic, cross-functional, and bottom-line-oriented" than ever before. He has succeeded admirably in opening up a new page in the theory and practice of marketing.

—*Philip Kotler*
   S. C. Johnson & Son Distinguished Professor
   of International Marketing, Kellogg School
   of Management, Northwestern University

Emancipate yourselves from mental slavery;
None but ourselves can free our minds.

—Bob Marley, *Redemption Song*

MARKETING HAS FASCINATED ME since I was seventeen years old and discovered the second edition of Philip Kotler's *Marketing Management*. Almost a decade later, Northwestern University's Kellogg Graduate School of Management admitted me to its marketing Ph.D. program. While the doctoral program exhilarated me overall, one aspect of it frequently troubled me— we seldom discussed marketing. With a few exceptions, notably Jim Anderson, George Day, Philip Kotler, John Quelch, Jagdish Sheth, Lou Stern, and Fred Webster, most marketing academics did not focus on the issues important to practitioners.

To learn the messy practice of business, I plowed into the consulting world. As a marketing consultant to large firms, I interacted primarily with marketers, not general managers and certainly not CEOs. Most marketing departments in these firms had no prominent seat at the CEO's table. Even now, top executives view marketing as a hit-or-miss vocation without any deep capabilities, thanks partly to marketing education. Business schools continue to organize themselves by functional departments, whereas most businesses have become cross-functional. By distancing themselves from "strategy" to justify their existence as a separate academic discipline and business school department, marketing professors have adopted a narrow tactical focus. Consequently, marketers often do not aspire to engage CEOs and top management on the larger strategic issues that interest them.

Fortunately, the executive development programs at IMD (International Institute for Management Development) offered me the opportunities to interact with general managers and CEOs. Time and time again, CEOs demonstrated their hunger for marketing knowledge and their enthusiasm for connecting with customers. However, they had no idea how marketers could help them address their most pressing issues. Who can blame them? CEOs want to know about managing brand portfolios, but most marketing academics research brand extensions. CEOs want to stop all price promotions, but academic journals publish numerous studies on the effectiveness of price promotions. CEOs are grappling with channel migration, but most channel research focuses on individual channel members. CEOs wish to unleash radical value innovation on the marketplace, but marketing research expounds upon incremental product development. Almost exclusively, academic research in marketing is U.S.-based, but CEOs must manage global corporations.

I do not mean to suggest that the academic marketing fraternity lacks incredibly smart, well-trained, analytical, and hardworking professors or good, managerially relevant academic research. But let us be honest: For the most part, the marketing discipline does not focus on the strategic marketplace challenges that CEOs face today. Therein lie the origins of this book.

This book views marketing from the trenches and, as the reader has probably already grasped, as such it is intensely personal and opinionated. I urge the reader to look beyond this, and instead focus on the ideas that are presented. I am passionate about marketing and business. I hope that this book will help practitioners across business functions and stimulate debate among marketing academics. If it achieves those two goals, then it has connected with its customers.

Acknowledgments

This book is a product of more than fifteen years of researching, teaching, and consulting in the field of marketing. Over these years, I have learned that very few ideas are truly original, but rather are inspired by what we have learned, heard, or seen before. True learning occurs when we disassociate the source from the idea and make it our own.

It has been my good fortune to have many talented professors, colleagues, clients, and students. While this book carries my name, I wish to emphasize that it represents what I have learned as a student, colleague, teacher, and consultant.

Clearly, I stand on the shoulders of the many business school professors whose ideas have influenced me over the years. Professors James C. Anderson, Peter Drucker, Gary Hamel, W. Chan Kim, Philip Kotler, C. K. Prahalad, and Louis W. Stern have shaped the development of my own ideas on business through their writings or interactions with me. In many ways, I have borrowed shamelessly from them, sometimes openly, sometimes adapting. As a matter of style, I have decided not to reference every sentence because I write here primarily for practitioners and secondarily for my peers.

This book was initiated during my sabbatical, a wonderful year that I split between Harvard Business School and London Business School. At these institutions, my marketing colleagues encouraged me by sparring on these very issues facing marketing as a discipline. I am especially indebted to Susan Fournier, Dave Godes, Doug Holt, Rajiv Lal, Elie Ofek, John Quelch, and Kash Rangan at Harvard, and to Tim Ambler, Paddy Barwise, Shantanu Dutta, Kathy Hammond, Bruce Hardie, Mark Ritson, Craig Smith, Nader Tavassoli, and Naufel Vilcassim in London, now my new home.

Over the years, I have coauthored articles and cases with Inge Geyskens, Jacques Horovitz, Brian Rogers, Lisa Scheer, and Jan-

Benedict Steenkamp, all of whom have been wonderful collabora-
tors and friends. Our work infuses this book, and I have drawn
the chapter on market driving largely from an article coauthored
with Lisa Scheer and Philip Kotler. I am grateful to Rebecca Chung,
Josiane Cosendai, Sophie Linguri, and Michelle Perrinjaquet of
IMD for their tireless efforts in helping assemble this book. I received valuable comments from Vithala Rao and three reviewers.
Kirsten Sandberg of Harvard Business School Press was wonderful in
her continuous support and encouragement of this book. Everyone
whom I interacted with at the Press was extremely professional.

The companies that let me test my ideas in the real world are
too numerous to list. However, Akzo Nobel, Bell Atlantic (now
Verizon), Caterpillar, Dow Chemical, Goodyear, IBM, Motorola,
Nestlé, RPG Enterprises, and Sara Lee have been especially sup-
portive. I am grateful to Leif Abilgaard and Martin Uunila of
Akzo Nobel, Thomas Bata and Carlos Silva Lopes of Dow Chem-
ical, Stelios Haji-Ioannou of easyJet, Jeff Bartman and Dan
Sweeney of IBM, Frank Cella of Nestlé, George Farah of Philip
Morris International, Pradipta Mohapatra of RPG Enterprises,
Linda Hopkins of Tax-Free World Association, and Mariann
Wenckheim of 20/20 for their encouragement.

I have had the delightful opportunity to lecture thousands of
participants at conferences and in various M.B.A. and executive
programs. These "students" have often taught me as much as I
have offered them. I interacted most intensely with participants in
IMD's Program for Executive Development (PED) and Managing
for Marketing Success (MMS) between 1995 and 2003. In addition, the students of Harvard Business School M.B.A. class of
2003, Section I, and the London Business School Sloan Masters
program of 2002–2003 were fertile testing grounds for many of
the book's ideas.

Perhaps my greatest debt is to IMD, a wonderful business
school in Lausanne, Switzerland, where I spent eight transformational years. I entered as a marketing professor specializing
in distribution, with little idea of how managers actually run a

business. IMD turned me into a professor of business, specializing in marketing. My fifty-four IMD faculty colleagues selflessly shared their intellectual firepower with me, welcomed me as a member of the family despite my many idiosyncrasies, and carried my share of the teaching load while I wrote this book. I had the honor of working with each one of them and I thank them all for making this book possible.

ONE

From Marketing as a Function to Marketing as a Transformational Engine

Markets always change faster than marketing.

IN *The Practice of Management,* Peter Drucker wrote, "The business enterprise has two and only two basic functions: marketing and innovation. Marketing and innovation produce results; all the rest are costs."[1] Today, many CEOs of major companies are disappointed over marketing's inability to produce measurable results. Increasingly, they view their marketing department as an expense rather than an investment, and fewer marketers are rising through the ranks to become CEOs. While companies unabashedly declare their wish to get closer to customers, marketing is actually losing power to other functions in the corporation.

What happened? How did marketers lose their influence, and marketing its organizational relevance? More important, how can marketers capture the imagination of CEOs and marketing recapture its strategic role in the firm? Ironically, while the marketing function has been declining, the need for marketing has never been greater. However, to rescue themselves from the corporate obscurity that comes from responsibility for implementing tactics—the traditional four Ps of product, place, price, and promotion—marketers must start driving overall strategic change. They must help CEOs lead organization-wide transformational initiatives that deliver substantial revenue growth and increased profitability.

The Decline of Marketing

After the postwar 1950s boom, marketing quickly rose to power. Customers were trusting and abundant, distribution channels were fragmented and weak, new product launches were less frequent and more substantial, and prices were under little pressure.[2] In such an environment, mass media, especially network television, was a powerful tool for reaching large numbers of homogeneous consumers. Marketing led both top- and bottom-line growth for companies.

Over the past two decades, marketing as the company's growth engine has sputtered amid increased market fragmentation, strong global competitors, product commoditization, increasingly shorter product life cycles, skyrocketing customer expectations, and powerful channel members. As a result, the ability of marketing to deliver significant growth has been severely constrained and marketing productivity has declined. Not surprisingly, in many companies, doubts have begun to surface about the value of contemporary marketing.[3]

A study of 545 U.K. companies revealed that just 18 percent of executives rated marketing's strategic effectiveness in their company as better than good while 36 percent rated it as fair to poor.[4] Another study of senior executives indicated considerable dissatisfaction with the marketing skills of brand managers (overall effectiveness, 48 percent; strategic skills, 60 percent; innovation, 92 percent; risk profile, 48 percent; and speed, 56 percent).[5]

Ambitious marketers are therefore finding it difficult to reach the CEO position.

A 2001 study of the FTSE 100 index firms in the United Kingdom revealed that just thirteen chief executives had marketing backgrounds compared with twenty-six who rose through finance.[6] The study also found that the number of CEOs from marketing backgrounds had declined over the past three years. Furthermore, even in consumer goods companies that presumably value marketing efforts, accountants outnumbered marketers as CEOs.

British Airports Authority CEO Mike Hodgkinson argued that his accountancy training offers two advantages over someone with a pure marketing orientation. "I can speak the shareholders' language and the training gave me a disciplined approach to issues."[7] Marketers are often not considered capable of getting the company through tough times with their "spend" rather than "make-and-save" mentality. It is no wonder that Niall FitzGerald, head of Unilever, describes himself as "an accountant by training, a marketer by instinct."[8]

True, some companies have had unrealistic expectations of marketing given the more competitive landscape. Still, many CEOs, unable to count on their marketing departments for results, have had to turn instead to operations and finance, cutting costs and reengineering the supply chain to increase profitability and mergers and acquisitions to grow revenues. Consequently, marketing's share of voice at the corporate level has declined. Research now demonstrates that, at large companies, only 10 percent of executive meeting time is devoted to marketing.[9]

As the attention and imagination of CEOs have shifted to other functions, marketing academics have bemoaned marketing's declining influence within the firm. Don Lehman, the director of Marketing Science Institute, a leading academic research think tank devoted to marketing, recently observed: "Marketing as a function is in some danger of being marginalized. . . . Some think that marketing people do little more than blue-light specials and coupons."[10] Fred Webster, a noted marketing professor, argued that marketing has surrendered its strategic responsibilities to other functions that do not systematically prioritize the customer.[11]

Numerous conferences have been organized to help reinvigorate the discipline. To earn the respect of CEOs and CFOs, the established academic marketing interest groups have launched a campaign to document the importance of marketing by attempting to demonstrate the return on investment (ROI) from marketing expenditures. The feeling is that, consumed by a focus on shareholder value, CEOs and companies are unable to see the value of marketing. Therefore, in this line of reasoning, marketers must find metrics that will document the positive impact of their activities on shareholder value.

The search to demonstrate the ROI of marketing misses the point and reinforces the perception that marketers still misunderstand their CEO's expectations. Of course, CEOs want to increase the efficiency of current marketing activities, namely the tactical four Ps. However, CEOs really seek strategic leadership from marketers in exploiting new business opportunities, building strong brand and customer franchises, increasing the organization's overall customer responsiveness, redefining industry distribution channels, enhancing global effectiveness, and reducing such risks as industry price pressures. It is about marketers doing better things rather than simply doing things better.

Getting Marketing Back
on the CEO's Agenda

In an annual survey of CEOs conducted by The Conference Board, nearly seven hundred CEOs globally were polled about the challenges facing their companies in 2002.[12] CEOs identified "customer loyalty and retention" as the leading management issue ahead of reducing costs, developing leaders, increasing innovation, and improving stock price, among other issues. In the same survey, "downward pressure on prices" emerged as the top marketplace issue, rated ahead of challenges such as industry consolidation, access to capital, and impact of the Internet.

This survey clearly reveals that CEOs already see their most important challenges as marketing ones—they just don't believe that marketers themselves can confront them. The marketing function may have lost importance, but the importance of marketing as a mind-set is unquestioned in firms.

CEOs know that their firms must become more market-oriented, market-driven, or customer-focused. But a true market orientation does not mean becoming marketing-driven; it means that the entire company obsesses over creating value for the customer and views itself as a bundle of processes that profitably define, create, communicate, and deliver value to its target customers. Only demonstrated customer value can assure firms of fair, perhaps even premium, prices and customer loyalty.

The Ubiquity of Marketing Activities

If one believes that everyone in the organization should serve the customer and create customer value, then obviously everyone must do marketing regardless of function or department.[13] In fact, most of the traditional activities under the control of marketing, such as market research, advertising, and promotions, are perhaps the least important elements in creating customer value.

The accounting department is marketing when it develops an invoice format that customers can actually understand. The finance department is marketing when it develops flexible payment options based on different customer segments. The human resources department is marketing when it involves frequent flyers in helping to select in-flight crew. The logistics team is marketing when it calls on a major customer to coordinate supply chains. The operations department is marketing when its receptionists smile at guests during hotel check-in. In all these activities, what role does the marketing department typically play? None. And so, substantial reductions in the size of marketing departments may be simultaneously associated with a greater number of marketing activities performed and a higher market orientation throughout the company.[14]

With the activity of marketing dispersed across the organization, marketing is not the sole responsibility of the marketing department. For example, new product development in the automobile industry requires coordination among marketing (by defining the important attributes), product development (by designing a car that satisfies customer needs), purchasing (by providing realistic cost-benefit trade-offs when developing cars), manufacturing (by actually making the car), and external suppliers (who increasingly must deliver preassembled subsystems, not merely raw materials or parts).[15] But who coordinates the activities across all of these functions to deliver a consistent customer experience?

The Networked Organization

Three mutually reinforcing changes are enabling faster and more coherent coordination of the customer value-creating activities within organizations.[16] First, companies are thinking in terms of processes rather than functions. Second, they are moving from hierarchies to teams. Finally, they are substituting partnerships for arms-length transactions with suppliers and distributors. The tightly specified, vertical, functional, divisional, and closed organization is slowly becoming relatively loose, horizontal, flexible, dynamic, and networked.[17]

Ultimately, a customer receives the outcome of several cross-functional processes. Cross-functional teams break down silos and enhance critical processes such as new product development, customer acquisition, and order fulfillment. In these teams, formal leadership resides with the appointed team leader, but informally, leadership passes among team members based on their expertise and the problem at hand. Such teams actually do much of the work of organizations today.[18]

Marketing in the Networked Organization

The evolving networked organization demands that functional specialists and country experts learn how to communicate with other functions and nationalities. Consequently, organizations are emphasizing integration over specialization.[19] But traditionally, marketing has systematically prioritized specialization over generalization, rewarding its academics and practitioners alike for knowing more and more about less and less.[20]

Nowhere is this excessive specialization more apparent than at business schools. Academic research in marketing typically attacks irrelevant, esoteric problems with highly sophisticated methodologies. To distinguish themselves from the strategy area, they are plunging deeper into tactical implementation issues. Anyone who attends an academic marketing conference will observe numerous papers presented on "promotions," a euphemism for "price cuts." What should have been a "field of dreams" has turned into a "field of deals." Whereas marketing departments continue to churn out thousands of marketing undergraduates who find jobs mostly in sales, they have little to say that interests CEOs.

In all its specializing, marketing has not aspired to lead major transformational projects that involve cross-functional, multinational teams sponsored by the CEO. Other functions have rallied around transforming initiatives such as Total Quality Management (TQM) and reengineering led by operations, Economic Value Added (EVA) and Mergers and Acquisitions (M&A) guided by finance, and the Balanced Scorecard driven by accounting.[21] What, if anything, can marketing do?

Marketing as a Transformational Engine

For marketers to capture the imagination of their CEOs, they must break from the tactical four Ps and associate instead with organization-wide transformational initiatives worthy of the CEO's agenda. Only initiatives that are strategic, cross-functional, and bottom-line oriented will attract the CEO's attention, and only by leading such initiatives will marketers elevate their role in the organization. Marketing must never limit its scope to implementation issues.[22] It must aspire to participate in those conversations that shape the firm's destiny.

Since CEOs can focus on only a few major initiatives at any given moment, they usually choose those that require improvement on multiple dimensions simultaneously—greater service, lower costs, improved quality, greater customization, and more focused communications.[23] So marketers should target problems that involve multiple products, countries, brands, channels, and/or functions. True transformational leaders think across multiple dimensions and levels of abstraction.

A cross-functional orientation requires marketers to understand the entire value chain thoroughly, including engineering, purchasing, manufacturing, and logistics, as well as the enabling functions of finance and accounting—and not simply advertising, promotion, and pricing.[24] When experienced marketers ask me which executive marketing program would improve their skills, I direct them to a course on finance or operations. Only by deeply understanding all other functions can marketers guide activities across the entire value chain. Transformational marketing efforts should focus on initiatives that

- profitably deliver value to customers;
- require a high level of marketing expertise;
- need cross-functional orchestration for successful implementation; and
- are results-oriented.

As professors Sheth and Sisodia observe, despite being several times greater than capital expenditures in many companies, sales and marketing expenses do not receive the same level of rigorous evaluation that capital expenses do.[25] The belief is that a finance person managing a brand would probably take more time to determine how much to spend to support it and how to measure the effects of the spending than a marketer, who would just ask for more money.[26] Today, shareholders great and small are pressuring corporations and their CEOs to deliver against short-term profit and revenue objectives while maintaining the overall strategic direction. Marketing initiatives must have a substantial, demonstrated, top- or bottom-line effect to excite the CEO. Any lag between a marketing activity and its effect should not excuse marketers from measuring those effects whenever possible. Faith-based marketing is no longer an option.

The CEO's Marketing Manifesto

Figure 1-1 divides the CEO's Marketing Manifesto into seven organization-wide transformational initiatives that marketers could lead. These initiatives pass the three tests outlined above: Each is strategic, cross-functional, and bottom-line oriented. While all seven transformations may not apply to all firms, at

FIGURE 1-1

The CEO's Marketing Manifesto

CEOs
- Sponsor marketing initiatives
- Be the customer champion
- Be the quality controller

Marketers
- Be more strategic
- Be more cross-functional
- Be more bottom-line oriented

1. From Market Segments to Strategic Segments
2. From Selling Products to Providing Solutions
3. From Declining to Growing Distribution Channels
4. From Branded Bulldozers to Global Distribution Partners
5. From Brand Acquisitions to Brand Rationalization
6. From Market-Driven to Market-Driving
7. From SBU Marketing to Corporate Marketing

least one will apply to every firm. Current projects within a company may actually address one or two, in which case the respective chapter should help provide strategic and implementation tools. The firm may not have considered one of these initiatives before, and so this book will help managers to go beyond best practice to next practice.

From Market Segments to Strategic Segments

In the face of increasing price pressure and declining customer loyalty, more than anything what CEOs seek from marketing is differentiation, especially differentiation that is difficult for competitors to imitate. As Franklin D. Raines, chairman and CEO of Fannie Mae, observed: "People talk about mortgages as commodities. But . . . nothing has to be a commodity. Not even mortgages. . . . Indeed, our strategy is to transform mortgages from commodities. . . . We are not talking about mere branding, we mean creating real differentiation that consumers value."[27]

Traditionally, marketing has relied on market segmentation and marketing mix to create differentiation. Market segmentation is the process of dividing the market into clusters of customers in such a way that each market segment is best reached through a unique marketing mix of the four Ps. However, creating differentiation across segments exclusively through the four Ps is too limiting. Instead, marketing needs a framework that inspires greater strategic insights, that examines the cross-functional implications of serving different segments of customers, and that allows an identification of where, deep in the organization, any differentiation is being created.

To meet this need, I propose the concept of strategic segments. To create meaningful differentiation through strategic segments requires dedicating unique value networks to serving individual strategic segments. A value network, sometimes also referred to as a value chain or business system, is the orchestration of all marketing and nonmarketing activities necessary to create value for the customer. Replicating a value network is more difficult than copying a marketing mix. Therefore, the concept of strategic segments helps identify opportunities for deep differentiation.

Chapter 2 will examine the transformation from market segments to strategic segments. Adopting the strategic segments framework will help marketing address CEO-level questions regarding segmentation such as, Can one organization serve two different segments? Where in the value network is differentiation necessary to serve the varied segments? When is differentiating on the four Ps enough? How can one distinguish between strategic segments versus market segments?

The segmentation dilemma at the CEO level is determining where in the value network the firm must build differentiation to effectively serve the different segments without losing the potential synergies of serving a portfolio of segments. If the value network segregation for the strategic segments is too shallow, then it will lead to customer dissatisfaction. On the other hand, too deep a segregation in the value network may destroy opportunities for economies of scale.

From Selling Products to Providing Solutions

In a global marketplace, customers are awash in supplier choices, and differentiation based on products is usually unsustainable. For example, Gillette spent almost a billion dollars and seven years to develop the triple-blade Mach 3 razor. The U.K. retailer Asda needed only two months to copy it. Given relatively undifferentiated products, consumers will pay more only for demonstrated value. CEOs want their companies to enhance customer loyalty and alleviate pricing pressures by offering customers solutions instead of products.

After attending presentations by the CEOs of Sun Microsystems, AMD, Microsoft, and others at COMDEX (the most prestigious trade exhibition in the technology world), a reporter observed that any of those CEOs could have uttered the following line from Hewlett-Packard CEO Carly Fiorina's keynote: "The latest and greatest [is] . . . not what you need most. . . . While point products are cool, what you need most are solutions . . . a partner who can help make all the pieces you've already got work better together, who can manage your systems seamlessly across global networks." [28] Imagine that, from an industry famous for falling in love with its gizmos.

The traditional marketing technique of simply offering another standard product under a "brand name" is currently inadequate to lock in customers. Today, customers are time starved, impatient, and demanding. They presume product quality and demand solutions, personalization, meaningful choice, and easy-to-do-business-with companies. Companies as diverse as Baxter International, W.W. Grainger, Home Depot, and IBM have recognized these demands. For example, Home Depot's research indicates that traditional "Do-It-Yourselfers" are evolving into "Do-It-For-Mes." As a result, Home Depot is intensifying service and training personnel to ask potential shoppers, "What project are you working on?" rather than "What product are you looking for?"

Chapter 3 will study the transformation necessary within organizations that desire to move from selling products to providing solutions for customers. Solution selling creates many challenges that tend to land on the CEO's desk. How can we move the company's mind-set from developing "better" products to solving customer problems? How can we obtain company-wide coordination from the different parts of the organization that have traditionally competed against each other? How can we assess the value of solutions for customers, and then subsequently price such solutions?

Firms aspiring to provide solutions encounter challenging dilemmas in creating true customer solutions and maintaining profitability. At some stage, solution-selling firms have to confront the reality that impartially serving customer needs may sometimes demand incorporating competitors' products and services into the solution. In addition, delivering solutions entails significant additional customization costs for the seller, while many solution customers believe they are entitled to volume discounts.

From Declining to Growing Distribution Channels

Distribution channels today are in flux. Many traditional channels are declining and innovative new ones are emerging. Dell in the personal computer industry and First Direct in the insurance industry have seized market leadership by adopting direct distribution strategies. In contrast, Charles Schwab developed the financial supermarket, concentrating on distribution in a traditionally vertically integrated industry. By offering a vast selection of mutual funds from a variety of suppliers, Schwab more effectively serves self-sufficient investors.

The Internet's rapid development has accelerated the number and diversity of distribution channels by introducing concepts such as Amazon, eBay, ebookers.com, FreeMarkets, Kazaa, NCsoft's Lineage, and priceline.com. Most of these new online and offline channels are technology intensive and their competitive advantage over existing channels usually involves superior efficiency and greater reach. In some extreme cases, such as music, the efficiency and reach of online distribution has disrupted the entire industry's business model.

Traditionally, industries such as automobile and financial services as well as companies such as Caterpillar, Delta, and Compaq have stressed their loyalty to existing channels and have opposed changing their distribution structure. For example, consider the automobile industry, where products have changed dramatically over the past hundred years but distribution has remained essentially untouched. Furthermore, like many existing distribution networks, automobile dealers are protected by tight contracts.

Demands from CEOs for revenue growth combined with the greater efficiency and reach of new distribution formats make it impossible for companies to ignore these emerging high-growth channels. For example, even Levi's, who has long spurned the advances of mass merchandisers such as Wal-Mart or Tesco and sued them for selling its jeans at discount prices, has decided that it can no longer ignore them. It is introducing a new line of jeans targeted specifically at such supermarkets and mass merchandisers.

Chapter 4 examines the challenge of transforming traditional distribution networks and positioning oneself in the growing channels of the future. Since distribution structure decisions are relatively long term and have legal ramifications, channel migration requires firms to confront a number of issues that pique CEO interest. Should the firm be an early entrant or a fast follower into new channels of distribution? How can it migrate into new distribution channels while managing existing ones? How can the firm manage the ensuing channel conflict? Which industry players are best positioned to exploit new channel opportunities?

New distribution channels present a dilemma for a company. During the transition period, despite the rapid growth in new channels, existing channels still account for the lion's share of the industry and the company's revenues. Moving too fast into the new distribution formats can unleash destructive channel conflict. On the other hand, hesitancy can lock companies into declining distribution channels and high distribution costs. Players in industries as diverse as entertainment, financial services, personal computers, and travel are still struggling to strike the right balance.

From Branded Bulldozers to Global Distribution Partners

Beyond new distribution formats, existing distribution channels have consolidated and become increasingly sophisticated. FMCG companies, including the most famous household names, have been taken aback by the dramatic reversal in their fortunes due to the retailers.[29] Historically, retailers were local, fragmented, and technologically primitive, and as such, powerful multinational manufacturers such as Coca-Cola, Colgate-Palmolive, Gillette, and Procter & Gamble behaved like branded bulldozers, freely pushing their products and promotion plans onto retailers, who were expected to accept them subserviently.

Within a span of two decades, all this has become history. The largest retailers, such as Carrefour of France, METRO of Germany, Tesco of the United Kingdom, and Wal-Mart of the United States, have global footprints. The worldwide revenues of these retailers exceed those of the large branded manufacturers and the retail industry is still in the early consolidation stage. As retailers have bulked up, they have moved from a position of vulnerability to one of power relative to their suppliers. This shift in power and the global purchasing practices of retailers has brought enormous price pressure on the most sophisticated of all marketers—the leading consumer packaged goods manufacturers.

The brand management system that worked so well in the past seems ineffective in dealing with large, professionally managed retailers. The typical brand manager is too inexperienced, too narrowly focused on the brand, and too short-term oriented, as well as lacking the internal authority and resources to be a strategic partner with the purchasing counterpart at a global retailer. In response, companies have been forced to introduce category management (combining the management of all brands within a particular category to ensure greater coherence in strategy) and customer development teams (bringing together representatives from different brands, categories, functions, and countries to present a single face to a retailer). Unfortunately all of these changes have not helped the perception of CEOs that marketing departments are bloated with much duplication of functions at the brand, category, country, customer, and corporate levels.

Chapter 5 investigates the necessary organizational and cultural transformation of manufacturers as they move from being branded bulldozers to global distribution partners with powerful distributors. The volume sold through global retailers demands CEO participation in these partnerships. For example, Wal-Mart alone accounts for more than 17 percent of Procter & Gamble's worldwide turnover. Developing global manufacturer–distributor partnerships raises many issues including how to generate trust, how to manage global retailer demands, and how to develop global account management structures that provide an efficient and an effective interface.

The global account management dilemma for manufacturers is that prices for their nearly identical products can differ by as much as 40 to 60 percent between countries. Global distribution partners make such manufacturer products and prices "naked" by demanding a single worldwide price. Unfortunately, for most manufacturing companies operating in numerous local markets, customer ignorance was their biggest profit center![30]

From Brand Acquisitions to Brand Rationalization

Powerful distributors are using their tremendous negotiating clout against suppliers to aggressively push them into granting trade promotions, slotting allowances, and failure fees, besides, of course, the usual price concessions. As a result, marketers have increasingly diverted resources to various forms of promotions to move volume. In 1997, the percentage of total sales volume for select items in U.S. supermarkets that sold on promotions was 35 percent for fresh bread, 36 percent for diapers, and 62 percent for refrigerated orange juice. Similarly, marked-down products that accounted for just 8 percent of department store sales three decades ago have now climbed to about 20 percent.[31]

Even consumer durables and emotional products are not exempt. For example, for the big three U.S. automakers, incentives now amount to $3,764 per vehicle or 14 percent of the selling price of a vehicle.[32] Without strong brands and competitive products, even short-term promotions may backfire, as happened in the fall of 2001 when the big three automakers furiously launched zero percent interest financing to draw American customers into their showrooms. It turned out that the customers came into the showroom, compared cars, and disproportionately bought Toyotas and Hondas even though these Japanese companies were not offering similar low interest rates. No wonder Chrysler CEO Dieter Zetsche, who is trying to wean Chrysler away from incentives, observed: "I see it as a drug. It might give you short-term relief, but long term it is extremely harmful."[33]

CEOs are questioning why marketing efforts are being allocated primarily to short-term sales inducements rather than long-term investments in building brand equity. Why has distribution pushback onto manufacturers been so successful in obtaining price concessions? To a large extent the answer lies in mushrooming brands. Companies like Akzo Nobel, Electrolux, General Motors, Goodyear, and Unilever have until recently had too many brands in their portfolios, most of them obtained through acquisitions over the years. While each portfolio contains strong global brands, a significant number of the brands are both weak and local.

Distributors and retailers excel at playing weak manufacturer brands against each other and holding name-brands hostage. CEOs are demanding that marketers brutally examine the brand portfolio, and then delete, merge, or sell weaker brands to concentrate on the few truly differentiated brands.

Chapter 6 examines the transformation in brand portfolio strategy, moving from brand acquisitions to brand rationalization. How does a company decide which brands to delete? What is the role of each brand in the portfolio? How can brands be consolidated? Where in the organization should the locus of decision making for each brand reside?

The dilemma of brand rationalization is how to delete marginal brands without losing their associated customers and sales. Successful brand rationalization entails shrinking the brand portfolio while growing sales and profitability through greater focus on the remaining brands.

From Market-Driven to Market-Driving

At the top of every CEO's agenda is growth through innovation. CEOs understand that, without innovation, companies risk their future growth and profitability, and so they devote considerable resources to launching new products. An estimated thirty thousand new products were launched in the U.S. last year in the packaged goods industry alone. Despite the $20 to $50 million average cost of a product launch, approximately 90 percent of new products fail.

Sadly, most of these launches involve incremental innovations such as new product lines for the company, line extensions such as new flavors, or improvements to existing products. Less than 10 percent of all new products are truly innovative or "new to the world." Not surprisingly, between 50 and 80 percent of consumers in the United States and Western Europe believe that, in the past two years, no one has made any valuable innovation in many product categories (for example, housing, clothing, furniture) and service categories (for example, insurance, hospitals, education, government).[34]

Marketers unfortunately make two errors in pursuing the CEO's innovation agenda. First, marketers tend to interpret innovation narrowly as simply new product development. Second, most marketers believe that new product development starts with consumer research, but this market-driven approach usually results in incremental product innovation rather than truly breakthrough business concepts.

CEOs are insisting that their organization think of innovation beyond new products, services, or even processes. More specifically, their mandate is to generate radical market-driving concepts, such as NTT DoCoMo's i-mode, Sony's PlayStation, Nestlé's Nespresso, and Zara's catwalk fashions at cheap prices—products that change an industry's rules and boundaries. 3M is often a poster child of the incumbent that creates new customer needs through market-driving innovations (Post-it notes) rather than by satisfying expressed market-driven desires.

Chapter 7 explores the transformation from market-driven to market-driving. It asks questions essential to the CEO's agenda of changing an industry through innovation. What processes encourage radical innovation? What marketing strategies do we need for market-driving innovations? How do we manage simultaneous incremental and radical innovation?

The dilemma with market driving is to strike the proper balance between satisfying current customer needs better through market-driven processes and creating new market demand through market-driving processes while not being too far ahead of customers.

From SBU Marketing to Corporate Marketing

Consistent with marketing's historical focus on the tactical four Ps, in most organizations marketing has been consigned to the strategic business unit (SBU) level. Rather than being a partner for the CEO in developing strategy content, marketing's role is being increasingly subjugated into responsibility for short-term demand stimulation.[35] Therefore, few companies exist where the corporate marketing function or role is substantial.

Currently, many CEOs believe that marketing is failing at the strategic level because marketing efforts are not aligned with the strategic goals and overall strategy of the firm. In the face of pressure to perform and demonstrate results, as with many complex challenges, managers are frequently in search of quick fixes. Rather than build long-term value for consumers and enhance the company's success formula, marketers try to raise market share and sales through dubious temporary tactics such as more promotions, greater salesperson effort, and pushing inventory onto distributors. It is a short-term, paint-by-numbers approach.[36]

Marketing's lack of productivity is often blamed on overutilization of short-term tactics and an overemphasis on customer acquisition and market share gains, while paying inadequate consideration to the profitability of the customers acquired or shares gained. Moreover, CEOs are uncertain even about the marketing gains. As one CEO of a food ingredient company remarked to me: "We spend all this money on marketing and what do we have to show for it? Perhaps I would be happy if at least we were competing on price but now we are competing on costs."

CEOs want marketing to become a strategic partner, and many companies appoint chief marketing officers (CMOs) because SBU-level marketers usually lack the clout needed to lead when organization-wide marketing transformations cut across several SBUs. Transforming efforts such as brand portfolio rationalization, radical market concept innovation, solution selling, or global distribution partnerships require corporate marketing as the engine.

Chapter 8 examines the transformation from SBU marketing to corporate marketing. It answers such questions as, How can marketing create value from the corporate center? What is the role of corporate marketing? What initiatives should the CMO sponsor? What opportunities for marketing synergies and leverage exist?

The dilemma for corporate marketing is the belief in many companies that all marketing is local. Marketers must demonstrate that they can create value from the corporate center and partner with the CEO while balancing the legitimate local interests of SBUs.

Cultivating Organizational Respect for the Customer

CEOs are not alone in their frustration. Behind closed doors, marketers will likely complain that their CEOs do not understand the marketing function and do not sufficiently engage in the sales and marketing processes;[37] or that others see them as a big cost center, a means of keeping up with the competition;[38] or that marketing is like a charity: well funded in good times but the first to be cut in the bad.[39]

Many marketers feel that CEOs have unrealistic expectations about what marketing can do and do not sufficiently elicit marketing's input into corporate strategy. Promotions—that is, price cuts—often proliferate because marketing must sell whatever the factory produces. This is common in the automobile industry. The leadership at Chrysler, Ford, and General Motors has not addressed fundamental issues such as surplus manufacturing capacity, overlapping brands, and product differentiation. Without built-to-order systems, tension thickens between car salespeople who have to move current stock, and consumers who want exactly what they can imagine—not what stands on the showroom floor.

Some CEOs erroneously believe that hiring world-class marketers from other companies will turn their company into a market-driven one but they cannot simply graft marketing expertise into an organization that is not already market-oriented.[40] Companies like Unilever and Nestlé have great marketers on staff, but their marketing succeeds because the whole company, including the CEO, focuses on customers.

CEOs Leading from the Front, Rather than the Top

Unfortunately, CEOs often lose touch with their customers. One CEO of a major car company had never bought a car at a dealership and therefore could not understand customer frustration. Contrast that with Henry Ford's sensibility: "When one of my cars breaks down I know I am to blame."[41]

To appreciate the customer experience, CEOs and top management must learn to lead from the front rather than from the top. At Southwest Airlines, senior executives must spend time regularly in customer contact areas to interact with and witness other employees' interaction with customers. Stelios Haji-Ioannou, CEO of easyJet, frequently flies in his economy class–only planes. Top executives at Sony tried to set up their own VCRs using the accompanying instruction booklet. This exercise led to the development of an easier menu-based application. While one CEO of a chemical company frequently logs customer complaints against his own company to assess responsiveness, how many other CEOs can even find the customer service numbers for their products?

The CEO should be the customer champion, a quality controller who regularly tests the systems. Symbolic gestures communicate this role most effectively to employees. For example, if an executive of Mandarin Oriental Hotel Group observes a full ashtray while awaiting an elevator, he will empty it. On full flights, Cathay Pacific bumps its board members to provide seats to paying customers. At one point, different offices competed to see who could bump the most board members, thereby demonstrating their customer orientation.

Beware of Make-Believe Marketing Metrics

To get respect, some marketers have rushed to quantify each activity in terms of profitability and shareholder value. After all, what cannot be measured, cannot be managed, let alone add value, right? Yet, we must avoid make-believe metrics.[42] We can more easily measure the effects of promotions on sales and profits than those of advertisements, but that does not mean that we should rely more on promotions. Coca-Cola would not be a globally recognized brand today without a century's worth of advertising.

Everyone in the organization, including marketers, must be bottom-line oriented. If profits fall short, then the company cannot continue serving customers or attracting resources to serve even more customers. While sales and profits tell us how well the firm has performed in the past, we must add indicators—marketing metrics like brand equity, customer satisfaction, and customer loyalty—that inform us about the company's current health and its prospects.[43] The CEO plays an important balancing role. Robert E. Riley of Mandarin Oriental Hotel Group notes, "As managing director, I take ultimate responsibility for the brand— as any CEO must. . . . In every organization, ultimately the CEO must decide on the final balance between short-term financial objectives and the requirement to build the brand with a long-term perspective."[44]

By building and using metrics that matter, one can clearly connect investments in marketing to the ultimate goal of satisfying customers profitably. These marketing metrics should help address important questions about the company's marketing effectiveness, such as: Are we servicing our customers better? Have we truly differentiated our products in a clearly visible way that matters to customers? Is our differentiation generating profits for us? Does our price premium reflect the additional value delivered to customers? Are we satisfying our customers better than our competitors? Are we exploiting market opportunities faster than others? Do our people understand how we create value for our customers? Must distributors carry our products to maintain legitimacy in the industry? These questions will help a firm understand how well marketing is performing.

Unfortunately, the executive suite usually fails to ask them. Most boards of directors devote precious little time to such marketing- and strategy-related questions and focus instead on past financial performance and proposed budgets, of which the latter rarely materialize. On the boards that I sit on, I have always argued that we should carefully review marketing metrics such as customer satisfaction, brand equity, and customer loyalty. Let us bring the customer into the boardroom.

Discovering Consumer Capitalism

The dot-com bust and the failures of Enron, Tyco, and Worldcom have helped to shift the organizational arena in ways that will potentially benefit marketing and the customer point of view. Real customer value creation—not share price driven—strategies are back in vogue. After the financial engineering of the late 1990s, companies will do well by rediscovering the purpose of the corporation conceived in the 1950s and 1960s.

In 1954, Peter Drucker noted that the customer determines what a business is and is the foundation of a business.[45] A Harvard Business School professor, Ted Levitt, argued persuasively that the "purpose of a business is to create and keep a customer."[46] Profit, he contended, was a meaningless statement of corporate purpose. Without a clear view of customers, and how to serve them effectively, there could be no profits.

FIGURE 1-2

Sales Versus Marketing Orientation

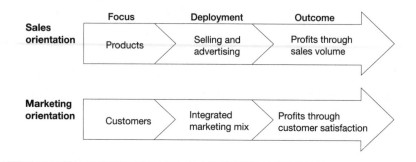

In the 1960s, Philip Kotler popularized the marketing concept that profits are not the objective but the reward for creating satisfied customers (see figure 1-2). Whereas a sales-oriented company makes products and then seeks customers through sales and advertising, the marketing-oriented firm finds customer needs and then deploys an integrated marketing mix (made up of the popular four Ps) to satisfy them.[47]

We must reaffirm the fundamental purpose of a corporation: to serve customers over time and not to maximize shareholder wealth. I call this consumer capitalism, where companies generate a fair profit to reinvest in the business and to continue serving customers. Lee Scott, CEO of Wal-Mart, described Wal-Mart's entry into financial services as an opportunity: "I'd like to do it more along the Wal-Mart way than other people's. Rather than pricing off the market and [saying] if the market's at 70 percent margin, we could be at 50 percent and make a lot of money and still be cheaper, I'd rather say, what is a fair return on doing that?"[48] To illustrate, Wal-Mart plans to offer payroll check cashing at a flat $3 charge compared to its rivals' 3 to 6 percent commission.

Consumer capitalism outshines North America's shareholder capitalism (maximize shareholder value) or Europe's more diffuse stakeholder capitalism (balance the needs of employees, share-

holders, communities, and environment). Companies must redis-
cover mission statements like that of Aravind Eye Hospital in
India: "To eradicate needless blindness by providing appropriate,
compassionate, and high-quality eye care to all." Johnson & Johnson has rallied around a one-page credo for over fifty years:

> *Our first responsibility is to the doctors, nurses and patients,*
> *to mothers and fathers and all others who use our products*
> *and services. In meeting their needs everything we do must be*
> *of high quality. We must constantly strive to reduce our costs*
> *in order to maintain reasonable prices. Customers' orders*
> *must be serviced promptly and accurately. Our suppliers and*
> *distributors must have an opportunity to make a fair profit.*[49]

The purpose of companies is to serve their customers' needs
and create value for them. Creating customer value requires the
entire organization to function in a coordinated manner, not just
the marketing department. If we consider the pathologies of
power—seeking unilateral control, guarding turf, withholding
information, and nonparticipation—with the many other problems of assigning ownership to a particular group, then we clearly
see that responsibility and accountability for marketing belongs
jointly to the CEO and the top team, senior line managers, and
marketing specialists.[50]

Conclusion

Whereas the challenges facing marketing are many, the good news
is that marketing has perhaps never had a more auspicious time to
take leadership through organization-wide transformations that
have top- and bottom-line impact. The forces altering the marketing
landscape compel companies to strengthen their marketing efforts.
As a former CEO of Procter & Gamble stated, "We are not banking on things getting better, we are banking on us getting better."

Companies now realize that they increasingly draw value from intangible market-based assets, not physical ones. Which would affect Coca-Cola's market value more: a loss of all its factories overnight, or the erasure of its brand name from human memory? Clearly, the latter would hurt more. Brands, customers, and distribution networks are the crown jewels in any company, and marketers are their main custodians.

At the dawn of the twenty-first century, marketers face the challenge of change. Power in organizations is moving away from those with marketing expertise tied to specific countries and industries. As industry and national boundaries are blurring, the ability to think across industries, transcend culture, and find universals is emerging as the new necessity.[51] The demand from CEOs is for foresight rather than hindsight, for innovators, not tacticians, and for market strategists, not marketing planners. Marketers must learn to lead with imagination driven by consumer insight and not rely on market research for predictions. As marketers, are we ready to face these challenges? We have nothing to lose except hierarchies, national and functional boundaries, and, most of all, the four Ps.

From Market Segments to Strategic Segments

If you went out of business, would anyone miss you?

M ARKETING'S BASIC MISSION is to create a difference between a company's offering and that of its competitors on an attribute important to customers. To create differentiation, marketers use *segmentation*, *targeting*, and *positioning*, or STP. Market segmentation is the process of dividing the market into homogeneous groups of customers who respond similarly to a particular marketing mix of the four Ps—product, price, place, and promotion—the essential tactical tools for positioning the firm's offer to the targeted segment. Not surprisingly, any marketing practitioner can comfortably converse in terms of market segments, target markets, and positioning.

One of the biggest frustrations of CEOs is their marketers' inability to create such perceived differentiation among offerings. The tactical orientation has led marketers to rely too heavily on the marketing mix, which has limited how deeply they can differentiate in strategic segments. This deeper differentiation is critical to create distinguishing benefits that are sustainable and avoid commoditization.

In contrast to the relatively shallow market segment differentiation created through the exclusive use of the four Ps, deep differentiation is achieved by building the firm's source of competitive advantage into the value network that serves a particular strategic segment.[1] The value network—the cross-functional orchestration of activities necessary to effectively serve the chosen segment—includes differentiation based on the four Ps.[2] But it also goes beyond marketing, to encompass differentiation on other functions such as R&D, operations, and service.

This chapter begins by describing how marketers view segmentation. The remainder of the chapter, however, will be devoted to advancing a new way to conceptualize segments based on the distinction between market segments, which require unique four-P constellations, and strategic segments, which require unique value network configurations. This distinction between market and strategic segments has far-reaching consequences for an organization and its source of competitive advantage.

To address the cross-functional implications of serving strategic segments, rather than limit themselves to the tactical four Ps, marketers must think more broadly in terms of the valued customer, value proposition, and value network, which I refer to as the three Vs. Conceptualizing strategic segments and using the three Vs model makes marketing more malleable and able to address important questions such as: How does a firm create sustainable differentiation? What are the cross-functional implications of serving a particular segment? What positive or negative synergies exist in serving combinations of different segments? Where should the value network be sliced to serve different segments? How unique is our marketing concept? What are sources of our differential advantage in terms of competences, processes, and assets? These are the strategic issues with respect to segmentation and differentiation that are going to excite CEOs, not the tactical four Ps that marketers traditionally focus on.

Market Segments: Divided by the Four Ps

Let us start by examining how marketers have traditionally conceptualized market segments and used them in practice. Conceptually, marketers begin by identifying market segments, then selecting the appropriate segment(s) to target, and finally positioning the company's offer within the targeted segment(s) using the four Ps. Of course, in practice, segmentation is a messier process.

Market Segmentation

Customers within any market rarely have similar needs and expectations. To uncover the various segments into which customers fall, the segmentation process identifies variables that will maximize the differences between segments while simultaneously minimizing the differences within each segment. Creative segmentation can help a company get closer to its customers by developing the appropriate differential marketing mix for each segment, through changes in one or more of the four Ps.

The ultimate segmentation scheme from the customer's perspective is mass customization, where each customer is a distinct segment. A popular example of mass customization is Dell Computers. Dell has the ability to configure each of its personal computers in response to an individual customer's needs. For many other companies, the adoption of flexible production systems, quick-response supply chains, and shorter product development cycles has resulted in a relatively low cost for variety, enabling these companies to get closer to the ideal of mass customization. Competitive pressures are also forcing companies in this direction. As the CEO of a European company remarked a few years ago: "In the 1980s we looked for the customer in each individual. In the 1990s we must look for the individual in each customer."[3] However, most companies still must trade off between the company's logic, where economies of scale push for larger and larger segments, and the customer's logic, which drives companies toward recognizing the unique needs of the individual customer.[4]

The variables on which segmentation can occur are potentially numerous. In this sense, segmentation is an art. It is a lens through which to view the population of customers in an industry. Markets must be continuously segmented and resegmented to arrive at a scheme that delivers actionable segments. Actionable segments share three characteristics: (1) distinctiveness, that is, different segments respond differentially to the marketing mix; (2) identity, that is, the ability to reasonably profile which customers fall within which segment; and (3) adequate size, so that the development of tailored marketing programs for individual segments is economically viable for the firm.

Segmentation variables can be broadly classified into two categories: *identifier* and *response*. Identifier variables begin by segmenting the market based on who the customers are, in the hope that the resulting segments behave differently in response to marketing mix variables. This is called *a priori segmentation*. Examples include segmentation schemes that are based on sex, age, education, and income in consumer markets, or size of firm, industry, and geographical location in business-to-business markets. In contrast, *post hoc segmentation* starts by using response variables to divide the market on the basis of how customers behave, and then hopes that the resulting segments differ enough in terms of customer profiles to enable identification. An example would be segmenting telecommunication customers based on those whose primary concern is price versus those who are fixated on reliability or service quality. Figure 2-1 lists some commonly used segmentation variables.

In practice, managers need both a priori and post hoc processes to fine tune their understanding of market segments. Unfortunately, many firms frequently rely too heavily on a priori segmentation variables. For example, size of the firm is a popular means of segmenting customers in business markets. However, the resulting three segments of small, medium, and large firms, while easy to profile, rarely differ enough in terms of their needs

FIGURE 2-1

Common Market Segmentation Variables

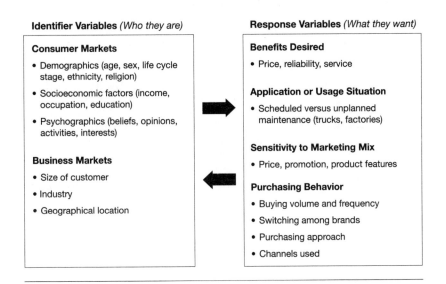

Identifier Variables *(Who they are)*

Consumer Markets

- Demographics (age, sex, life cycle stage, ethnicity, religion)
- Socioeconomic factors (income, occupation, education)
- Psychographics (beliefs, opinions, activities, interests)

Business Markets

- Size of customer
- Industry
- Geographical location

Response Variables *(What they want)*

Benefits Desired

- Price, reliability, service

Application or Usage Situation

- Scheduled versus unplanned maintenance (trucks, factories)

Sensitivity to Marketing Mix

- Price, promotion, product features

Purchasing Behavior

- Buying volume and frequency
- Switching among brands
- Purchasing approach
- Channels used

or behavior. Some small firms are looking for the same benefits as some large firms, and vice versa.

Targeting

Targeting or target market selection is the process of deciding which market segments the company should actively pursue to generate sales. Firms choose between adopting undifferentiated, differentiated, or concentrated targeting strategies. An undifferentiated strategy attempts to target all customers with the same marketing mix. The most famous example is Henry Ford's alleged 1908 declaration about the Ford Model T: "You can paint it any color, as long as it is black." While this seems like an anathema to the marketing concept, there are conditions under which it is appropriate. If standardization lowers the cost of delivering the value proposition to unprecedented levels and opens up the industry to large numbers of new customers, then an undifferentiated strategy can be powerful.

A differentiated strategy simultaneously targets several market segments, each with a unique marketing mix. For example, Ford Motor Company today has a portfolio of brands, including Aston Martin, Ford, Jaguar, Land Rover, Lincoln, and Volvo, to attack various segments in the automobile market.

Finally, a concentrated strategy selects one segment and concentrates on serving it, as Porsche has historically done with its over-forty, male, college graduate, with income over $200,000 per annum segment. However, Porsche subsegments using psychographics: *Top Guns* are driven, ambitious types who expect to be noticed and care about power and control; *Elitists* are old-money blue bloods who consider a car to be transportation, not an extension of one's personality, no matter how expensive; *Fantasists* are Walter Mitty types who escape through their cars and feel guilty about owning one; *Proud Patrons* consider ownership an end in itself, a trophy for hard work; and *Bon Vivants* are worldly jetsetters and thrill seekers whose cars heighten the excitement in their already passionate lives.[5]

Positioning

Positioning is about developing a unique selling proposition (USP) for the target segment. A company's unique selling proposition should be both unique, that is, differentiated from other competitors, as well as selling, that is, appealing to the target customers. It is the reason that the firm exists in the marketplace and why consumers would miss the company if it ceased operations. A well articulated USP should be capable of being briefly communicated by completing the sentence: "You should buy my product or service because . . ." In completing this sentence, the answer should be driven by customer benefits, not product features. Much of the disappointment of CEOs is rooted in the failure of marketers to answer this question in a compelling manner. The inability to do so results in either a price negotiation with the customer or a loss of the sale.

Volkswagen in the United States targeted a younger, more educated, more affluent demographic, and an adventurous, confident psychographic of customers who enjoy driving and even disobey speed limits. It positioned itself rationally as "affordable and German engineered," and emotionally as a "different driving experience more connected to the road and world." Compared to Nissan, Honda, Mazda, and Toyota, customers perceive VW to be more drivable, more substantial, more individual, and more spirited. Compared to BMW, Saab, Mercedes-Benz, and Volvo, VW is more approachable, more likeable, a better value, and more human.[6] The point: Companies must be very specific in terms of their intended positioning or unique selling proposition if they are to have any hope of being able to stand out among the clutter of choices confronting customers.

Complex Segmentation: Midas Style

Symptomatic of marketing's tactical orientation is the received wisdom on segmentation summarized above. The concept of market segments is about determining how to change the marketing mix, the four Ps, to serve different segments. Market segmentation helps the marketing manager determine which marketing mix to deploy to serve each unique segment.

Segmentation in companies is a more complex and messy process than in textbooks. To reveal how market segments operate in practice, let us examine Midas and the automobile repair business.[7] Midas offers consumers walk-in service for repairs on brakes, mufflers, and exhaust pipes. It segments its customers using three identifying variables: (1) age of the car, because the older the car, the more likely the customer will need Midas; (2) size of the car, since the bigger the car, the higher the value of the sale and the higher the margin; and (3) sex of the driver, since women are more likely to buy additional services. In response to this segmentation, it changes its marketing mix based on the customer and the characteristics of his or her car.

The market segmentation at Midas does not stop there. It has also discovered two service segments of customers, car lovers and utilitarians, based on service expectations and needs. The car lovers see their car as a prized possession, while the utilitarians tend to view their car as merely a means to take them from one place to another. Both segments want the same basic value proposition from Midas: fast, reliable, one-time repair. However, to completely satisfy both segments, Midas varies the additional services that surround this value proposition.

The service personnel interacting with the car lover focus the discussion on the car, offer opportunities to observe the repair while the car owner is waiting, provide old parts in the packaging of the new parts to show tangible evidence that the parts have been changed, and follow up with phone calls every six months to remind the customer that it is time for another check-up. The utilitarian would consider all of these services to be annoying. Instead, the service personnel talk to these customers about their lives, offer them a newspaper or a game to play while waiting, reassure them that the little noise is now gone, and guarantee the car for X number of miles without the problem recurring.

Strategic Segments: Divided by the Three Vs

Market and service segments such as the above, which only require changes in the marketing mix, can be distinguished from strategic segments. Strategic segments are those segments that require distinct value networks, rather than just changes in the marketing mix. For example, Midas caters to the strategic segment that wants "fast mechanical repair" in the auto repair business, as opposed to the "guaranteed repair" offered by factory-authorized car dealers, "specialty repair" offered by the independent workshops, "heavy-duty accidental repair" performed by body shops, or the "do-it-yourself repair" for the automobile enthusiast. Each of these strategic segments is associated with a unique set of key success factors.

The identification of strategic segments helps the business unit manager determine which value network to deploy. If a company wishes to serve two different strategic segments, then it must develop two unique value networks. Instead of simply aligning the four Ps, as is the case with market segments, serving different strategic segments requires the alignment of other functions such as R&D or operations. As a result, instead of the four Ps, I find it more appropriate to think in terms of the three Vs—valued customer, value proposition, and value network.[8]

Let us use the airline industry to illustrate in greater depth the concept of strategic segments and the three Vs model. In Europe, the leading low-cost airline is easyJet, which is modeled after Southwest Airlines in the United States.[9] EasyJet has seen extraordinary success since November 1995, when it offered to fly travelers from London to Glasgow for a one-way fare of £29 with the slogan: "Fly to Scotland for the price of a pair of jeans!" Under the colorful leadership of its founder Stelios Haji-Ioannou (who prefers to be addressed by his first name only), easyJet has become a thorn in the sides of the traditional European Flag Carriers such as British Airways, Air France, KLM, and Swiss. Comparing the Flag Carriers and easyJet on the three Vs highlights the power of strategic segments.

Valued Customer—Who to Serve?

On the first V—valued customer, or who to serve—the traditional Flag Carriers like KLM and Swiss target everyone; however, their most valued customers are business travelers. In contrast to business travelers who pay from other people's pockets, easyJet targets those customers who pay from their own pockets. While these tend to be predominantly leisure travelers, there are business people such as entrepreneurs and small business owners who also pay from their own pockets. Altogether, this is a large segment in Europe and one that was unhappy with the industry offerings until low-cost airlines such as easyJet and Ryanair emerged. These two segments are strategic segments because serving them effectively requires distinct value networks, rather than simply a differentiation of the marketing mix.

Value Proposition—What to Offer?

Value proposition, or what to offer to the valued customers, reveals stark differences between the two segments. Business travelers, whose bills are paid by their companies, are demanding, both in terms of services, such as seat comfort and business class, as well as freebies, such as free newspapers, meals, and frequent flyer miles. More legitimately, they also need seat selection, travel agents, and a worldwide network to save time, make seamless connections, and have the flexibility to change flights to accommodate their hectic schedules.

In contrast, while leisure travelers may enjoy the above services, when given the choice, they will forgo all of them for a lower price. Four questions developed by Professors Kim and Mauborgne provide a framework for understanding the creation of easyJet's value proposition, and should be addressed by every company.[10]

1. *Which attributes that our industry takes for granted should be eliminated?*   This question forces companies to reflect on whether each of the attributes offered creates value for their valued customers. EasyJet's conclusion was that free meals and travel agents could be eliminated. Instead, it sells snacks on the plane and 95 percent of its seats are sold through the Internet, while the remaining 5 percent are processed through their call center.

2. *Which attributes should be reduced to below industry standards?*   This question pushes companies to consider whether the industry has overdesigned its products and services for their valued customers. EasyJet concluded

that it could reduce flexibility in flight changes and seat selection offered to passengers. All fares at easyJet are nonrefundable. However, if another flight is available, passengers may change flights by paying a penalty of £10 per leg plus the difference in fares between the two flights. Seating is on a first-come, first-served basis. At check-in, passengers get a group boarding number tag, such as 1–25 or 26–50, so that they will arrive early for a good seat. Then, when boarding is announced for the passengers' group tag, they take any available seat, thereby accelerating the boarding process. At other airlines, aircraft often wait for passengers with preassigned seats who lack incentive to board quickly.

3. *Which attributes should be increased to above industry standards?*   This question presses companies to understand the compromises that the industry currently forces its customers to make. For example, compared to the rest of the industry, easyJet strives for lower prices, greater punctuality, and a younger fleet of airplanes.

4. *Which new attributes should be created that the industry has never offered?*   This question forces companies to think about what new sources of value creation exist within the industry. On this dimension, easyJet decided to offer only one-way fares, refunds if there is a delay of four hours or more, and ticketless travel.

The value proposition of easyJet can be graphically contrasted with that of the Flag Carriers using a tool called the value curve.[11] As can be seen from the value curves in figure 2-2, the Flag Carriers are superior to easyJet on almost every dimension. But consider the attributes that are most important to air travelers. First, they want to reach their destination safely. The low price of easyJet raises particular concern in this respect. How can easyJet make safety, which is an intangible benefit, tangible? New planes are the obvious answer. Second, they want to arrive on time. By offering

FIGURE 2-2

Value Curves of easyJet Versus Flag Carriers

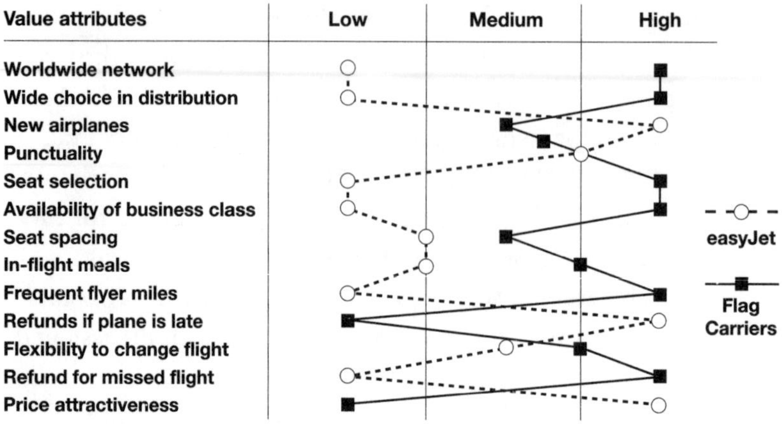

Value attributes	Low	Medium	High
Worldwide network			
Wide choice in distribution			
New airplanes			
Punctuality			
Seat selection			
Availability of business class			
Seat spacing			
In-flight meals			
Frequent flyer miles			
Refunds if plane is late			
Flexibility to change flight			
Refund for missed flight			
Price attractiveness			

- - -○- -   easyJet

━━━■━━━   Flag Carriers

refunds if the plane is more than four hours late, which is rather difficult for the short hauls that they operate on, easyJet makes punctuality a perceived benefit. Along with these two benefits, it offers low prices and in return asks its customers to trade off all other attributes that they may get from a full-service airline. It has stripped the value proposition to its bare bones, beating the competition only on the absolutely necessary dimensions of the value proposition for its valued customers.

Value Network—How to Deliver?

On the third V—value network, or how to deliver the value proposition to the valued customer—easyJet has systematically redefined each component to deliver low prices at a profit. It achieves distribution savings of about 20 to 25 percent over other full-service carriers by not using travel agents, encouraging Internet sales, not participating in industry reservation systems such as Sabre, and not issuing paper tickets. Ten percent of its budget is spent on marketing, but it gets a much bigger bang for its buck by having in-your-face, attention-grabbing, opportunistic advertising that generates loads of free publicity. In addition, through the use of a sophisticated yield management tool it can maximize the revenues for each flight based on dynamic matching of supply and demand. As demand for a flight goes up, prices increase, and vice versa.

While the transformations in the marketing and distribution components are important, much of the savings in its value network is generated through radically streamlined operations (see figure 2-3 for a comparison of the value networks of easyJet with those of Flag Carriers). EasyJet's operations are optimized for low costs through fast turnaround (the amount of time the plane is on the ground between flights) and greater utilization of airplanes. The exclusive use of a single type of airplane, the Boeing 737, reduces spare parts inventory, as well as training costs for pilots and maintenance personnel. It increases flexibility in interchanging

FIGURE 2-3

Value Networks of easyJet Versus Flag Carriers

		Purchasing	Operations	Marketing	Distribution
Flag Carriers		Integrated	• Multiple types of planes • Short- and long-haul routes • Prime airports (hubs) • Worldwide network • Assigned seating	• Segmented customers • Varied meal services • Frequent flyer program	• Travel agents • Worldwide reservation systems
easyJet		Outsourced	• Single type aircraft • 149 versus 109 seats • Short-haul routes • Point-to-point lines • Rapid turnaround • No business class • No preseating • No in-flight meals	• No market research • No frequent flyer programs • Use of plane for advertising • Attention-grabbing advertising campaigns • Variable pricing • One-way ticket only	• No travel agents • No tickets • No use of "Sabre" • Direct sales (phone and Internet) • Reservation agents on commission

planes, strengthens bargaining power with the vendor, and makes the yield management system easier to operate since the configuration of each plane is identical. The elimination of the kitchen and business class enables it to fit 149 seats on a Boeing 737 compared to 109 for the competition. The lack of preassigned seating increases punctuality and turnaround time.

Reinventing the Value Network.   At a more abstract level, there are five cost principles behind the construction of easyJet's value network:

1. Avoid fixed costs whenever possible. For example, there are no secretaries in the organization. Even the CEO, Ray Webster, must open his own e-mails!

2. If there are any fixed costs, make them work harder than the rest of the industry. For example, easyJet planes are in the air for 11 hours a day, compared with the 6.5-hour average for the industry.

3. Eliminate generally accepted variable costs whenever it makes sense, such as travel agents.

4. Keep any variable costs to a minimum, such as airport fees.

5. Examine whether variable cost factors associated with services can be converted into revenue generators, as easyJet has done by selling snacks on the plane.

While perhaps not as applicable as they are for easyJet, these are principles that all firms could adopt.

Drive Growth and Innovation Using the Three Vs

Comparing easyJet and the Flag Carriers along the three Vs generates several interesting propositions related to strategic segments (see table 2-1).

TABLE 2-1

easyJet Versus Flag Carriers on the Three Vs

	Flag Carriers	easyJet
Valued Customer "Who to Serve?"	Everyone, especially business class	People who pay from their own pockets and some who don't typically fly
Value Proposition "What to Offer?"	• Flexible • Full-service • High prices	• One-way fares • No frills • Low prices
Value Network "How to Deliver?"		
Purchasing	Integrated	Outsourced
Operations	• Multiple types of planes • Short- and long-haul routes • Worldwide network	• Single type of plane • Short-haul routes • Select destinations
Marketing	• Segmented customers • Varied meal services • Frequent flyer program	• Treat all customers the same • "Focused"
Distribution	Travel agents/all channels	Internet/direct sales only

Differentiate Deeply Based on the Value Network

Much of the competitive advantage of each type of company lies in distinct value networks. British Airways may try to offer easyJet's low fares, but it will never make a profit doing so. So it launched GO, a low-price subsidiary, to compete with easyJet and Ryanair. However, when GO was part of British Airways (BA), the temptation was to constantly seek synergies in the value chain. Because these two airlines were serving different strategic segments requiring divergent value networks, any attempt to exploit synergies hurt both subsidiaries. The so-called synergies, or shared portions of the value network, were neither optimized for the low costs necessary for GO, nor the full service necessary for BA. As a result, BA divested GO and let it try to survive as an independent firm until easyJet eventually acquired it. In contrast, if one is serving two market segments, then much of the value network may be shared.

Firms need to align the three Vs. One cannot serve easyJet's valued customers with the easyJet value proposition and have the value network of the traditional full-service airline company. The margins would simply be too small to generate a profit. Alternatively, one could not offer the full-service value proposition of the traditional airline with the value network of easyJet. The customer expectations with respect to service would never be met. When developing the three Vs, a company should ask: (1) To what extent does our marketing concept differ from others in the industry? (2) To what extent do elements of our marketing concept mutually reinforce each other?[12]

Unlike decisions to serve new market segments, entering a new strategic segment requires a new value network, and is thus a major decision for the company often requiring the approval of the board of directors. For example, KLM operated its low-cost carrier, Buzz, as a separate subsidiary and even looked for outside investors to help fund the expansion of Buzz. Yet, because there were no synergies between KLM and Buzz, Buzz was ultimately sold to Ryanair, despite the fact that low-cost air travel is the fastest growing and only profitable segment in the European airline industry.

Explore Different Value Network Options for Unique Segments

Many companies are struggling with the question of where to slice the value network to serve different segments. Consider the major food companies such as Danone, Nestlé, and Unilever, which sell famous branded products like Danone yogurt, Nescafé coffee, and Magnum ice cream through retailers. The increasing power of retailers combined with time-starved, affluent consumers has eroded grocery sales of branded products from 52 percent to 33 percent of the total consumer spending on food from 1982 to 1990 in the United Kingdom.[13] On one hand, private labels pushed by powerful retailers have increased their share from 33 percent to 46 percent. On the other hand, time-impoverished consumers with greater disposable income have helped increase the share of eating out from 15 percent to 21 percent.

In response to these consumer patterns, the multinational food companies have begun manufacturing private labels for major retailers as well as launching into the food service business by developing products and packaging specifically targeting hotels, restaurants, and cafeterias. As food companies try to serve the consumer segments that buy private labels or eat out, the issue of value network segregation is constantly raised.

Within these companies, the executives responsible for managing food service often complain that their business has completely different research and development needs and does not receive adequate attention from the firm, despite being the high-growth sector in the company. They argue that the food service business is a strategic segment requiring a unique value network. Other executives in the same companies argue that the food service business is a market segment that can be managed effectively in combination with the branded products business. Their perspective is that each should have a dedicated sales force and unique packaging, but R&D and manufacturing should be shared between the two. As this example demonstrates, there is a continuum

FIGURE 2-4

Value Network Options for Market Versus Strategic Segments

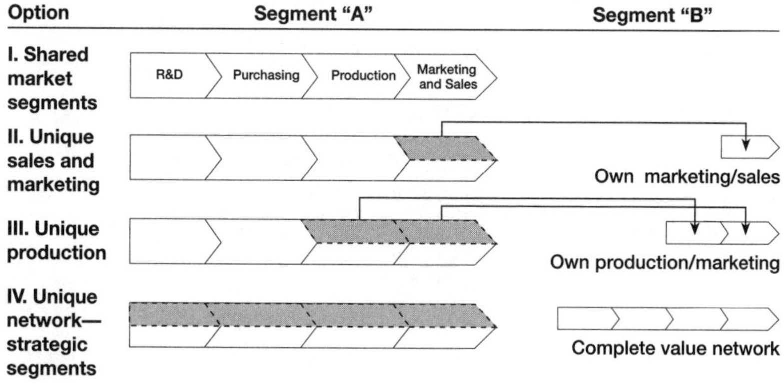

Option	Segment "A"	Segment "B"
I. Shared market segments	R&D ⟩ Purchasing ⟩ Production ⟩ Marketing and Sales ⟩	
II. Unique sales and marketing		Own marketing/sales
III. Unique production		Own production/marketing
IV. Unique network—strategic segments		Complete value network

between strategic and market segments. Figure 2-4 shows the different value network options for market versus strategic segments.

Analyze the Financial Implications of Serving Segments

Similar, but in my experience more heated, arguments occur on whether the private labels and branded businesses represent strategic segments. The issue is more difficult here as both the branded products and the private labels are usually sold to the same retailers. Thus the incentive to share logistics, sales force, and marketing is significant. However, the value network for profitable private labels differs significantly from that of branded products.

Table 2-2 offers a disguised example from the consumer packaged goods industry benchmarking the value networks of the most successful private label manufacturer against the leading branded manufacturer. Both companies were focused, that is, the branded manufacturer did not engage in manufacturing private labels for retailers and the private label manufacturer did not sell any products under proprietary brand names. On average, the price for the end consumer of the private label product was 35 percent lower (hence the consumer price index of 65 for private labels versus 100 for branded manufacturer).

Compared to branded products, the average retailer margin on private labels was larger in terms of percentage (50 percent versus 40 percent) but smaller in terms of absolute dollars ($32.50 versus $40). Both the private label manufacturer (4.5/32.5) and the branded manufacturer (9/40) had operating profit margins of around 15 percent on sales. However, they achieved this by optimizing the value network in completely different ways.

The private label manufacturer had almost no research and development and instead relied exclusively on copycat innovations. It utilized cheaper raw materials and aggressive buying

TABLE 2-2

Value Networks of Private Label Versus Branded Business

	R&D	Purchasing	Manufacturing	Marketing, Logistics, Sales	Manufacturer Operating Profits	Reseller's Gross Margin	Average Price
Private Label Value Network	• Copycat • Reverse engineer 0	• Cheaper raw materials • Bidding 12	• Fewer SKUs • Longer lead-time 9.5	• KAM • Copy packaging 6	4.5	32.5	65
Manufacturer Branded Value Network	• New products • New functionality 2	• Joint development of proprietary materials 15	• Wide range of SKUs • Quick response 14	• Extensive brand investments • Large sales force 20	9	40	100

practices. Since it supplied only a few very large retailers, the number of stock-keeping units (SKUs) were relatively small and the rather transparent purchasing pattern of its customers allowed longer lead times in manufacturing. This helped run an efficient supply chain that lowered costs significantly. In addition, all the retailers were served through a single key account manager (KAM), and few resources needed to be devoted to developing packaging as they adopted me-too packaging.

The branded manufacturer invested in research and development to generate new products and functionality for consumers that sometimes required partnering with suppliers to develop proprietary materials. It had an expensive manufacturing system that was set up to produce a wide range of SKUs to satisfy the many different retailers and target segments served. Differentiation was also built into the system through quick response capabilities. However, the largest additional cost was in building the brand through expensive advertising and promotional campaigns as well as a large, well-educated sales force.

In contrast to these two value networks, a third company's sales were derived equally from private labels manufactured for major retailers and its own manufacturer brands. Many of the latter were among the leading brands in their respective countries. Unfortunately, because its value network was integrated, the company was actually just about breaking even, despite being among the largest players in the industry.

Sharing the value network compromised the integrity of the branded product since retailers were extremely savvy at transferring benefits (quality, innovations, packaging) from the branded line into their private label, while paying the private label price. However, in continuous process industries such as toilet paper or aluminum foil, value network separation at the level of purchasing and manufacturing would severely compromise production efficiencies.

Given the distinct nature of the two value networks, the company was advised to choose among the following three options:

1. Concentrate exclusively on being either a branded or a private label player.

2. Become primarily a branded player, but accept private label manufacturing only under very strict criteria: meet a hurdle rate of return on sales, use only excess plant capacity, and do not "borrow" packaging or recently introduced innovative features of the company's branded product.

3. Completely separate the private label business from the branded business and let each optimize its own value network.

After much debate, the company chose the last option rather successfully.

Over and over again, in the face of nimble new competitors such as Charles Schwab, Dell, easyJet, Hennes & Mauritz, and Wal-Mart, companies must confront the issue of slicing the value network after analyzing the financial implications. Usually, they cannot change because their corporate mind-set clings to the old value network. British Airways, Continental, Delta, KLM, and Lufthansa all chose to divest their low-cost airlines, despite the latter competing in the faster growing, more profitable, and ultimately higher market capitalization segment.

Drive Marketing Innovation Using the Three Vs

Marketing innovation can be conceptualized using the three Vs model by asking three questions:

1. *Are there customers who are either unhappy with all of the industry's offerings or are not being served at all?* Through posing this question, one can find tremendous opportunities to exploit. Think of all the HIV-positive people in Africa. The value networks of the major multinational pharmaceutical firms—characterized

by sophisticated R&D, expensive insurance reimburse-ment–driven pricing practices, high marketing costs, and large profit margins—will never be able to generate a solution for them. Instead, these patients are waiting for a visionary to develop an "easyJet" value network that will deliver effective treatment to them. Or consider Progressive Insurance's successful focus on high-risk individuals whom no other insurance company will cover.

2. *Can we offer a value proposition that delivers dramatically higher benefits or lower prices, compared with others in the industry?*   Virgin's ability to pamper its passengers with massages and manicures is an example of a strategy driven by higher benefits. Or consider Zara's strategy of copying catwalk fashions and offering them to customers faster and cheaper than the designers themselves can bring them to the market. The value curves are a clever way of clearly differentiating one's value proposition. A graphic value curve is hard to fudge, forcing one to confront whether, and where, the firm's value proposition is truly differentiated.

3. *Can we radically redefine the value network for the industry with much lower costs?*   Dell in the personal computer business, Formula 1 in the hotel industry, and IKEA in furniture retailing are diverse examples of companies that have achieved this.

The four value proposition questions presented previously and the three questions above help conceptualize opportunities for marketing innovation in the industry. And using the three Vs to generate innovation clarifies that innovation is not the exclusive territory of technical R&D and product development people. Rather, marketers and strategists can contribute to innovation by discovering underserved or unhappy segments, offering new value curves, and reinventing industry value networks.

Exploit the Three Vs–Related Growth Opportunities

By combining the three marketing innovation questions from the previous section with an in-depth understanding of a company's three Vs model, the company's strategic growth map can be developed.[14] Understanding where customers are not being served helps determine which markets and industries the firm should operate in or "who to serve." Clarity in the winning formula and economic logic create the potential to offer dramatically different value propositions and help determine "what to offer." Finally, the value network, or "how to deliver," explicates the timing (when to move into which markets) and vehicles (how to get there) that will help enable the firm's growth moves (see figure 2-5).

Stelios Haji-Ioannou has innovated and diversified into at least two new businesses since starting easyJet. EasyInternetcafé is the first chain of large Internet cafés in the world.[15] These cafés, open twenty-four hours a day and located all over Europe (as well as one in New York), allow consumers to surf the Internet on flat screens using high-speed connections for about £1 an hour. EasyCar is an Internet-reservation-only rental car company, which offered, at least initially, Mercedes A-class vehicles exclusively, for a price as low as £9 per day.

Of course, Stelios has incorporated many of the ideas from easyJet into his two new businesses by constantly asking: What are our core competences (things we know), strategic assets (things we own), and core processes (things we do)?[16] The core competence of easyGroup is redefining the value chain of an industry at a significantly lower cost. Its strategic asset is the "easy" brand as a consumer champion. Its core process is yield management–based pricing systems. All of these are unique to the company, create value for the consumer, and can be transferred to other businesses.[17] They are the platforms for exploiting growth and diversification opportunities.

FIGURE 2-5

easyGroup Diversification

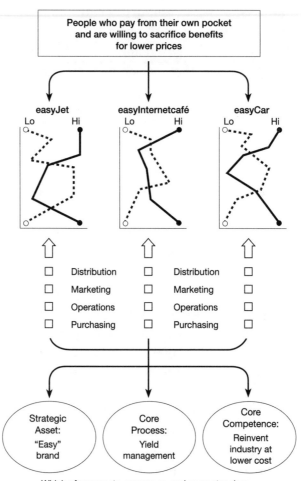

Align the Three Vs

People who pay from their own pocket and are willing to sacrifice benefits for lower prices

easyJet	easyInternetcafé	easyCar
Lo · · · Hi	Lo · · · Hi	Lo · · · Hi

☐ Distribution   ☐ Distribution   ☐
☐ Marketing   ☐ Marketing   ☐
☐ Operations   ☐ Operations   ☐
☐ Purchasing   ☐ Purchasing   ☐

Strategic Asset: "Easy" brand

Core Process: Yield management

Core Competence: Reinvent industry at lower cost

Which of our assets, processes, and competencies:
• are unique?
• are transferable to other industries?
• create value for customers?

Marketing Innovation Questions	Strategy/Growth Questions	easyJet Responses
Valued Customer Are there customers who are unhappy with the current industry offerings or not being served?	**Markets** Which segments and geographies?	European focus, short haul in airlines.
	Industries Which product service categories?	Airlines, Internet cafés, rental cars.
Value Proposition Can we have a value proposition that is dramatically different from the industry?	**Winning Formula** How will we win—image, price, customization?	Lowest price in industry and consumer champion image.
	Economic Logic How will we make money?	High utilization of assets through dynamic pricing in high-fixed-costs businesses.
Value Network Can we reinvent the value network at a radically lower cost or higher benefit?	**Timing** Speed and sequence of our moves?	Fast into high-traffic "winner-takes-all" markets. Dominate a city before moving to a new one.
	Vehicles How to get there—joint ventures, internal growth, alliances?	Internal growth focus— small opportunistic acquisitions.

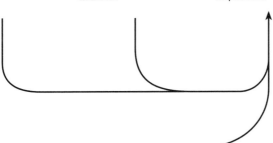

Checklist for Marketers
on the Three Vs

Valued Customer

- *Who are our valued customers?*

- *Are there customers who are unhappy with all the current offerings of the industry?*

- *Are there customers who have a need but are not being currently served by the industry?*

- *Are we trying to reach customers who are unaware that they need our product? If so, how are we going to create the need?*

- *Who is the user? The buyer? The influencer? The payer? What are the preferred criteria of each and their power in the buying decision?*

- *Is the target segment large enough to meet our sales objectives?*

- *What is the growth rate of the target segment?*

Value Proposition

- *What are the core needs we are trying to address with our value proposition?*

- *Does the value proposition fit the needs of our valued customers?*

I have used the easyGroup of companies to illustrate the idea of strategic segmentation versus market segmentation and how to use the three Vs model for innovation and growth. This is not to imply that the easyGroup is without its challenges. EasyInternet-cafés are still struggling to find a profitable business model. Easy-

- *What benefits are we actually delivering to the customers?*

- *Is our value proposition differentiated from the competitors or are we positioning in a crowded space?*

- *Are our value proposition claims reinforced by underlying product and service features?*

- *Are we positioning on attributes that we can defend against competitive attacks?*

- *Are we positioning on too many benefits to be credible?*

Value Network

- *Can we serve the valued customers with the value proposition at a profit?*

- *Do we have the necessary capabilities to deliver the value proposition? If not, could we acquire or partner with them?*

- *Would serving the valued customers have negative consequences on our existing customers or businesses? If so, how are we going to control for this?*

- *Which high-cost or low-value-added activities could be eliminated, reduced, or outsourced in our value network?*

- *Where are the advantages of scale in our value network? Can we maintain scale while not losing flexibility?*

- *How different is our value network from the rest of the industry?*

- *What is our break-even point? Could we lower it by slightly varying the value network?*

Jet is in the process of assimilating the GO acquisition. In addition, both easyJet and easyCar have moved away from the single type of aircraft and car models. Having a single supplier made the firm a hostage when it came to purchasing additional capacity. Thus Stelios is willing to trade off somewhat higher operating costs for lower aircraft or vehicle acquisition costs. The implications of this decision will not be known for some time.

Conclusion

CEOs often fault marketers for not clearly communicating the value proposition of the firm and how it differs from that of the competition. The value curve tool and the three Vs approach can help marketers by constantly forcing them to ask the hard questions regarding segmentation, targeting, positioning, and the business model for delivering the value proposition. (See "Checklist for Marketers on the Three Vs.")

Understanding strategic segmentation and then conceptualizing and responding to it using the three Vs model helps illuminate critical issues facing many companies. As companies enter and operate in related segments of businesses, are they facing strategic segments or market segments? How far back in the value network should they separate the two businesses? Is it enough to separate marketing, or should marketing and distribution be segregated? Or does one need a completely distinct value network for the new segment? How can marketing be used to generate innovation and growth in the industry? These are challenges related to segmentation that are currently on CEOs' agendas. The resolution of these questions has strategic, cross-functional, and bottom-line implications. By using the three Vs lens to answer these questions, a company can find new strategic segments, build deep differentiation, and drive innovation and growth while transforming industries at the same time.

THREE

From Selling Products to Providing Solutions

Customers buy holes, not drills.

IN MANY INDUSTRIES, especially in business-to-business (B2B) markets, suppliers of "products" struggle to withstand commoditization. Competitors rapidly copy new features, effectively destroying product differentiation, and sophisticated buyers refuse to pay any brand premium—at least not a premium that would cover the required additional marketing costs to build and maintain it.

Companies confronting commoditization have few strategic options. They can become a low-cost provider in their industries, but that requires relentless cost-cutting, generally by moving production overseas to low-cost locations, trading low margins for (hopefully) higher volume, revealing cost structures to customers, and favoring sales over any real marketing function. In the commodity business, purchasing agents tend to drive customer interactions and as customers hold the power; sellers have little pricing flexibility. In response to this pressure, many companies instead aspire to become solution providers, by integrating bundles of their products with services for the customer. The business imperative for providing solutions is relatively clear. Compared to products, solutions include a large service component and therefore are less comparable. Over time, the seller masters the customer's business processes. This makes changing suppliers difficult and costly for the customer and thereby increases customer loyalty. Furthermore, since selling solutions usually requires integrating a large number of products and services, the typical sale generates larger revenues.

Not surprisingly, the growth and profit mantra of industries as diverse as chemicals, financial services, health care, information technology, logistics, pesticides, telecommunications, and travel is to become a problem-solver for the customer, not simply a producer of products. Even Sun Microsystems, whose CEO Scott McNealy once said that service is what companies sell when they cannot sell products, now claims, "Sun's Internet expertise, combined with innovative yet reliable end-to-end solutions and professional consulting services, makes Sun the ideal partner for delivering IP-based services!"[1]

Transforming the organization into a solutions provider is tricky. Few executives truly comprehend the enormity of the challenge, let alone what "solution provider" really means. But some companies are well on their way. Notably, IBM has successfully made the transition from mainframe giant to PC maker to end-to-end IT solutions provider.

The Turnaround of IBM by Selling Solutions

After leading the market for years, IBM hobbled into the 1990s.[2] The company could no longer command price premiums as its competitors narrowed the gap in perceived quality. Between 1991 and 1993, IBM recorded losses of $16 billion; in 1993 alone it lost $8.1 billion on sales of $62.7 billion. Wall Street pressured

IBM to spin off undervalued divisions as its stock price tumbled and losses mounted.

On April 1, 1993, Lou Gerstner became chair and CEO of IBM, after stints at RJR Nabisco and American Express, both quintessential marketing outfits. Many observers in and outside IBM doubted whether IBM's first outsider could succeed, especially without a technology background. Some computer publications even polled their readers: "Do you think Lou Gerstner is the right man to lead IBM's turnaround?"[3]

Gerstner soon identified IBM's destructive practices, unnoticed when it was the technology leader with growing revenues. In R&D, IBM strove for the new and disdained outside technology. A classic sales-driven organization, sales reps pushed whatever R&D gave them. Over the years, many of IBM's strengths, such as employee loyalty and a sales-driven culture, became its weaknesses. The company's culture had grown insular, and the "IBM way" to do everything stifled experimentation. Worse, IBM's people knew how computers worked but not what they did for customers. Gerstner, who had authorized purchases of IBM equipment at American Express, had a good understanding of this difference.

Gerstner made customer contact a priority, frequently going on the road himself to listen to customers without the IBM bureaucratic filter. He also wanted all employees to do the same. The IBM corporate office buildings symbolized the company's insularity, bureaucracy, and lack of cost control. Gerstner saw the two IBM skyscrapers in New York and Chicago, designed by I. M. Pei and Mies van der Rohe respectively, as more suited to lawyers or investment bankers than an industrial giant like IBM. He emptied them and issued laptops so that employees could work from home or in the field.

What Gerstner heard was that customers lacked the expertise and the resources to integrate their hardware and software. They wanted solutions to their problems, but were stymied by the shortage of IT professionals and the rapid rate of technological change.

In response, Gerstner quashed plans to dismantle and sell IBM's different businesses. IBM's value, he argued, was in delivering vertically integrated products and services to the customer. IBM had products in every corner of the networking world—large-scale mainframe systems that hosted massive databases, high-performance servers, and application software. He changed IBM's focus from selling hardware products to bundling hardware with software and service into a total technology solution. No other company could do what Team IBM could do.

In 1996, to demonstrate that services were now IBM's strategic priority, Gerstner formed IBM Global Services (IGS) to deliver customer solutions by connecting and improving information flow among different businesses. By 2002, IGS had become a $36.4 billion business, a major contributor to IBM's 2002 revenues of $81.3 billion and profits of $3.6 billion.

To communicate his new mandate, Gerstner's speeches emphasized customer service and identifying what customers wanted. Accustomed to hearing about the "great IBM technology," this message left many long-standing IBM employees cold. In response, Gerstner reasoned, "Technology changes much too quickly now for any company to build a sustainable competitive advantage on that basis alone. . . . [What matters is how] you help customers use technology."

Transforming the Three Vs to Sell Solutions

IBM's success has led other companies, including Cisco, Compaq, Sun Microsystems, and Unisys, to attempt similar transitions to selling solutions. Even Microsoft, the ultimate product company, claimed in a presentation to the banking industry, "Our goal is not to sell software products but to sell solutions to help the banking industry better serve its customers."[4]

Despite some success, none of these imitators has managed the transformation as well as IBM. Why is the transition so chal-

TABLE 3-1

The Products-to-Solutions Three Vs Transformation

	Product Focus	Solutions Focus
Valued Customer	Almost all customers	Segment focus
Value Proposition	"Better" products with service	End-to-end solutions that reduce customer costs and risks or increase revenues
Value Network		
R&D	• New technology focus • Stand-alone products • Proprietary products	• Customer problem focus • Modular products • Open, standards-based
Operations	• In-house manufacturing of products • Limited supply-chain complexity	• Partner with best providers and be product agnostic • Many interdependent partners requiring high coordination
Service	Cost center, bundled free with products	Profit center, unbundled from products
Marketing	• Cost-plus product pricing • Product sales • Salesperson as order taker • Geographical coverage • Volume-based commissions	• Value-based pricing • Multiyear service contracts • Salesperson as consultant • Industry experts • Service-based commissions
Distribution	Products sold through many channels	Become a value-added reseller (VAR)

lenging? Table 3-1 employs the three Vs model articulated in the previous chapter to show that becoming a solutions provider requires a significant modification of each element of the marketing concept.

Target Customers Who Will Pay for Solutions

In its 2000 annual report, the networking company 3Com stated, "There are products, and there are solutions. A product performs a function. A solution fulfills a human need. People want solutions."[5] Obviously, people prefer solutions rather than products—but not everyone will pay for them. The critical difference between customer needs and customer demands is that demands are needs that customers are able, and willing, to pay for. Since providing solutions requires customization and is therefore costly, a company aspiring to sell solutions must be meticulous in defining the valued customer for a solution.

Selecting the valued customer requires a thorough understanding of a solution's value proposition. A solution involves more than simply bundling together related components and is not just a fancy name for cross-selling one's own products and services. A true solution is defined by and designed around the customer's need, not around an attempt to sell more of the supplier's current products.[6] Solution selling, therefore, requires a high degree of collaboration between the supplier and the customer in defining the customer's need. After that, products and service components are integrated into a distinctive offering.

Given a set of products and competences, the customers and problems that will be served through solutions can be tightly specified. For example, IBM's global services are focused on three areas: (1) front-end systems, to help redesign the customer interaction process through automation; (2) plumbing, which integrates systems since customers often have products from different vendors; and (3) outsourcing, where IBM runs the entire system. Because of the need for an in-depth understanding of the customer's business operations and systems—which can be expensive and time-consuming to acquire—these services primarily target large customers.

To outsource an activity is usually a general management, or sometimes even a top management, decision. Therefore, the decision to purchase a solution is usually made by general managers rather than purchasing agents. Resistance is often encountered from the traditional buyer of "products," the IT professionals, who fear that their jobs will be outsourced to IBM.

For example, in 2002, American Express signed a seven-year, $4 billion contract that shifted 2,000 IT professionals and computers to IBM.[7] Rather than the standard outsourcing contract, American Express agreed to pay IBM only for the technology used every month. Consequently, American Express expects to save hundreds of millions of dollars over the life of the contract; and with IBM running the system, it expects to upgrade its technology five times faster.

Customers rarely develop budgets for purchasing solutions. Therefore, the seller must convince the client's top management that the firm needs a particular solution and that managers should budget for it. As shown in figure 3-1, the best prospects for purchasing a solution already want to outsource or are exploring possibilities. In contrast, customers who are already outsourcing have committed to a supplier and therefore may be more difficult to win. Solution selling also needs a salesperson different from the usual "order taker." The solutions salesperson must be more of a "consultant," able to interact with general managers, and capable of convincing the buyer to purchase a whole solution, not just a product or service.

FIGURE 3-1

Identifying Prospects for Solutions

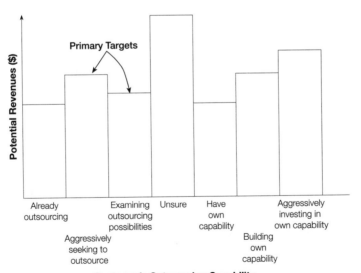

Create Customer Value Through Three Types of Solutions

The "right" customer for a solution will derive value from faster deployment, seamless operations, a focus on core activities, fewer up-front costs, reduced support costs, and decreased use of internal resources. Solutions providers create customer value by: (a) helping customers increase revenues; (b) assuming customer risk and responsibility for part of the business; or (c) reducing customers' total costs of consuming the product or service. While some powerful solutions tend to perform on all three dimensions, most solutions have one of these dimensions as the primary motivation.

Enhance Customer Revenues Through Solutions.   Hendrix Voeders BV, an operating company of Nutreco, had an 8 percent market share of the Dutch animal feed market for pigs, poultry, sheep, cattle, and milk cows.[8] While most companies competed on price, Hendrix Voeders priced its feed about 10 to 15 percent higher and competed instead on services. Its 150-person consulting force—separate from the sales force—provided services that helped deliver either an incremental animal weight gain of 5 to 10 percent or an increase of 4 to 5 percent in live births.

Delivering this productivity gain required a sophisticated data management system that allowed farmers and consultants to monitor the animals' progress. Each animal was individually numbered and its feed consumption and weight gain was tracked daily. This precision allowed microadjustments in nutrients, medicine, and physical environment. For example, as a result of its sow monitoring system, Hendrix can help a sow that usually produces 18 to 24 piglets a year produce one or two more. The additional 10 percent price premium for Hendrix's feed becomes relatively trivial.

Over the years, Hendrix Voeders has developed 1,500 feed products to meet animal nutritional needs through each phase of life. They have moved from being a supplier of bulk feed to providing a complete service to the farmer. For example, during an animal's early growth phases, Hendrix can provide most of the essential supplies, from feed, milk substitutes, vitamins, and mineral mixes. At the other end of the cycle, it would arrange for the slaughter and sale of animals and the processing of meat. Its slogan? "If the farmer does well, Hendrix does well."

Decrease Customer Risks Through Solutions.   Quarries have traditionally used packaged explosives, usually sausage-shaped, for blasting.[9] To set up a blast, workers drill holes on the rock face over several days. On the day of the blast, they spend about five hours loading these holes with the packaged explosives, often racing to complete their work during the permitted hours. The process blasts rock far away from the site, then large backhoes and trucks harvest and transport it to the crusher, where the rock is broken into smaller, more uniform pieces. The rock is then stored according to grade, and is ready for sale to the customer.

Drilling and blasting costs were a significant portion of a quarry's total operating costs. With strict controls on the storage and handling of explosives, quarries typically ordered just enough explosives for one blast, and had them delivered on blast day. The labor-intensive process allowed only a few quarries to compete in the industry, which is noted for large overcapacity.

A well-designed blast, however, could break the rock face into a pile of more uniform pieces—avoiding the large boulders that required secondary breakage before crushing—and would not throw rock more than thirty meters from the face, a danger as well as a waste of explosives. The rubble would then be much more easily harvested by the backhoes.

In 1985, ICI Explosives in Australia started supplying emulsion explosive in bulk from the back of a truck, rather than in the usual sausage packaging. After a customer placed an order, a Mobile Manufacturing Unit (MMU) containing intermediate chemicals arrived at the quarry, mixed the constituent chemicals on site, and delivered the resultant bulk emulsion explosive down predrilled blasting holes.

ICI also converted blasting from an empirical art to a precise science through laser profiling of the rock face and better blasting geometries. The improved consistency of the emulsion explosive and the detailed rock profiling reduced drilling time, thereby trimming overall drilling costs. Through better blast performance, ICI improved rock yield and reduced downstream processing costs.

ICI then began offering service contracts of "broken rock" to quarry customers, billing for their services based on the amount of broken rock of a certain defined size (as measured by the weighbridge), not for the amount of explosive supplied. The benefits for both the customer and ICI Explosives included:

- making the explosive part of an overall service, not a commodity;

- enabling ICI to make unconstrained deliveries to quarries since the component raw materials were nonexplosive until mixed; and

- giving the customer a fully charged set of blast holes, without excess explosive to store until the next blast.

Reduce Customer Costs Through Solutions. W.W. Grainger, the largest U.S. distributor of maintenance, repair, and operating (MRO) supplies with over five hundred thousand MRO products and sales of $5 billion, established Grainger Integrated Supply Operations (GISO) in 1995 in response to requests from customers (primarily manufacturing companies) for materials-management expertise and consulting.[10] Grainger Integrated Supply Operations was aimed at businesses seeking to outsource their entire indirect materials management process, to reduce costs related to process, product, and inventory. Grainger employees work on-site, managing different services related to indirect materials for the clients, such as business process reengineering, inventory management, supply chain management, tool crib management, and information management.

At first, GISO was available only to customers who ordered a minimum of $1 million of product per location per year. For such customers, the savings resulting from Grainger managing the procurement process for indirect materials was substantial in absolute terms. Consequently, Grainger could more easily earn an adequate return on investment on large clients like AlliedSignal, American Airlines, General Motors, and Universal Studios. Over time, it has reduced the threshold for participation.

To be a solution seller, W.W. Grainger established a technological platform of extranets, intranets, and private networks that allow GISO employees to access twelve thousand suppliers and over five million products. They use these networks to communicate with suppliers and to evaluate prices, product availability, and technical data. They can thus reduce redundancy and improve efficiency in the supply chain, thereby cutting costs. Companies who outsource their entire MRO process to GISO report cost reductions of 20 percent, a 60 percent decrease in inventory, and process-cycle phase improvements of between 50 and 80 percent. Additionally, this means customer employees who normally managed these MRO processes are now free to focus on core business. GISO has documented that this increases employee productivity as well as reduces defects for the customer.

Solution-selling strategies that are based on reducing customer costs take a holistic view of total customer costs rather than focusing simply on product costs. W.W. Grainger does not compete by reducing the prices of the products that the customer purchases. Instead, it focuses on lowering the customer's total costs (for example, products, handling, inventory, waste, and labor) of consuming MRO supplies.

Similarly, IBM promises significant costs reduction to those clients who sign multiyear contracts and outsource most of their IT operations to IBM. For example, in March 2002, IBM won a $500 million contract to provide the IT backbone for Nestlé's Globe project.[11] Nestlé, the world's biggest food company, is planning to centralize more than one hundred IT centers around the world into just five, as part of a plan to cut costs by $1.8 billion over five years. IBM will provide servers, storage systems, and database software for the five Globe data centers: two in Bussigny, Switzerland, and others in Sydney, Frankfurt, and Phoenix.

The IBM contract is part of Nestlé's attempt to set up a common IT platform that will allow it to consolidate and standardize its global business processes without losing its decentralized management structure. Over the years, Nestlé has duplicated IT and marketing support functions in most of the countries it operates. One of the main aims of the Globe project is to harmonize supplier, customer, and product data for Nestlé worldwide.

The Globe project, launched by CEO Peter Brabeck, could boost Nestlé's EBITDA (Earnings Before Interest, Taxes, Depreciation, and Amortization) by more than a quarter to 15.2 percent by 2006, for a compound growth in earnings per share of 15.1 percent between 2003 and 2006.

Design Products for Service

To support the new value proposition, top management must reevaluate almost every component of the value network. As a product-driven organization, IBM was focused on selling products, with services being a tactical weapon employed as needed to close sales. As a solution-driven company, service is the "product" that the customer is purchasing and the products are bundled in as needed.

For IBM to become a true solutions provider meant that its historical pride in developing the best quality stand-alone products became less critical for success. Instead, companies wishing to sell solutions have to concentrate on helping customers solve problems by integrating different products. Hence, solution sellers focus on product modularity and develop "plug-and-play" products that can easily integrate with their own, complementary, and even competitors' products.

To deliver on the promise that the system will perform seamlessly, companies must design products with ease-of-service in mind, since the solutions provider often supervises the system's operation on site.[12] If the products are expensive to service, then the contracts may become unprofitable. This is in stark contrast to the product-driven company, where servicing and replacement parts can generate considerable profits.

Select an Appropriate Product-Agnostic Posture

IBM and other companies often combine their previously incompatible products and services to create seamlessly operating systems that they market as "solutions." They then look for customers with problems that might fit their proprietary solution. In contrast to such systems selling, real solution selling involves working with a customer to uncover their problems and then designing a customized solution (see figure 3-2). The pre- and post-sales efforts are considerable and require a strong relationship with the customer.

No company can maintain a technological advantage in all the products necessary to complete solutions. In addition, customers may have their own brand preferences, based on legacy systems. For proud product companies, the most gut-wrenching change is to become product agnostic, allowing the customer to specify any brand of hardware, even competitors, as part of its solution.

FIGURE 3-2

Solution-Selling Matrix

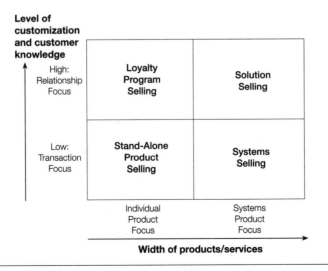

A company that recommends its own products even when they are not optimal for a particular application or customer reverts to selling products and systems rather than solutions. For example, a London department store chain that features home furnishings decided that consumers desired solutions to their home decoration problems. Therefore, the store deployed personal shopping assistants to help consumers. Unfortunately, the personal shopping assistants could recommend only furnishings in the store, which greatly reduced the assistants' efficacy.

Those people assigned to the solutions-selling unit in product-oriented companies often must choose between product logic and solution logic.[13] In client interactions, they need to assume a consultant identity to act in the client's best interest first, and in the product division's second. However, product divisions often expect the solutions unit to maintain a staff identity, demonstrating loyalty to the company brands. If the product logic dominates the solution logic, then the firm loses its ability and credibility to provide customer-centric solutions.

Product-Agnostic IBM?   IBM has attempted to make IGS hardware agnostic by blending technology from different sources like Sun or Hewlett-Packard and recommending the best for each application. In 1999, all IBM executives signed a "business partner charter" in which they pledged to bundle IBM products and services with competitors' superior products. Today, IBM boasts the "industry's most extensive Business Partner network"— seventy-two strategic software partners, including SAP and Siebel Systems. Its marketing and distribution muscle make it an attractive integrator for smaller software companies.

Partnering allows IGS to access more potential customers and provide a more complete palette of services to existing customers. Bob Timpson, general manager of IBM developer relations, summed up the partner rationale: "In the current world, you can't have just your own hardware, software, and sales force. You have to be part of a larger ecosystem."[14] Of course, one must always raise questions about brand integrity and performance guarantees on competitors' products.

Product agnosticism has lent credibility to IBM as a technology expert. As a solutions provider, IBM actively discussed how customers could leverage technology to improve their operations, innovation, and distribution channels. By blending technology from different sources, IBM built systems that responded to specific customer business needs. This product-agnostic customer focus has built trust between IBM and its customers.

Becoming a solutions provider is a journey, not a destination. IGS is still not truly agnostic regarding other hardware and software brands. If the customer wants a different platform, IGS will provide it, but reluctantly. Furthermore, IBM will keep its pledge to bundle products from competitors that are better, but only if that competitor is an approved IBM Business Partner, which is not an easy status to achieve. To help, IBM has instituted an incentive system for its consultants whereby their bonuses depend less on selling IBM products and more on meeting goals within the services business.

Does Having Great Products Hinder Solution Selling?   Following IBM's success, Hewlett-Packard (HP) has made at least three unsuccessful attempts to adopt a similar customer solutions strategy by integrating its vast range of products and undoubted technical capabilities.[15] Hewlett-Packard's merger with Compaq is its latest crack at becoming a more effective competitor against IBM.

Besides its highly decentralized culture, part of the problem for HP is its great engineering background and all the wonderful products it has created as a result of that. A culture of great engineering can become a handicap in making the transformation to solutions, since the company often falls in love with its products instead of its customers and their problems. In fact, one may argue that it is preferable for a solutions provider not to have proprietary products as it forces the firm to create customer value purely through integration.

Accenture, formerly Andersen Consulting, is an example of an information technology solutions provider with no products of its own in the classic sense. Instead, Accenture consultants look at the customer, map out the customer's processes, and then reengineer and automate them. The consultants spend their time understanding the client and its work practices instead of trying to sell products. When the time comes to select the hardware, Accenture can be relatively neutral. In fact, most customers do not specify a particular brand of hardware. Since usually more than one box can do the same function, Accenture buys from the most appropriate vendor for the deal. Accenture's only products are concepts and methodologies—this makes it particularly powerful as a solutions provider.

Price to Capture the Value of Solutions

Unlike products, setting the appropriate price for a solution is difficult, especially since no two solutions are identical. Even if the solution is identical, its value to different customers may differ considerably. The price must be delicately balanced between the value of the solution to the customer and the cost of providing it for the supplier.[16] If the price is too high, the customer may decide to buy individual components and develop their own solution. If the price is too low, then the supplier will not be adequately compensated for the effort that went into delivering it.

To avoid pricing solutions too low, the valued customer and value proposition must be clear. The value of the solution for the customer must be greater than the cost of its discrete components. The value should not lie in a quantity discount achieved by consolidating sales with one vendor. Solutions providers earn greater margins because the price of the whole package exceeds the prices of the discrete components.

Part of the value created for the customer accrues from the different pricing options offered by the solutions provider. Since most solutions deliver value over time, customers may differ considerably in how they pay for the value created based on their financial and risk profile. The options vary from a one-time, upfront payment (turnkey solution), a series of payments as the value is delivered (pay per use or milestone payments), a recurring monthly or yearly charge (periodic payments), or even revenue-sharing and equity participation.[17] In addition, there may be all types of fees for service, maintenance, operating, license, and consulting. These pricing strategies may be used separately or in combination and are a far cry from the dollars per box, pound, or ton mentality in most business markets.

Move from Free to Paid Services

There are several different ways to perceive the role of services in companies. Traditionally, in product companies, services are bundled free and are therefore a cost center. For example, companies often ask Cisco to provide information on becoming more e-business oriented and Cisco does not charge any fees for such advice. It believes that the equipment orders that result from sharing their expertise far outweigh the cost of providing such consultancy services.[18]

At IBM in the 1960s and 1970s, the margins on mainframes were so high that IBM could bundle all its services in them. As it became a solutions provider, IBM started unbundling the services and charging individually for them. One of its most successful strategies has been pursuing large multiyear service contracts, which has become a model for competitors such as HP.[19]

As the Cisco and IBM examples demonstrate, companies take different positions along the following continuum regarding the role of services: (1) provided free in support of products; (2) partial cost recovery; (3) full cost recovery; (4) independent profit center in support of products; or (5) an independent business unit that supports and utilizes competitors' products.[20] Solutions providers fall into the final category. Companies usually do not jump from free services to solutions; instead they tend to go through one or more of the intermediate stages.

Making the transition from free to paid services is difficult because companies struggle to make customers realize the value and the costs of the free services that they receive. Part of the difficulty lies in the fact that all customers do not equally value these free services. Some customers consume significant amounts of free services while others barely use them. Consequently, charging for these previously free services is an effective way to segment customers, as heavy users of services now have to pay for them whereas those customers who do not consume services receive more competitive prices. Yet, convincing heavy users to start paying for services is not easy, as Internet business models—which are based on providing free services to end users in exchange for ancillary revenue streams such as advertising (Yahoo!, for example)—have discovered.[21] The best way to approach this problem is by using the matrix in table 3-2 developed by two professors, James Anderson and James Narus. The process begins by selecting a segment and then listing under each heading in the first column the services currently offered to that segment as a standard (that is, for free), those offered as options for additional fees, and the new services that the company is contemplating offering. For

TABLE 3-2

Service Offering Matrix

Service Element Status	Offer as "Standard"	Offer as "Optional"	Do Not Offer
Existing "standard" services: 1. _____ 2. _____ 3. _____	Retain in standard offering	Recast as value-added option	Prune from standard offering
Existing "optional" services: 1. _____ 2. _____ 3. _____	Recast to enhance standard offering	Retain as value-added option	Prune option
New services: 1. _____ 2. _____ 3. _____	Augment standard offering	Introduce as value-added option	Keep on shelf

Source: Adapted from James C. Anderson and James A. Narus, *Business Market Management: Understanding, Creating, and Delivering Value* (Upper Saddle River, NJ: Prentice Hall, 1999), 176. Reprinted by permission of Pearson Education, Inc., Upper Saddle River, NJ.

each standard, optional, or potential new service, one should then ask whether this service should be: (a) offered for free (that is, "standard") because most customers place a value on it; (b) offered as an option because only some customers place a value on it; or (c) removed from the offer because very few customers place any value on it or the cost of providing it outstrips the value for customers. Once this decision has been made, the matrix suggests how each service should be managed.

Given the difficulty of persuading customers to pay for existing free services, it is easier to begin the process by innovating and developing new services, which are offered for a fee as a way of conditioning customers into paying for services. Simultaneously, one can send phantom invoices (usually with the words "do not pay") to unprofitable customers whenever they consume a free service so that they begin perceiving the value thereof. Companies that find ways to communicate value can convert freeloaders of services into paying customers over time. Finally, one can also develop two versions of a service: a free one and an enhanced version for a premium. For example, Hotmail accounts with limited functionality are free, whereas paid accounts come with full functionality.

For many product companies, services now account for a significant, fast-growing portion of their revenues.[22] Of Otis Elevator's $5 billion revenues, two-thirds come from service and maintenance fees. ABB Service manages more than 100 large, full-service contracts worldwide for maintaining its or competitors' equipment.

Build Solution-Selling Capabilities

Effective solution selling requires developing new capabilities and significant investments of scarce resources such as time, people, and money. The lack of these requirements has stalled many firms in their transition from selling products to providing solutions.

Change the Mind-Set to Take Responsibility for Customer Outcomes

An agonizing change in mind-set is necessary in order to transition to solution selling. In a product-driven company, everything begins and ends with the existing product and its functions, and a constant search for new applications and new customers. If the product is not ideal for some customers or applications, then the firm either adds a new product feature or develops a new product.[23] Regardless, the company can solve only those problems that correspond with the company's own products.[24] In contrast, a solution-driven company starts with a customer problem and guarantees the desired customer outcome, which usually requires taking responsibility for the entire process at the customer's site.

For example, instead of selling gallons of paint to car manufacturers, one paint supplier manages the painting process and charges the automakers a fixed fee per painted car. In the earlier approach, the more paint that was wasted in the car manufacturing process, the greater the profits for the supplier since it meant that it sold more paint. But after taking over the painting process, waste in the painting process meant lower profits for the paint supplier since paint was now a cost in its capacity as a solution provider.

Map the Entire Customer Process

Solution sellers often create value by sparing the customer the hassle and cost of dealing with multiple suppliers, as well as by reducing the ordeal of integrating the components and services. To understand the value of seamless operations, for example, consider the following scenario of a customer attempting to resolve a problem. The software provider says the problem is in the hardware, the hardware provider says the problem lies with the network connection, the network support company says the problem is the

FIGURE 3-3

Customer Activity Cycle of Akzo Nobel's DIY Consumer

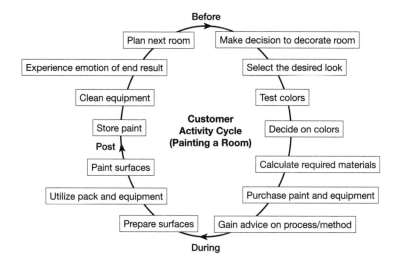

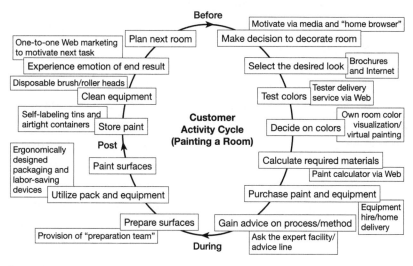

Source: Akzo Nobel.

phone line, while the telephone company says the problem is with the software. Solutions providers instead provide one contact point.

Providing a seamless solution for the customer requires mapping out the entire business process for the customer and developing a solution that makes it easier for the customer to consume the product. The seller's process must fit with the customer's process, and each customer may have a different process. Rather than focus on the product, the entire customer activity cycle related to consuming the product must be articulated.[25] As an example, figure 3-3 elaborates the process that a do-it-yourself painter must go through to paint a room.

Assess Customer Total Cost

As the Hendrix-Voeders, ICI Explosives, and W.W. Grainger examples demonstrate, solution sellers must thoroughly understand the operating economics of their customers. In addition to taking responsibility for the customer's outcome and mapping the customer's process end to end, the solution seller must document the customer's total costs of consuming the product.

Articulating the total costs requires outlining all the different acquisition costs (price, prepurchase evaluation, shopping time, paper work, expedition of the order, mistakes in order, and travel costs), possession costs (interest, taxes and insurance, storage, installations, handling, shrinkage, obsolescence, and quality control), and usage costs (downtime, parts and supplies, training, user labor, product longevity, replacement, and disposal).[26] Discussing this with a customer widens their focus from just the product price.

Consider Airbus's success over Boeing. Airbus can provide a fleet of different aircraft with the same cockpit design and similar flying traits.[27] Such similitude lowers costs since Airbus users do not need to retrain pilots whenever they switch aircraft, and airlines can schedule pilots to fly various planes. While Boeing can offer extremely attractive prices, the initial capital cost of a plane represents only a small part of the cost of each flight hour.

C. C. Tung, chairman of Orient Overseas Container Line, remarks, "We are training our staff to function more as logistics consultants than service providers . . . to avoid competing on price alone. . . . [Transportation] is a relatively small part of the our major customers' total logistics expenditures, so we are . . . helping them in other ways, such as reducing interest costs through minimum stocking [and] improving cash flow through speedy and error free documentation."[28]

Educate Customers About Total Costs

Unfortunately, customers are often unaware of the operating economics of their own business processes. Consequently, the solution seller must educate the customer. For example, Douwe Egberts, part of Sara Lee, has developed a freshly brewed coffee solution called Cafitesse for professional food service operators in Europe. A modular system incorporates high-speed brewing (a cappuccino in nine seconds) and reduced cleaning and maintenance, while producing little waste in terms of coffee, filters, or coffee remains. The coffee-brewing market, as one would expect, is extremely price sensitive, and focus is often on the price per kilogram of coffee. The coffee used in the Cafitesse solution does not compare favorably on a price per kilo basis but coffee by itself accounts for only about 20 to 30 percent (up to 40 percent in some cases) of the total costs of making a cup of coffee. The remaining elements are usually forgotten by, or hidden from, the customer, leading to erroneous cost comparisons between different coffee brewing solutions.

To help educate the customer, Douwe Egberts developed an extensive and transparent Excel spreadsheet. It calculates the current cost per cup for the customer using their existing solution and then compares that with the cost per cup using the Cafitesse solution. The comparison considers many different elements including cleaning time, depreciation, filters, power, water usage, waste of coffee brewed, and so on—elements that all are part of a cup of coffee, no matter how the customer chooses to brew it. The high-speed and lower-waste features of Cafitesse help reduce the cost per cup. As an example of waste, consider that 98.5 percent of a "normal" cup of coffee is water. If 20 percent of the brewed coffee is wasted when using a conventional coffee system, both coffee and water are important elements in the waste equation. By supplying the customer with a system that reduces waste, pricing turns into something more than just "per kilo" prices.

Customers are often surprised when confronted with the costs of their existing brewing method. The spreadsheet makes them more open to listening to Cafitesse's arguments. Looking at the total cost per cup of coffee, where Cafitesse compares rather favorably, changes the conversation with the customer from price to taste.

Similarly, W.W. Grainger conducts a detailed analysis for large companies to demonstrate that in consuming indirect materials, process costs account for approximately 70 percent of a product's total cost. One of its advertisements—"It took seven people to buy this hammer. The hammer costs $17. Their time costs $100"— helps educate purchasing agents that most of the monetary savings do not lie in pushing the supplier to lower product costs.

Develop Knowledge Banks

Solution selling is information intensive. To sell solutions, a company must have extensive information on each customer and their business processes, as well as the ability to slice the data in multiple ways. For example, as part of its customer relationship management (CRM) process, IBM maintains up-to-date estimates of the needs of its thousand largest customers.[29] These estimates include both current requirements as well as projections of their future needs. Customers are then ranked according to their growth rates and estimated lifetime value to IBM.

Often, companies sell a high level of customized information bundled around the original product. By becoming an expert in the consumption process through benchmarking across customers, the seller can deliver knowledge on how best to apply the product. The knowledge that Hendrix Voeders, IBM, ICI Explosives, and W.W. Grainger ultimately sell to their customers becomes the true distinguishing—and constantly growing, if well managed—core competence of the organization. The more a firm uses it, the more powerful it grows in the marketplace, and competitors cannot easily copy it.

To sell solutions effectively, a company must have a system that provides companywide access to otherwise isolated pools of expertise. IBM is investing in an online inventory of its knowledge so that the IBM intranet can function as a collaborative portal for its solution sellers. One feature is an "expertise locator" which could, for example, help an employee find a software engineer who can build a Linux database.

Transforming the Organization for Solution Selling

Solution selling clearly has critical implications for the organization. If the organization does not morph, then the solutions strategy will atrophy, especially in large companies. Consider IBM's transformation.

Corporate Fault Zones

Effective solution selling requires the salesperson to quickly diagnose the critical issues facing the client and then craft a customized and complete solution that fits the customer's requirements. To succeed, the salesperson must have a keen insight into their company's capabilities, as well as the ability to deeply understand the business of the customer. This may mean hiring outsiders, perhaps from the customer's industry, who have an extensive knowledge of the customer's business processes and costs.

IBM realized the challenge that a salesperson faced in selling a computer to a bank one day, to a retailer the next day, and to an oil and gas company on the following day. The only way a salesperson could accomplish this was by being an expert in the products rather than being an expert on customer problems. If the sales force were to evolve from being order takers to becoming consultants to customers, they needed to become industry experts.

If the IBM salesperson sold an IT solution to a large multinational customer, then delivery required mobilizing several country and product divisions. In a sense, the solutions provider guaranteed that many parts of many different units would collaborate.[30] But the seats of power in IBM belonged to product chiefs and especially the geographic heads. If you were the president of IBM France, it was like an ambassadorship. You had a huge organization with lots of staff work, secretaries, and bureaucracy. Thus, IBM's organizational structure impeded providing solutions to customers, while system integrators, who put together products from different vendors to solve customer problems, were gaining influence at IBM's expense. In response, Gerstner designated fourteen industry sectors for IBM to dominate (for example, financial services and retailing) and appointed individuals to lead each one.

Many of the new IBM industry heads were outsiders selected on the basis of having the personality and power to go head-to-head with the IBM geographic and product chiefs. The product and country heads became internal suppliers to these industry heads as the latter attempted to create customer solutions. A few country managers resisted reporting to the industry heads and some of them ultimately left the firm. Creating solutions for large multinational clients required coordinated efforts that cut across multiple products and countries. The firm reorganized the geographically assigned sales force along industry lines and developed new coordinating processes, such as transfer pricing to allow product units to sell internally, and structures, like strong regional leadership, to allocate resources to solutions.

The Transition Process

While it looks revolutionary in its implications, the change from a product company to a solutions company is an evolutionary process. It takes time and effort to convert product customers into solution buyers. During this period, the current as well as the future business models must be managed. Managing on these two levels presents a complex management challenge.

The traditional product- and country-based business units must continue to perform while the new team-based organization responsible for customer solutions floats on top of them. Dedicated customer solution teams will draw together elements from different business units to deliver on particular projects. During the transition, the previous clear-cut accountability, hierarchy, lines of authority, and dedicated resources will be under stress from the new business units, which are organized around fluid teams and opportunities, and managed by project owners who lack direct control over the necessary resources.[31]

Employees who will be providing customer solutions need expertise from relevant product groups, industry consultants, and country specialists to implement integrated solutions. For them, the company must function as a portfolio of resources, not business units.[32] But the traditional proprietors of these resources—the product and country managers—will view such sharing of scarce resources as unrequited costs and worse, as they lose their best customers to solutions teams.[33] Compensation committees must review incentive systems so that compensation plans for top managers stress contributions to the company, relative to their business units.

Transformational Leadership

To transition to solutions selling, companies need the type of transformational leadership that Lou Gerstner provided at IBM. Gerstner cut costs, overhauled the culture, and instilled the customer-centric mind-set. While revenues had been consistently high, IBM's internal fiefdoms made the costs of doing business even higher. Gerstner reportedly remarked when he first took over, "We're making $64 billion a year. By far, the most money spent in the information technology business is being spent with us. The problem is that it's costing us $69 billion to do it."[34]

Gerstner's transformational leadership played several important roles in IBM's turnaround. First, he brought his external viewpoints to an inward-looking, myopic culture. A former IBM customer, he understood market and industry issues enough to make IBM a much better partner to its customers. By focusing on customers rather than technology, he amassed a vital intellectual power over the rest of the organization.

Second, Gerstner realized that IBM needed senior management with no loyalty to IBM's past winning concepts and practices. He sought experts who could understand customers and cut costs.[35] Breaking precedent, he chose his vice president of marketing and vice president of communications from outside IBM, and then hired Chrysler's Jerry York as CFO to cut costs in a tough environment.

Third, since Gerstner appreciated IBM's brand strength and potential impact on the market and marketing process, he kept the company intact rather than divest underperforming units. Keeping the company intact was the single most valuable decision he made for shareholders.

Fourth, as an ex-McKinsey consultant, Gerstner recognized the importance of aligning structure with strategy and worked tirelessly to harmonize the various IBM units and minimize the turf wars. Gerstner's early successes endeared him to the IBM troops fairly rapidly.

Samuel J. Palmisano, IBM's current CEO, remarked, "The DNA of the IBM company is what it always stood for. But get rid of the bad in the DNA—rigid behavior, starched white shirts, straw hats, company songs . . . that caused us to become insular, focused on ourselves. Beating up your colleagues was more important than winning in the marketplace. Lou [Gerstner] did a lot to knock all that down."[36]

FIGURE 3-4

A Solutions Organization

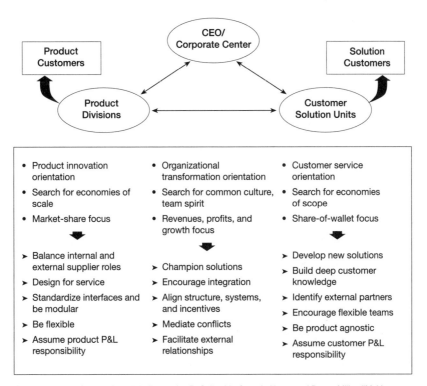

- Product innovation orientation
- Search for economies of scale
- Market-share focus

- Organizational transformation orientation
- Search for common culture, team spirit
- Revenues, profits, and growth focus

- Customer service orientation
- Search for economies of scope
- Share-of-wallet focus

➤ Balance internal and external supplier roles
➤ Design for service
➤ Standardize interfaces and be modular
➤ Be flexible
➤ Assume product P&L responsibility

➤ Champion solutions
➤ Encourage integration
➤ Align structure, systems, and incentives
➤ Mediate conflicts
➤ Facilitate external relationships

➤ Develop new solutions
➤ Build deep customer knowledge
➤ Identify external partners
➤ Encourage flexible teams
➤ Be product agnostic
➤ Assume customer P&L responsibility

Source: Adapted from Nathaniel W. Foote, Jay R. Galbraith, Quentin Hope, and Danny Miller, "Making Solutions the Answer," *McKinsey Quarterly* 3 (2001): 84–93.

With help from the corporate center, CEOs play an important role in championing the case for customer solutions. They must help with the collaboration process, to iron out the conflicts that rise to their attention. They may have to sponsor initiatives to change the resource allocation process within the company. Projects need to be ranked to ensure that the most valuable resources are chasing the most valuable solution-selling opportunities. Figure 3-4 summarizes the organizational architecture supportive of solution selling.

Solutions Checklist

Valued Customer and Value Proposition

- *Have we defined criteria to identify customers who are willing to pay for solutions?*

- *What is our primary value proposition to solution customers— increase revenues, lower total costs, or reduce risk?*

- *Do we offer customers various payment options such as pay per use, revenue, or cost savings sharing?*

- *Do we guarantee customer outcomes instead of product performance?*

- *Are we product agnostic?*

- *Do we truly make money off integration (charge more than the prices of the products bundled in the solution)?*

Solution Capabilities

- *Are we focused on developing modular products that interface easily with our own and competitors' products?*

- *Do we have the capability of guaranteeing system performance at customer sites?*

Conclusion

Jack Welch of General Electric noted: "The winners will be those who deliver solutions from the users' point of view. That is a big part of Marketing's job." However, as a company attempts to transform itself from a seller of products to a provider of customer solutions, it will observe that many of its strengths, such as a decentralized organization, great technology, and strong

- *Have we developed effective tools to assess customer value?*

- *Have our salespeople developed consulting skills and deep customer industry knowledge?*

- *Can we articulate customers' total costs and operating economics?*

- *Do we have the industry's best customer information and knowledge bank?*

- *Do we have strong project management skills?*

Organizing for Solutions

- *Do our product and country organizations support solution selling?*

- *Is the CEO championing the solutions initiative?*

- *Have we developed effective processes to allocate resources to solution projects?*

- *Does the organizational incentive system support the delivery of solutions to customers?*

- *How good are our coordinating mechanisms (for example, transfer pricing) for serving solutions to customers?*

product divisions, become precisely those things that stop the firm from making an effective transition.

Developing customer solutions entails having a thorough understanding of the customer activity cycle and customer total costs. Information on the differential economic benefits that each customer will receive from the solution provided is critical. To deliver the customer solution requires a broader skill set, the risk profile to take greater responsibility for performance at the customer site, more flexible operations and organization, and the ability to manage numerous partnerships with suppliers and competitors. Additionally, capturing the value of solutions delivered to customers requires offering flexible pricing options. The box "Solutions Checklist" provides a checklist for solutions. Considerable investments are needed to capture the learning acquired from each project. A proprietary database that is continuously updated with data on each customer, implementation process learning, and solution technology is essential.

The successful solutions company is a networked company. It has the ability to integrate diverse production skills and multiple streams of technology from a variety of companies, including itself. It must quickly see new opportunities to solve customer problems and exploit them through flexible structures and declining transactions costs. The ideal solutions provider has an organization that is people-, knowledge-, and process-intensive but asset-light. Its focus is on knowledge—learning about customers, collaborative learning with partners, and learning to leverage network partners' resources and competences. Instead of filling capacity or assets, it focuses on using knowledge to leverage its primary asset—people. This is what allows it to earn higher margins than its competitors.

To achieve all of this requires, most of all, a change in mindset. Without a focused effort from the top of the organization, the move to selling solutions is doomed to succumb to the overwhelming corporate inertia that haunts most large organizations. For the transformation to succeed, someone, most likely the CEO, must stake his or her career on it.

FOUR

From Declining to Growing Distribution Channels

Let us keep the cannibals in the family.

A S A NEW CHANNEL, the Internet complicated distribution not only by facilitating the delivery of digital goods and services like news and music but also by enabling dynamically priced transactions for just about any physical good or service—among perfect strangers. Electronic marketplaces have proliferated for business-to-business (B2B) sales (for example, FreeMarkets), business-to-consumer (B2C) retail, resale, and referrals (for example, Amazon), and consumer-to-consumer (C2C) resale and services (for example, eBay).

The Internet is but one of several technologies affecting distribution, and new channels inevitably startle managers at large, established firms. Should they rapidly develop new competences and exploit these emerging channels to reach new customers, often at lower costs, or should they wait until the format matures? Will they cannibalize current revenues or jeopardize long-standing reseller partnerships?

Such incumbent dithering allows upstarts like Amazon, Charles Schwab, Dell, Direct Line, easyJet, and IKEA to seize advantage and disrupt industry leaders through channel inflexions, or disruptions that overturn industry channel structure, in industries such as entertainment, financial services, communications, computing, publishing, software, and travel. Charles Schwab has developed the financial supermarket model by concentrating on distribution in a traditionally vertically integrated industry. Citigroup has aggressively shifted customers and transactions to ATM machines, while Direct Line has become the largest automobile insurance company in the United Kingdom by using telephone-based selling. Dell and easyJet have developed cost-efficient business models based on selling directly to consumers while disintermediating traditional retailers and travel agents, respectively. Michael O'Leary, CEO of Ryanair, notes, "Four years ago we sold 60 percent . . . through travel agents, who charged us about 9 percent of the ticket price. Then computerized reservations added about another 6 percent. So we were paying about 15 percent for distribution. Today, 96 percent of our sales are sold across Ryanair.com, and the cost is about a cent per ticket."[1]

Observing the success of these new entrants, incumbents are finally realizing the strategic role of distribution and the need to adjust their channel strategies. Under pressure to generate top-line growth in a tough economic and competitive environment, senior executives cannot overlook innovative channels that reach new segments and significantly cut costs.

But channel migration from the old to the new rarely happens without turmoil and top management support. Line marketing managers will simply not challenge entrenched internal and external constituencies without top management's support. Reconfiguring channels demands a CEO like O'Leary: "British Airways says you can't upset the travel agents. . . . Screw the travel agents! . . . What have they done for passengers over the years?"[2]

Channel Migration Strategies

When a new distribution channel emerges, managers must ask two essential questions: (1) To what extent does the new channel

FIGURE 4-1

Channel Migration Strategies

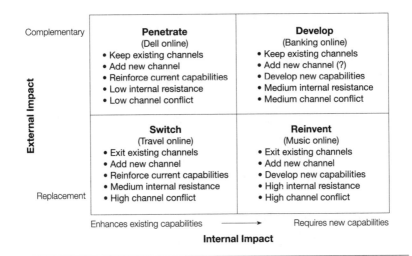

complement or replace existing industry distribution channels? (2) To what extent does the new channel enhance or devalue our existing capabilities and value network? The answers should help pinpoint the necessary channel migration strategy, the level of internal resistance, and the external channel conflict that one should anticipate, as well as provide insight into the migration process (see figure 4-1).

Replacement Versus Complementary Effects

Supermarkets that displaced "mom-and-pop" stores in the United States illustrate the replacement effects of new distribution channels.[3] The supermarket's value proposition of a better assortment, one-stop shopping, and substantially lower prices for a little more travel surpassed that of mom-and-pop stores. Consequently, the absolute number of mom-and-pops and their relative market share both declined.

In contrast, television and home video extended the distribution channels of the motion picture industry. When television first appeared in the 1950s, Hollywood studio market values fell dramatically. The same happened with cinema companies when home video first appeared. In each instance, managers and analysts overlooked two important issues.

First, the value proposition of the new distribution channel (television and home video) was different from, but not superior to, the existing channel (cinema theatres). Home video, for example, offers greater assortment, time flexibility, informality, and lower prices, whereas cinemas are venues for a "date" or "an evening out." The two distribution channels have clearly delineated value propositions for distinct customer usage segments and can therefore coexist.

Second, home video allowed consumers to watch movies when tired, dressed down, wanting solitude, or homebound by babies or illness, or when cinemas were closed or no longer running a particular film. Television and video expanded the market for motion pictures and provided substantial additional streams of revenues for the industry. Producers no longer relied solely on cinema revenues to break even. For example, in 2002, U.S. box office revenues were $10.1 billion, but combined sales and rental of VHS tapes and DVD discs exceeded $25 billion.[4]

Whether a new distribution channel complements or displaces existing distribution channels highlights the nature of channel migration. In replacements, the existing customer segments buy from the new channels of distribution and abandon the existing channels. In contrast, complementary distribution channels open up new segments of customers or new value propositions for existing products. Cannibalization, channel conflict, and resistance to change obviously occur more in replacement situations.

Replacement channels force incumbents to abandon existing channels and focus on new channels of distribution. The ability to purchase airline tickets or book hotel and car reservations over the Internet will not likely increase the number of vacations or business trips consumed. Instead, with the necessary information accessible online, many customers will simply not need a travel agent. No wonder three hundred storefront travel agents are closing per month, and the share of U.S. domestic airline reservations booked through independent travel agents has declined from 80 percent to less than 50 percent.

Replacement effects also obligate managers to determine which channels and segments are affected. For example, leisure consumers for airline travel are migrating faster to Internet channels than business travelers. Based on the firm's competitive position in each segment, one may decide to accelerate the migration, as easyJet does by offering discounts to customers who book on the Web, or decelerate by refusing to accommodate the new channel.

In contrast, complementary effects compel companies to move certain types of transactions and customers to the new channel of distribution. New channels add to the existing value network without substantially lowering the value of existing distribution outlets. Marketers must communicate these economics to distribution members who may irrationally fear any new outlet. Sharing independent market research demonstrating the complementary effects works especially well in reducing channel member anxiety.

Turning Core Capabilities into Core Rigidities

The emergence of a new type of distribution channel usually generates considerable excitement as companies see the potential for increased coverage, lowered costs, and/or greater control. Unfortunately, innovative new distribution channels also aggravate industry incumbents. Established companies often fear that new, especially radically new, distribution channels will harm them by obsolescing competences, devaluing their distribution network assets, ossifying their core capabilities, and eroding their industry leadership positions. To illustrate these repercussions, let us examine the channel transitions in the PC industry.

Channel Migration in the PC Industry.   In 1981, almost 80 percent of personal computer sales were through a combination of a direct sales force serving the large accounts and full-service PC dealers reaching the rest. Currently, direct sales and PC dealers account for less than 40 percent of the industry sales with the remainder flowing through a multiplicity of channels including value-added resellers (VARs), direct response pioneered by Dell, mass merchandisers dominated by Wal-Mart, warehouse clubs like Price Club/Costco, consumer electronic superstores populated by Best Buy and Circuit City, computer superstores led by CompUSA, and office product superstores such as Staples. In addition, there are numerous Internet operations of brick-and-mortar and pure play retailers. During the intervening years, channel transitions have played a major role in determining the changing fortunes of PC manufacturers such as Compaq, Dell, and IBM.

COMPAQ VERSUS DELL. Today, the worldwide PC market leaders are Compaq and Dell. However, as table 4-1 demonstrates, the business models of the two companies differ significantly. Compaq has a value network typical of branded products:

TABLE 4-1

Business Models of Dell Versus Compaq

	Dell	Compaq
Valued Customer	Knowledgeable customer buying multiple units	Multiple customer segments with varied needs
Value Proposition	Customized PC at competitive price	"Brand" with quality image
Value Network		
R&D	Limited	Considerable
Manufacturing	Flexible assembly, cost disadvantage	High-speed, low-variety, low-cost manufacturing system
Supply Chain	Made-to-order; one week, primarily component inventory	Made-to-stock; one month, primarily finished-product inventory
Marketing	Moderate sales response advertising	Expensive brand advertising
Sales and Distribution	Direct	Primarily through third-party resellers

relatively high R&D expenditures; low-cost, low-variety, large-run manufacturing systems; one-month finished products inventory; and third-party resellers. In the early 1990s—when IBM, with its large direct sales force, was ambivalent about third-party resellers—Compaq dedicated itself to PC sales through resellers, thereby endearing it to resellers, whose subsequent push catapulted Compaq into market leadership in 1992.

Dell primarily targeted corporate accounts but with built-to-order, customized PCs at reasonable prices. It invented a radically different value network combining minimal R&D expenditures, made-to-order, flexible manufacturing systems (which give Dell a slight manufacturing cost disadvantage compared to Compaq), one-week parts inventory, and an efficient direct distribution system. In the early 1990s, this direct distribution system took orders through toll-free telephone numbers and delivered through various courier services.

DELL'S RETAIL EXPERIENCE.   As the value curves in figure 4-2 indicate, the value proposition of serving customers through Dell Direct differs from that through retail stores. In 1991, to reach those small business customers and individual consumers who preferred to shop at retail outlets, Dell decided to expand its distribution to retailers such as Business Depot in Canada; CompUSA, Sam's Club, and Staples in the United States and Mexico; and PC World in the United Kingdom.[5] However, unlike the customization option available through the Dell Direct channel, since selling through retail stores required Dell to build for inventory, only a limited number of preset PC configurations could be offered in the indirect channel. Despite this limitation, channel expansion to retail stores brought immediate and impressive sales gains for Dell as revenues rose from about $900 million in 1991 to more than $2.8 billion in 1993.

Unfortunately, the sales gains through the retail channels did not result in additional profits. Dell's internal cost of selling fell from 14 percent in the direct channel to 10 percent in the indirect channel as retailers took responsibility for some channel functions. However, this did not fully offset the 12 percent margin that

FIGURE 4-2

Value Curves: Dell Direct Versus Retail

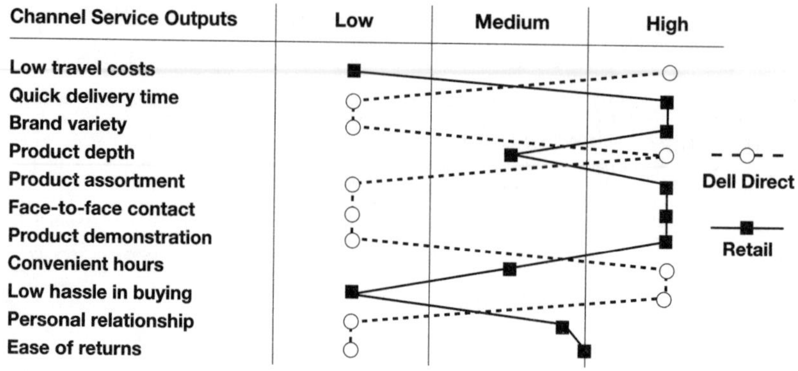

Channel Service Outputs	Low	Medium	High
Low travel costs			
Quick delivery time			
Brand variety			
Product depth			
Product assortment			
Face-to-face contact			
Product demonstration			
Convenient hours			
Low hassle in buying			
Personal relationship			
Ease of returns			

– –◯– –   Dell Direct

■——■   Retail

retailers had to be given for their sales efforts. As a result, it was 8 percent more expensive for Dell to sell through indirect channels. Given that its operating income was only 5 percent in the Dell Direct channel, it was losing 3 percent in the indirect channels. And the more volume Dell pushed through the retail channels, the more money it lost. In 1993, Dell posted its first loss of $36 million. By mid-1994, Dell decided to exit the retail channel and concentrate on direct distribution. This decision turned profits around to $149 million in 1994.

Beyond the economics, Dell sidelined many of its core capabilities and advantages when sales went through retail. Michael Dell explained,

> *Our direct model . . . turns inventory 12 times, while our competitors who sell through retail only turn their inventory 6 times. Even though customization increases our costs by 5%, we [can] get a 15% price premium because of the upgrades and added features. But for the standard configurations we offered through retail, we [could not] get any premium in the market. . . . Compaq, not us, got a 10% price advantage.*[6]

COMPAQ, DELL, AND INTERNET DISTRIBUTION.   In the mid-
1990s, Compaq and Dell explored how to exploit the Internet.
What made the Internet so exciting was the opportunity to have a
one-to-one dialogue with the customer (interactive capacity) and
then to respond with a unique, customized offer (responsive
capacity).Thanks to its value network, Dell exploited the unique
features of the Internet, and sales through the Internet were a natural extension of the "Dell Direct Model." It launched its Web site
in July 1996.

Compaq, on the other hand, struggled to exploit the Internet,
because to do so would force it to customize PCs and bypass dealers. However, delivering customized products at competitive
prices with high-volume, low-variety manufacturing systems is
tricky. How could Compaq promote sales through the Internet
without upsetting its resellers and jeopardizing its historically
strong relationships with them?

Compaq lagged Dell by almost three years in adopting direct
sales through the Internet. To limit direct competition, Compaq
initially designed a new line of PCs, Prosignia, for direct online
sales. When retailers objected, it offered this line through retail
channels as well. The Internet channel had turned Compaq's core
competences and distribution network assets—low-cost manufacturing systems and strong relationships with third-party
resellers—into core rigidities. By 1999, Dell overtook Compaq as
the U.S. market leader with online PC sales of $30 million daily.

Regardless of whether a new channel complements or displaces existing distribution channels at an industry level, it will
likely affect the core competences and distribution network assets
of existing players in different ways. Therein lies a large part of
the disruptive nature of new distribution channels: New channels
may help some companies leverage their core competences and
distribution assets, while it hinders other companies within the
same industry. How competences and assets are affected depends
on how a company competes within an industry. But the need to
develop new capabilities usually generates considerable internal

resistance as it devalues the power of those within the organization who run the existing value network.

The Reinvention of Music Distribution Business Models. As illustrated in figure 4-1, the most difficult channel migration strategy is to reinvent distribution channels. Reinvention is necessary in the face of both replacement effects and the need to develop new capabilities. In such cases, the importance of business model transformation cannot be overestimated. New distribution channels that are convenient and attractive from the consumer's perspective can languish without profitable business models. This situation currently pervades online distribution of digital products like movies, music, games, books, and software. In particular, online distribution of music is having a potentially dramatic, and some would say destructive, impact on existing industry business models.

THE MUSIC INDUSTRY COST STRUCTURE.   The average prerecorded music CD sells in the retail store for about fifteen dollars. Figure 4-3 attempts to break down its cost structure. Two things are particularly relevant when examining the industry's traditional value chain. First, distribution-related costs account for a relatively high proportion, 40 to 50 percent, of the total price. Second, predicting which products will be a "hit" is a relatively difficult proposition for the industry. So music companies guarantee retailers the right to return unsold product for full credit. Some 15 to 25 percent of the product comes back. The absolute costs of handling these returns, included in distribution and logistics, are enormous.

GRAMOPHONE COMPANY OF INDIA.   Given the cost structure of the CDs, and a similar situation in the book publishing industry, online sales is a rather attractive opportunity for these manufacturers. Consider the Gramophone Company of India, the largest music publisher in India.[7] Gramophone owns the rights to forty-five thousand albums or 50 percent of all Indian music ever recorded. However, it is only economically viable for the company to rerelease an old album and keep it in print if the demand

FIGURE 4-3

Cost Breakdown for a Compact Disc

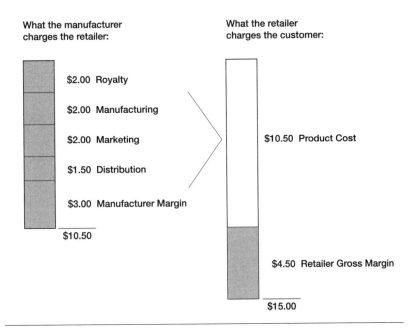

What the manufacturer
charges the retailer:

What the retailer
charges the customer:

$2.00 Royalty

$2.00 Manufacturing

$2.00 Marketing

$10.50 Product Cost

$1.50 Distribution

$3.00 Manufacturer Margin

$10.50

$4.50 Retailer Gross Margin

$15.00

justifies a production run of five thousand copies. As a result, between years 1995 and 2000, only 17 percent of the album catalog was being exploited, or in industry jargon, was in print. Sales were through brick-and-mortar retailers with about 15 percent of sales being returned as unsold stock. In terms of distribution, Gramophone Company, like other music companies, was squarely in the lower left-hand corner (box 1) of the distribution matrix of figure 4-4.

The emergence of the Internet brought with it the opportunity to sell directly to consumers and move to box 4. Since the Indian music retail industry is highly fragmented, mostly populated by mom-and-pop stores, channel conflict was not a major concern. For the music manufacturer, selling online had the benefits of not having to pay the retailer's margin, greater customer knowledge, and positive working capital. Since the mailing costs for CDs and cassettes were not high and consumers would pay some additional

FIGURE 4-4

Online Music Distribution Opportunity Matrix

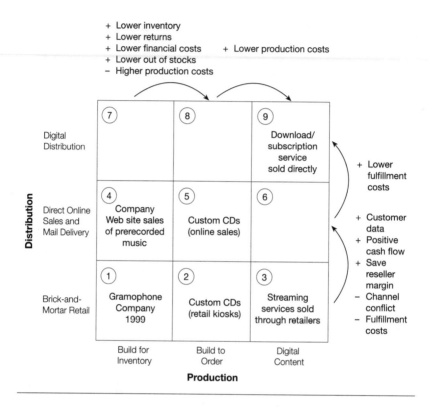

shipping costs, the fulfillment costs did not overwhelm the advantages of online sales. Expanding into direct online sales was easy.

A special division called HamaraCD investigated customized CDs where consumers could select songs from the manufacturer's Web site (box 5) or at a retail kiosk (box 2). The manufacturing costs of a custom CD were somewhat higher than a prerecorded CD but the additional benefits of no inventory, fewer returns, and allowing the entire catalog to be offered (no out-of-stock situation) more than compensated for this. Furthermore, consumers place a 50 percent higher value on custom CDs, allowing the manufacturer to charge a higher price.

THE SEARCH FOR A DIGITAL DISTRIBUTION MODEL.   Broadband Internet has opened up an entirely new, completely digital form of music distribution. By allowing customers to directly download or stream music off a server, both production and distribution costs decline dramatically (boxes 3 and 9). Suddenly, the music, an information product, is freed from the tyranny of the plastic CD box, a physical product, and the problems that come with managing physical manufacturing and supply chains. Unfortunately, worried about piracy and faced with the need to develop new business models, music companies were too slow to exploit digital distribution.

Time is now running out for music companies to find that new business model. The global recording industry has shrunk for the sixth consecutive year (down from 785 million CDs and cassettes in 2000 to 681 million in 2002), while the sales of recordable CDs have more than doubled between 1999 and 2001.[8] In fact, 2001 was the first year when more blank CDs than recorded CDs were sold.[9] Artist David Bowie observed, "The absolute transformation of everything that we ever thought about music will take place within ten years, and nothing is going to be able to stop it . . . you'd better be prepared for doing a lot of touring because that's really the only unique situation that's going to be left."[10]

While music executives and artists launched lawsuits against online music swapping, Apple Computer launched the iTunes music store in 2002. iTunes allows consumers to download music at 99 cents per track and burn it onto CDs or transfer it among three specified computers. In the first two months, customers downloaded over 5 million songs, proving that a simple, reasonably priced online service can attract consumers. When broadband is readily accessible and reliable, a subscription service that streams music to consumers anywhere, anytime becomes a viable business model. For the price of perhaps one CD a month, companies could offer unlimited music to consumers off a central server. This capability could change the music business from a packaged goods industry to an electronic distribution industry. However, to succeed requires transforming the existing industry business model.

The Channel Migration Process

Channel transitions, even for the better, are usually traumatic and difficult to reverse. Therefore, prior to launching into channel migration, it is prudent to do one's homework. Successful channel migration is composed of the following four-step process.

Step 1: Conduct a Distribution Strategy Audit of Existing Channels

Given the delicate interdependence that exists between the new and existing distribution channels, a company should assess how well it is performing in its current channels prior to entering any new ones. Why rush into new channels without understanding and developing strategies to resolve conflicts in the existing distribution network? Unfortunately, many companies see the new channels as a way to overcome or avoid problems. For example, consumer packaged goods firms initially thought that the Internet would allow them to bypass the powerful traditional retailers that controlled access to consumers.

Figure 4-5 demonstrates my distribution strategy audit tool that many companies have effectively used. It assesses the company's distribution network from both quantitative and qualitative perspectives.

To fully exploit this tool, companies must have implemented some level of activity-based costing (ABC). Activity-based costing helps get more precise estimates of the cost of serving through each channel. In one fast-moving consumer goods company in Brazil, the managers complained constantly about the price pressure that the large retailers were exerting. However, on conducting a relatively simple ABC analysis, they discovered that the manufacturer

FIGURE 4-5

Distribution Strategy Audit: Consumer Durable Goods Firm, Do-It-Yourself Sector

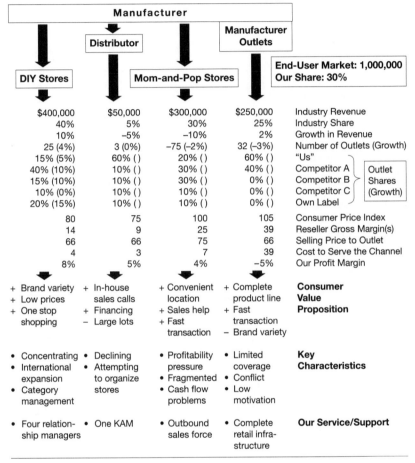

$400,000	$50,000	$300,000	$250,000	Industry Revenue
40%	5%	30%	25%	Industry Share
10%	–5%	–10%	2%	Growth in Revenue
25 (4%)	3 (0%)	–75 (–2%)	32 (–3%)	Number of Outlets (Growth)
15% (5%)	60% ( )	20% ( )	60% ( )	"Us"
40% (10%)	10% ( )	30% ( )	40% ( )	Competitor A
15% (10%)	10% ( )	30% ( )	0% ( )	Competitor B
10% (0%)	10% ( )	10% ( )	0% ( )	Competitor C
20% (15%)	10% ( )	10% ( )	0% ( )	Own Label
80	75	100	105	Consumer Price Index
14	9	25	39	Reseller Gross Margin(s)
66	66	75	66	Selling Price to Outlet
4	3	7	39	Cost to Serve the Channel
8%	5%	4%	–5%	Our Profit Margin

(Outlet Shares (Growth) — bracketed alongside Competitor A / Competitor B / Competitor C / Own Label)

+ Brand variety	+ In-house	+ Convenient	+ Complete	**Consumer**
+ Low prices	sales calls	location	product line	**Value**
+ One stop	+ Financing	+ Sales help	+ Fast	**Proposition**
shopping	– Large lots	+ Fast	transaction	
		transaction	– Brand variety	

• Concentrating	• Declining	• Profitability	• Limited	**Key**
• International	• Attempting	pressure	coverage	**Characteristics**
expansion	to organize	• Fragmented	• Conflict	
• Category	stores	• Cash flow	• Low	
management		problems	motivation	

• Four relation-	• One KAM	• Outbound	• Complete	**Our Service/Support**
ship managers		sales force	retail infra-	
			structure	

Conclusions

- We are weak in fast-growing DIY
- Mom-and-Pop stores are declining
- We are losing money in our own stores

Recommendations

- We need to devote more resources to DIY
- We need to give fewer resources to distributors
- We need to improve our own store profitability

profitability was highest in sales through large retailers. In fact, the manufacturer was actually losing money on sales through mom-and-pop stores despite the fact that these stores were paying the highest prices. The difference was in the manufacturer's cost to serve to the two channels. The mom-and-pop stores had to be supported with high levels of outbound sales efforts and service. In contrast, the large retailers were assigned only key account managers, purchased in large volumes, did not permit any in-store manufacturer help, and had their own inbound logistics service.

Step 2: Articulate the Strategic Logic for Channel Migration

A well-articulated strategic logic for entering a new or emerging channel of distribution is the bedrock of any channel migration decision. The following six questions are helpful in evaluating the opportunity presented by the new distribution channel.[11]

1. How attractive is the value proposition that the new distribution channel offers to our target segments?

2. Is the proportion of our target segment attracted to the new channel large enough to demand our attention?

3. Do we have a differentiated value proposition or an operational advantage in serving customers through the new channel?

4. Is our cost structure and value network optimized to serve customers through the new channel?

5. What can and will competition do with the new channel?

6. How will the new distribution channel change consumer channel preferences and strategies of existing channel members?

To understand the attractiveness of a new channel of distribution, managers should plot the value curves for each of the channels, ideally with some market research data from consumers. The value curves usually reveal that no "best" channel of distribution truly exists. Rather, each channel has its strengths and weaknesses, and a segment for which it is best suited. For example, in figure 4-2, Dell Direct is better for patient price buyers whereas retail is better for those who want to test products and get local service.

The first three questions look relatively obvious but new channel enthusiasts often miss them. Much of the misplaced optimism about the Internet resulted from such management zeal. Consider Priceline.com, a company that sells flights, hotel rooms, and rents cars on its Web site.[12] Priceline.com allows customers to name their own price for a flight on a particular date and then either accepts or declines the offer. Customers cannot specify the airline or the time of departure. Consumers benefit by getting very low prices in return for sacrificing some flexibility, and airlines benefit by selling excess capacity at prices above marginal costs. In 1999, Priceline.com decided to extend its model to groceries.

Despite the widespread belief at the time that many products would eventually be sold online, the grocery venture failed. To buy an airline ticket at a discount, once or twice a year, is worth waiting for acceptance of one's offer. Moreover, most major airline seats and services are identical; any airline will do. But in groceries, consumers treasure certain brands and replacements are not considered equal. Furthermore, computing a desirable discount price for a different basket of desired products on each purchase occasion was too much of a hassle. Given the high marginal costs and the ability to inventory most groceries, major brand manufacturers had little incentive to participate. The target segment and the related value proposition were too small.

Exploit Online Channels When Network Effects Exist.   Now that the Internet hype is over, one can take a more dispassionate look at where online selling can create value for consumers and marketers. The Internet's most important attribute is that it dramatically reduces transaction costs, or the cost of connecting people and businesses to one another. It adds the most value when connecting large numbers of consumers, sometimes referred to as P2P (person to person) or network effects. It's no wonder that eBay, the online auction site, is one of the most successful Internet business ideas. eBay's business model would not be as effective or as efficient without the Internet.

Other profitable businesses that capitalize on network effects of the Internet are massive multiplayer games (MMPG) and various matchmaking services. One example is Sony's EverQuest, where more than 432,000 subscribers pay $12.95 per month to indulge in a medieval role-playing fantasy against other online gamers.[13] Similarly, the Korean NCSoft has four million customers who play games such as Lineage that can involve hundreds of thousands of people at the same time. No more having to be a lonely kid!

Given the costs of fulfillment, it is hard to create profitable online models for physical goods where the costs of shipping are relatively high compared to the price of the product. Furthermore, there are many products that consumers wish to see, touch, and feel, and where online selling will have a limited impact. However, even here if network effects matter, such as when sending gifts to family and friends who live far away, online sales can be significant. Thus, while online sales in 2002 accounted for only 2.5 percent of the U.S. retail industry, U.S. consumers spent more than 17 percent of their year-end holiday shopping budgets online.[14]

Consider Cost and Competitive Moves.   The importance of the fourth question on cost structure and value network is emphasized by the earlier example of the differential effects of channel transitions on Compaq and Dell. The online music sales example also underlined the importance of examining the effects of new distribution models on costs and value chains.

What competition can and will do is an important consideration in developing strategy toward the new distribution channels. Voices within the organization will lobby for letting competitors move first, since early entrants usually bear the brunt of the backlash from existing channels. For example, when Delta initiated online selling and reduced travel agent commissions, many independent travel agents vowed to boycott them.

Insights from game theory in economics, which models interactions among independent players, can be particularly useful here. For example, suppose a manufacturer is considering direct online sales to consumers. It must balance the potential for additional sales and margins with the risk of upsetting its existing dealers. The optimal approach depends on two factors: (1) what management expects the major competitor to do with online sales and (2) the level of online sales expected.[15] Both of these require judgments since no one can accurately predict the level of sales through a new channel in the initial stages.

If online sales turn out to be small, then the firm should stay out of this channel and hope that its competitor initiates such sales. The competitor would suffer channel repercussions, and the firm could exploit this backlash to enhance its own position with existing channels. But if online sales turn out to be significant, then the competitor would gain important first-mover advantage. Of course, one must consider a whole host of other factors, such as the speed of change. If online sales take off slowly, then the second mover may still enter without significant volume loss while letting the first mover work out all the political and technological kinks.

Finally, distribution innovations such as the Internet change consumer shopping patterns. The ideal service outputs demanded by consumers from the distribution channel evolve over time, especially regarding channel discontinuities. Managers should periodically ask several key questions: (1) How well are existing channels serving the needs of existing customer segments? (2) How will consumer preferences for channels change, potentially warranting a different segmentation? (3) How will the strategies of all channel members and of competitors change? (4) How should we alter our distribution channel strategy to enhance our value network?

Step 3: Mobilize Support for Channel Migration

A strong strategic logic for channel migration can fail in the face of the powerful inertia that plagues most companies. Consider the example of Goodyear Tire & Rubber Company in the United States in 1992.[16] Goodyear had historically sold its tires to the replacement market through a network of wholly owned outlets and independent dealers. Goodyear did not distribute through service stations, mass merchandisers such as Sears and Wal-Mart, or warehouse clubs like Sam's Club. Its main competitor, Michelin, distributed aggressively through all channels.

Unfortunately, Goodyear's independent dealers were increasingly unable to compete against the buying power of warehouse clubs and mass merchandisers. As a result, an increasing share of the branded tire market migrated to these clubs and merchandisers. Since Goodyear was absent in the latter two channels, it had large coverage gaps in the branded tires marketplace. The decision of whether Goodyear should sell tires through Sears, Sam's Club, or Wal-Mart faced remarkable internal and external resistance.

The point is that new channels threaten both the sales volumes in the existing channel and the managers within the company who are responsible for them. Often the compensation of these executives is linked to the volumes in existing channels. But beyond the compensation issues, a rich personal network of relationships emerges between managers and their counterparts in existing channels. These friendships and associated levels of personal loyalty often lead to a desire to protect the existing channel members from any potential loss of volume. To succeed, firms need a well-thought-out implementation plan for channel migration. Such an implementation plan should address the following five questions:[17]

1. Is there a shared understanding of the problem or opportunity?
2. Is there a top management mandate for change?
3. Is there adequate bottom-up involvement?
4. Are there clear timetables and milestones?
5. Have we addressed the human problem of change?

Sharing the results of a distribution strategy audit and constantly communicating the strategic logic behind the channel migration builds shared understanding. Managers will more likely generate shared understanding by asking those with a stake in the decision to participate in the audit. As far as possible, however, one should have market research behind the conclusions to focus the discussion on facts rather than unsubstantiated opinions and passions.

If a change in distribution channels threatens the volume in the existing channels, then the new channel champion will face stiff resistance from managers of the existing channels. It helps channel migration efforts if such resisters have heard top management's mandate for change. The CEO should never declare existing distribution institutions sacrosanct. For example in 1996, Donald V. Fites, then chair and CEO of Caterpillar, publicly proclaimed, "We'd sooner cut off our right arm than sell directly to customers and bypass our dealers."[18] If consumer buying behavior, competitive environment, or the nature of the company's products change significantly, such statements reduce future degrees of freedom and lock the managers into particular types of distribution institutions rather than selling in those channels where consumers wish to buy.

Once a company has decided to exit or enter certain channels, managers should ask for suggestions about implementation to create broad bottom-up involvement. Furthermore, a major change in channel structure will affect the job descriptions and careers of managers interfacing with existing channels. To help these people cope with change, top management should adjust compensation, make training available, and offer new job assignments.

Finally, since channel migration may take several years, managers should use a timetable with milestones that plot how the company's sales should migrate across the various channels over time, to track progress and suggest course corrections.

Step 4: Actively Manage Channel Conflict

The addition of a new distribution channel, whether it is the Internet, an emerging low-cost indirect channel, or a new manufacturer sales force, brings with it the potential for additional sales volume, but at the cost of greater channel conflict. Channel conflict occurs because the existing channels perceive the new distribution channel to be chasing after the same customers with the same brand.

As happened at Compaq, the fear of channel conflict can paralyze a company. But some amount of channel conflict is healthy.[19] The lack of channel conflict in a company's distribution network is usually a sign of market coverage gaps. In fact, much of what channel members call conflict is healthy competition. Therefore, the objective of conflict management should not be to eliminate channel conflict but rather manage it so that it does not escalate to destructive levels.

From the manufacturer's perspective, channel conflict becomes destructive when the existing distribution channels reduce support or shelf space for the manufacturer due to the emergence of the new channel. For example, when Estée Lauder set up a Web site to sell its Clinique and Bobbi Brown brands, the department store Dayton Hudson reduced shelf space for Estée Lauder products. In extreme cases, an existing distributor may even drop the brand, as happened when Gap decided to stop stocking Levi's and concentrate on its own brands after Levi's began expanding its distribution.

Channel conflict becomes particularly destructive when parties take actions that hurt themselves in order to hurt the other party. In 2002, Albert Heijn, the largest Dutch supermarket chain, boycotted some of Unilever's brands to retaliate against the manufacturer. While this was resolved quickly, Albert Heijn could have lost brands such as Bertoli mayonnaise and Cif cleaning products, which have very high brand loyalty amongst Dutch consumers.

While none are a panacea, several channel conflict management strategies exist, which can help avoid destructive conflict during, and after, channel migration. These are part of the arsenal of any multichannel marketer.

Position Channels Against Segments.   Since different channels have unique value curves, they reach distinct segments. Thus the rationale for having multiple channels should always be built on a clear end user segmentation strategy. For example, when Avon, which has traditionally used half a million direct sales representatives in the United States to sell its line of cosmetics, opened retail kiosks in malls, it found that 90 percent of the customers buying at these kiosks had never purchased from Avon before.[20] The kiosks were reaching a new segment.

When the convenience store complains to the manufacturer about the prices at which Wal-Mart is selling its products, the manufacturer must explain that a convenience store cannot compete with Wal-Mart on prices for the price-seeking customer. Instead, the convenience store must compete on saving the consumer time on travel, shopping, and transaction processing, all at a reasonable price premium. They serve two different segments and each should specialize in its target segment. Of course, the brand owner should balance the number of distribution points within a particular distribution channel with the size of the segment that the channel reaches.

Dedicate Products and Brands to Channels. A popular method of managing channel conflict is to dedicate parts of the product line to different channels of distribution. Many designers have managed the conflict with their existing retailers by developing special products for their factory outlet stores in order to reduce the conflict with department stores. Similarly, many luxury brand companies, like Camus Cognac and Guylian chocolates, offer special pack sizes and products that attract travelers at duty-free airports to minimize the conflict with their regular main street retailers. On the Internet, manufacturers can offer the SKUs that retailers are usually not willing to carry. At the extreme, some manufacturers dedicate different brands to different channels, sometimes referred to as channel brands. For example, MyTravel, a tour operator in Sweden, formerly distributed its Ving brand directly and developed the Always brand for travel agents. Likewise, Merrill Lynch allowed third parties to sell only Mercury funds while Merrill funds were restricted for in-house sales.

While having unique channel products or brands is sometimes seen as a resolution to the channel conflict problem, it is often unsustainable. Unless the product or the brand is targeted only to those customers buying in a particular channel or is unpopular, other distribution channels will quickly demand access to them. It took many years of pleas by travel agents before the highly successful Ving brand was offered to them. The expansion of Ving to travel agents brought an immediate increase in volume, and research indicated that 80 percent of those customers buying Ving through travel agent had never purchased Always or Ving previously. Similarly, in 2003, Merrill decided to close down the Mercury brand by consolidating those funds within Merrill Lynch.

Expand Channels and Sales Simultaneously.   Having a new "hit" product helps facilitate channel migration. Goodyear managed the migration to the mass merchandisers with only a reasonable amount of conflict by restricting the distribution of its new Aquatred tire to the independent dealers. This allowed the independent dealer to protect their profitability and sales volume through the higher margin, higher value Aquatred tire. Expanding channels when revenues are growing is easier as existing dealers are less likely to see absolute declines in sales and profits.

Adopt Dual Compensation and Role Differentiation.   To lessen channel conflict, some manufacturers agree to compensate the existing channels for sales through the new channel. While it may be perceived as just buying off the support of the existing channels for the channel migration, it can be useful if the existing distribution is given a role to perform in supporting the new channel. For example, when Allstate started selling insurance directly off the Web, it agreed to pay agents a 2 percent commission if they provided face-to-face service to customers who got their quotes off the Web. However, since this was lower than the 10 percent commission that agents typically received for offline transactions, many agents did not like it. Yet, it did help lower the negative backlash.

Many manufacturers will be unable to avoid selling on the Internet directly as consumers are seeking that distribution solution. Yet, they lack the logistical ability to fully satisfy the consumers. Using the existing channel partner can be a useful complement. Maytag, for example, joined forces with its retail partners to offer online sales. After the consumer decides on an appliance, she is shown the availability and pricing information from a local dealer who provides the fulfillment and installation. Similarly, Levi Strauss discovered that handling online returns was too costly, and that consumers preferred returning products to a physical store anyway. Consequently, it discontinued sales from its Levi's and Dockers Web sites and let J.C. Penney and Macy's sell Levi's on their sites.

Avoid Overdistribution.   The temptation for manufacturers is to expand the number of distribution points to increase sales. However, generally, the greater the number of points distributing a brand, the less support each distribution point will give to the brand. Thus, manufacturers, especially of prestigious goods requiring a high level of service, must be careful not to overdistribute their products. Having too many channels chase too few consumers can have a deleterious impact on sales.

Bang & Olufsen (B&O), a major Danish high-end player in the electronics industry, easily distinguished by its distinctive Bauhaus-inspired designs, was on the verge of bankruptcy in the early 1990s. It had too many retailers selling B&O products next to rival brands, and as a result, the focus was frequently on price. Unable to make adequate margins, retailers lowered their service in support of B&O products, which further weakened the brand's position as a luxury lifestyle product. Between 1994 and 1997, B&O cut a third of its dealers in Europe and dropped from 200 to 30 dealers in the United States. It then invested in improving the remaining dealers by setting up partially owned and franchise boutiques dedicated solely to B&O. Greater control and more dedicated retailers helped reposition B&O as a top-of-the-line audiovisual brand and sales rebounded despite having fewer dealers.

Treat Channels Equitably. Notwithstanding all of the above, in the face of multiple channels typically selling at different price levels, there will be channel conflict. Some retailers will be upset that the prices they pay the manufacturer are higher than those charged to other retailers or to the direct sales force. They will often feel that the manufacturer is favoring other channels at their expense. While they may never fully overcome these concerns, the best antidote is to treat channels equitably and in a transparent manner. If the manufacturer's prices differ across channels, it should be based on how the particular channel member performs. Tesco and Wal-Mart do receive lower prices, but it is because they engage in practices (buying large quantities, allowing electronic transactions, not demanding in-store help and promotions) that lower the manufacturer's cost to serve them.

Conclusion

The emergence of a new distribution channel raises several questions regarding the company, its competitors, the existing channels, and customers (see "Checklist for Channel Migration"). Any robust channel migration process must address them.

Innovation in distribution channels typically promises some combination of opportunities for serving overlooked customer segments, offering new value propositions, or the use of a more cost-efficient business model. For example, office superstores like Office Depot found a niche because of the poor service that other office product dealers were giving to small business customers. Priceline offered a new value proposition of cheaper airline fares for those who were willing to relinquish brand and departure time preferences.

Focused on defending existing distribution assets and value networks, established companies tend not to counterattack when a new innovative distribution channel challenges them.[21] When industry distribution structures change, traditional industry leaders repeatedly neglect the fastest-growing market segments. New

Checklist for Channel Migration

Customers

- *What service outputs will the new channel provide?*
- *Which segments will the new channel target?*
- *Which markets will the new channel operate in?*
- *How much additional industry volume will the new channel generate?*

Channels

- *How will the relative importance and power of existing channels change?*
- *How will existing channels react strategically to the new channel?*
- *What level of conflict will the new channel generate?*

Competitors

- *Which competitors will enter the new channel?*
- *What changes in channel incentives to existing members will competitors try?*
- *How will relative market share positions change?*
- *What are the competitive implications of being the leader, fast follower, or laggard in the new channel?*

Company

- *Which products and services will flow through the new channel?*
- *What will be the cost to serve through the new channel?*
- *What new competences do we need to enter the new channel?*
- *How will we manage channel conflict?*

distribution opportunities rarely fit the way the industry approaches the market, defines it, or organizes its value network to serve it. Therefore, innovators in distribution have a good chance of being left alone for a long time. The problem confronting managers of established firms is that they must cannibalize their own profitable businesses for questionable returns from emerging channels. But if they don't do it, their competitors will, and it is always better to have all the cannibals in the family.

In evaluating the urgency for channel migration, one must consider the speed at which channels are changing. The internal rate of change in distribution strategy must match the external rate of change in consumer channel preferences. Channel migration within established firms only happens when the CEO is willing to sign off on it. The engine must be consumer shopping patterns and preferences but the CEO must grease the wheels. As one CEO in the process of changing channels remarked to me, "We have finally decided to stop selling where we want to and instead have begun to sell where customers want to buy." History suggests that most companies cling too long to declining distribution networks.

FIVE

From Branded Bulldozers to Global Distribution Partners

No company is an island.

HISTORICALLY, POWER IN distribution channels has rested upstream with brand marketers such as Philip Morris and Sara Lee, manufacturers such as Ford Motor Company and Caterpillar, or franchisers such as McDonald's and PepsiCo. In contrast to these multinational suppliers, most retailers, dealers, and franchisees were local and fragmented. There was within each country a large owner-operated sector in distribution, which in retailing is romantically referred to as "mom and pop." Retailing, and more generally distribution, therefore acquired an image of being a simple, unsophisticated business, undeserving of attention from superior trained minds, be they academics or M.B.A.'s from prestigious schools.

In such an environment, supplier organizations were optimized for trade relations with small, vulnerable, and local distribution partners. In terms of structure, manufacturer and franchiser organizations typically coalesced around products and countries. And in terms of policies and practices, these suppliers were predisposed toward utilizing their superior coercive power over resellers in order to achieve distribution objectives.

Over the past two decades, there has been a remarkable shift in power downstream from suppliers to distributors and retailers. The increasing power of resellers has been driven by the rise of horizontal buying alliances, megaformats such as category killers and superstores, as well as mergers and acquisitions. Some of the most significant M&A activity has been cross-border mergers. The worldwide revenues of the largest retailers such as Ahold, Carrefour, and Wal-Mart now exceed, or at least compare favorably with, those of the leading branded manufacturers.

With distribution consolidation, fewer customers now account for a large proportion of the manufacturers' sales. A study of thirty-seven consumer packaged goods manufacturers in 2000 indicated that, on average, the top five international customers accounted for 32 percent of sales, up from 21 percent five years ago and expected to increase to 45 percent over the next five years.[1] When the five largest global retailers account for almost half of a supplier's business, they have tremendous negotiating clout over their suppliers.

Since manufacturer prices for the same product can vary by as much as 60 percent among countries, global retailers are increasingly demanding uniform worldwide prices, much to suppliers' dismay. John Mentzer, president and CEO of Wal-Mart's international division, declared, "We are using global sourcing to get the best products worldwide, to have the best stock worldwide, to leverage our supply chain and to get what we call transparent pricing worldwide. Transparent pricing to us is the same pricing adjusted for freight, duty, and local differences."[2]

The retailer's adoption of a global pricing policy can dramatically affect the manufacturer. For example, Carrefour, the second-largest retailer in the world, which operates in thirty-three countries, insisted that a leading packaged goods company use the lowest price in any country as the global price for each international SKU. The consumer packaged goods firm estimated that if Carrefour was allowed to pick the lowest price for every international SKU, it would lower their annual revenues from Carrefour by 7 million euros on a turnover of 100 million—and most consumer packaged goods firms hardly make a 7 percent after-tax return on sales.

Serving end users through powerful international distributors or retailers requires manufacturers to reorient their organizations around customers and relationships, not countries and products. As this chapter reveals, using global retailers effectively demands transformation in strategy, organization structure, information systems, human resource management, and, above all, a fresh mind-set.

Predictably, managers who attempt such changes themselves face stiff external and internal resistance. CEOs of major manufacturing and franchising companies often cannot fathom their channel partners' perceived lack of trust in them. Furthermore, the necessary organizational changes tend to disrupt the delicate power equilibrium between individuals and divisions within the firm. The current CEO of a packaged goods company articulates this transformation challenge well: "The fact that we are a multidivisional, multifunctional, multinational, multiproduct and multiplant company is not the customer's problem."

To transform the organization, the company needs ample resources and a committed change leader, often the CEO or someone whom the CEO openly supports. Today, CEOs themselves often wrestle with global retail issues because of the aforementioned price pressures threatening the overall bottom line.

The Challenge from Global Retailers

The growth of global retailing has been substantial. For example, Ahold, Carrefour, and METRO each operate in more than twenty-five countries; Aldi, Auchan, Rewe, Tesco, and Wal-Mart operate in ten or more. While most of these examples feature the packaged goods industry where changes have been the most traumatic for suppliers, we can see these trends—distribution consolidation, increased globalization, increasing point-of-sale power, and value migration downstream—in industries as diverse as apparel, chemicals, entertainment, financial services, paints, and personal computers. Consider the following cross-border examples:

- Global retailers who operate under their own name include Amazon, Toys "R" Us (with over 1,600 stores in 27 countries), Hennes & Mauritz in fashion retailing (with 840 stores in 17 countries), and IKEA in furniture (with over 150 stores in over 30 countries).[3] Outside the United States, Blockbuster video has more than 2,600 stores in 27 countries and Starbucks Coffee has 900 stores in 22 countries.[4]

- The British retailer Kingfisher, an emerging global retailer that has grown through acquisitions, operates a portfolio of brand names. In the home improvement sector, Kingfisher has about 600 stores in 15 countries including B&Q in the United Kingdom, Castorama and Brico Dépôt in France, Réno-Dépôt in Canada, NOMI in Poland and Koctas in Turkey. It also owns about 650 electrical retail stores in 7 countries including Darty and But in France, Comet in the United Kingdom, New Vanden Borre in Belgium, BCC in the Netherlands, ProMarkt in Germany, and Datart in the Czech and Slovak Republics.[5]

- Tech Data Corporation's 1998 acquisition of German-based Computer 2000 AG created a *Fortune* 100 company. It generated annual sales of $15.7 billion in the fiscal year ending January 31, 2003, distributing microcomputer related hardware and software products from vendors such as IBM and Cisco to more than 100,000 technology resellers worldwide.[6]

The Retailer Challenge to Manufacturers

The emergence of global players has transformed retailing into a sophisticated, technologically intensive, and systems-driven business enviable by NASA's standards. Not satisfied as mere merchants, retailers have developed quality store brands.[7]

Powerful global retailers are demanding more from their branded multinational suppliers—gains from scale, synergies, and speed. This translates into demand for differentiation through unique offers and distinctive marketing concepts; efficiency gains through standardized back office functions; and gains in knowledge from branded suppliers like Nestlé or Unilever that have relatively greater multinational expertise in new business development in emerging markets.

In every part of the world, global customers expect coverage, speed, consistent and high-quality service, as well as extraordinary attention. This expectation requires manufacturers to provide a single point of contact, uniform terms of trade, as well as worldwide standardization of products and services.

The retailers' global procurement strategies push manufacturers into offering price concessions and enhanced fees such as trade promotions, slotting allowances, and failure fees. For example, one small Chinese supplier of bedding to Carrefour complained, "We must pay 4 percent of our annual sales each year just to keep our contract. On top of that are so-called holiday fees of around Rmb 2,000 each five times a year [and] a flat Rmb 10,000 fee called 'running the store fee.'"[8]

Global customers hate to learn that they were not offered the lowest prices. They demand more uniform, more transparent global prices. However, under the pretext of local cost or competitive considerations, multinational manufacturer prices for the same or similar products differ dramatically across countries, leading to amusing, if not awkward, situations. For example, in 2000, Tesco, then about a $30 billion dollar retailer, acquired a small thirteen-store supermarket chain in Poland called Hit, which was obtaining better prices from its suppliers than Tesco was. Pity the poor supplier representatives who had to explain the logic of their worldwide pricing structure to Tesco management.

The Challenge of Global Integration for Retailers

Historically, retailers, especially food retailers, have subscribed to the view that all retailing is local. Daniel Bernard,

Chairman and CEO of Carrefour, observed, "Retail is the image of the country in which it lives. You must adapt your food and other products to the local culture."[9] Because of this decentralized view, global food retailers are still learning to leverage their global operations. While they may make more decisions centrally on private labels and category management, for example, their actual level of global integration is quite low. Most global food retailers have not yet centralized worldwide purchasing functions. Currently, they fancy overriders—basically a percentage kickback from the supplier to the retailer's headquarters on the supplier's worldwide sales to the retailer.

Carrefour, like many other global retailers, is attempting to integrate its global operations. Yet, as of today, it cannot provide detailed benchmarking data across all thirty-three countries. At last count, the data was available for only twenty-three countries. In terms of purchasing, Carrefour has integrated its nonfood merchandise but still handles food sourcing locally.

Regrettably for manufacturers, retailers recognize that global integration is their key challenge. The chief executive of Ahold observed, "In the next three years, the various supermarket chains must find more synergies. Their sourcing will be completely centralized, with one center for procurement of perishable goods, which connects with the foodservice operation." The ubiquity of this view among global retailers means that life will only get tougher for brand manufacturers.

Developing a Relationship Mind-Set

To implement global account management, suppliers and their global retail partners must develop a shared relationship-building mind-set. Unfortunately, human nature leads us to exploit our relative power over other players. As figure 5-1 indicates, when suppliers are strong and resellers are weak, the former tend to bulldoze the latter. Historically, manufacturers have done just that, pushing their brands and promotion plans onto retailers for

FIGURE 5-1

Manufacturer-Reseller Relationship Matrix

Manufacturer — **Strong**	"Branded Bulldozers"	"Tug-of Wars"	"Strategic Partnerships"
Manufacturer — **Weak**	"Opportunistic Mating"	"Shelf-Space Bidders"	"Assortment Fillers"
	Weak	Strong and Adversarial	Strong and Cooperative

Reseller

Source: Adapted from Peter M. Freedman, Michael Reyner, and Thomas Tochtermann, "European Category Management: Look Before You Leap," *McKinsey Quarterly* 1 (1997): 156–164.

implementation. But as retailers have become powerful and adversarial, they have turned vulnerable manufacturers into shelf-space bidders.

Clearly, the relationship between retailers and manufacturers must change to reflect this new reality. Using the framework of figure 5-1, powerful manufacturers have moved from being "branded bulldozers" to a "tug-of-war" relationship with retailers. The challenge is to ultimately change this relationship into a "strategic partnership." The relationship between Procter & Gamble (P&G) and Wal-Mart is an excellent example of how a relationship evolves through these three phases.[10]

Two Tough Companies Learn to Dance Together

Word has it that P&G and Wal-Mart are two tough negotiators. Historically, P&G has wielded its enormous sword to dominate the trade, using its comprehensive consumer research to secure increased shelf space for its brands. Before retailers developed sophisticated point-of-sale systems to generate their own data, they could not dispute P&G's findings. Over the years, P&G established its reputation as a "self-aggrandizing bully of the trade."[11]

For its part, Wal-Mart asked its suppliers for rock-bottom prices, extra service, and preferred credit terms. In 1992, it instituted a policy of dealing directly with manufacturers, and only those that invested in customized electronic-data-interchange technology and put bar codes on their products. Manufacturers that depended on the volume and growth that Wal-Mart delivered played by the policy.

As one might expect, P&G initially dictated to Wal-Mart how much P&G would sell, at what prices, and under what terms. In turn, Wal-Mart threatened to drop P&G merchandise or give it poorer shelf locations. There was no sharing of information, no joint planning, and no systems coordination. Prior to 1987, no corporate officer of P&G had even contacted Wal-Mart. According to Sam Walton, the founder of Wal-Mart, "We just let our buyers slug it out with their salesmen."[12]

In the mid-1980s, this adversarial relationship began to change. On a now-legendary canoe trip, Sam Walton and Lou Pritchett, P&G's vice president of sales, agreed to reexamine the relationship between the two companies. They gathered the top ten officers of each company for two days to develop a collective vision of the future. Within three months, they established a team of twelve people from different functions in each company to convert that vision into an action plan. It examined how the companies could use information technology to increase sales and lower costs for both parties.

The result was a sophisticated efficient consumer response (ECR) partnership. This partnership enables P&G to manage Wal-Mart's inventory of any given product, such as P&G's Pampers diapers. Procter & Gamble receives continuous data via satellite on sales, inventory, and prices for different sizes of Pampers at individual Wal-Mart stores. This information allows P&G to anticipate Pampers sales at Wal-Mart, determine the number of shelf racks and quantity required, and automatically ship orders. Electronic invoicing and electronic transfer of funds complete the transaction cycle. The short order-to-delivery cycle enables Wal-Mart to pays P&G for the Pampers soon after the consumer buys the merchandise.

This partnership has created great value for consumers in the form of lower prices and more availability of their favorite P&G items. Through cooperation, the two giants have eliminated superfluous activities related to order processing, billing, and payment; reduced the number of sales calls; and dramatically reduced paperwork and opportunities for error. The orderless order system also lets P&G produce to demand rather than to inventory. Furthermore, Wal-Mart simultaneously reduced its inventory of Pampers and the probability of stock-outs, thereby avoiding lost sales for both parties. By collaborating, the two have turned a win-lose into a win-win proposition of reduced costs and greater revenues for both parties. Today, Wal-Mart is P&G's largest customer, generating about $7 billion in sales, or greater than 17 percent of P&G's worldwide revenues.

Over the last fifteen years, these two giants have developed a partnership based on mutual dependence: Wal-Mart needs P&G's brands and P&G needs Wal-Mart's access to customers. Naturally, the relationship has undergone the trust-building growing pains that are a benchmark for manufacturer-retailer symbiosis: Wal-Mart trusts P&G enough to share sales and price data and to cede control of the order process and inventory management. Procter & Gamble trusts Wal-Mart enough to dedicate a large cross-functional team to the Wal-Mart account, adopt everyday low prices (thereby eliminating special promotions), and invest in a customized information link. Instead of focusing on increasing sales to Wal-Mart, the P&G team concentrates on increasing sales of P&G products through Wal-Mart, maximizing both companies' profits.

Create Trust, Not Fear, in Distribution Relationships

The P&G and Wal-Mart partnership illustrates that exploiting power in distribution channels pays in the short run but not in the long, for three reasons.[13] First, extracting unfair concessions will burden a firm as power positions change over time. For instance, when Migros, a supermarket chain in Switzerland, was founded, the large branded manufacturers refused to supply it rather than upset their traditional mom-and-pop retailers. Without branded products, Migros adopted an exclusively private label format. Today, Migros is the largest retailer in Switzerland with private labels accounting for 90 percent of its total sales volume. Most major brands, such as Coca-Cola and Nescafé, can't be found on its shelves.

Second, when companies systematically exploit their advantage, the victims ultimately resist by developing countervailing power. For example, by banding together, automobile dealers and franchisees successfully lobbied lawmakers in Europe and the United States to pass particularistic legislation that restricts franchisers like Ford or McDonald's from sanctioning or sacking them. Apparel designers such as Giorgio Armani, Hugo Boss, Liz Claiborne, and Donna Karan opened their own outlets to escape bulldozing department stores that unilaterally returned products, took discounts off manufacturer invoices, and delayed payments.

Third, only by developing mutual trust and collaborating closely can manufacturers and their resellers deliver the greatest value to end users. While managers frequently use the word trust in distribution channels, they often fail to define it precisely. Trust involves dependability and faith.[14]

A dependable distribution partner is honest and credible. For example, one manufacturer signed onto a retailer's global promotion that cost more than a country-by-country promotion would have.[15] However, the retailer then failed to execute the promotion effectively in all its stores around the world.

Dependability alone does not suffice. Someone who promises to punish his partner and then does so is honest and credible, but not trusted. In trusting relationships, the parties believe that each cares about the other's welfare and will take into consideration the effects of its actions on the other party—that both will act in good faith.

Dealers and retailers who trust the manufacturer are less likely to seek alternative sources of supply, more likely to produce sales, and more forgiving of the manufacturer.[16] For example, in the consumer durable industry, dealers who trusted their manufacturers generated 78 percent more sales for the manufacturer.[17]

Given the benefits of trust, even those suppliers who can potentially behave like branded bulldozers should attempt to build trusting relationships with resellers. However, managing distribution relationships based on trust instead of power requires a leap in mind-set and culture (see table 5-1).

TABLE 5-1

The Power Versus Trust Game

	The Power Game	The Trust Game
Modus Operandi	Create fear	Create trust
Guiding Principles	• Pursue self-interest • Win-lose	• Pursue what's fair • Win-win
Negotiating Strategy	• Avoid dependence by playing multiple partners off against each other	• Create interdependence by limiting the number of partnerships
	• Retain flexibility for self but lock in partners by raising switching costs	• Both parties signal commitment through specialized investments, which lock them in
Communication	Primarily unilateral	Bilateral
Influence	Through coercion	Through expertise
Contracts	• "Closed," or formal, detailed, and short-term	• "Open," or informal and long-term
	• Use competitive bidding frequently	• Check market prices occasionally
Conflict Management	• Reduce conflict potential through detailed contracts	• Reduce conflict potential by selecting partners with similar values and by increasing mutual understanding
	• Resolve conflicts through the legal system	• Resolve conflicts through procedures such as mediation or arbitration

Source: Adapted from Nirmalya Kumar, "The Power of Trust in Manufacturer-Retailer Relationships," *Harvard Business Review* (November–December 1996): 92–105.

Adopt Fairness Principles in Relationships

To develop trust, the more powerful party must treat the weaker one fairly. Fairness encompasses two distinct types of justice: distributive justice, or fairness of outcomes received, and procedural justice, or fairness of policies and practices.[18]

Distributive Justice.   Distributive justice refers to a party's perception of the fairness of earnings and outcomes that it receives from the partnership. It refers to "pie sharing" or the division of benefits and burdens between partners. Compensating channel partners appropriately by allowing them a fair return can have long-term benefits that are not immediately apparent. For example, a few years ago, Buick cars consistently received higher customer satisfaction ratings than Oldsmobile, even though they were built at the same General Motors plant. Why? Buick was paying its dealers fifteen dollars per hour more for warranty work than Oldsmobile. When customers visited Oldsmobile dealers with a small problem, the dealers responded, "All cars do that;" Buick dealers fixed it. How dealers treat the customer factors into customer satisfaction.

Procedural Justice.   Procedural justice refers to "due process" or the fairness of a party's procedures and policies regarding its vulnerable partners. Procedurally fair systems in distribution rest on six principles:

1. *Bilateral communication* is the willingness of the firm to engage in two-way communication with its channel partners. The more powerful companies in the distribution channel tend to listen less to the other members in the system. Companies that develop trust establish practices that solicit input from channel partners. For example, at Anheuser-Busch Companies, the chairman meets with the fifteen-member wholesaler panel at least four times a year, to hear suggestions and complaints.

2. *Impartiality* is the consistency of the company's channel policies across all channel partners. While every channel partner can't be treated identically, partners can be given equitable opportunities.

3. *Refutability* is the ability of the smaller or more vulnerable partners to appeal against the more powerful party's channel policies and decisions. Manufacturers such as Caterpillar, DuPont, and 3M have dealer advisory councils at which dealers can air their concerns.

4. *Explanation* is providing one's partners with a coherent rationale for channel decisions and policies. It calls for greater transparency.

5. *Familiarity* is an understanding of the local conditions under which channel partners operate. Before Marks & Spencer enters into a relationship with a new manufacturer, it visits the manufacturer's plants several times and hosts meetings among its buyers, merchandisers, and designers.

6. *Courtesy* is treating a partner with respect. After all, relationships between companies are actually relationships between teams of people. Managers who recognize this fact are changing how they assign personnel to various accounts. Sherwin-Williams, the paint manufacturer, lets managers from Sears, Roebuck and Company help select the Sherwin-Williams people who will handle the Sears account.

Distributive justice and potentially large returns usually attract companies to a relationship, but procedural fairness holds the relationship together. Retaining partners by giving them higher margins than what they get from competitors is expensive because competitors quickly match them. Developing procedurally fair systems requires greater effort, energy, investment, patience, and perhaps even a change in organizational culture, but will more likely lead to sustainable competitive advantage.

Implement Efficient Consumer Response (ECR) Initiatives

ECR is a strategic initiative in which the retailer and manufacturer work closely together to eliminate excess costs and serve the consumer cheaper, faster, and better. In 1992, supermarkets and their suppliers embraced ECR as a powerful tool to optimize the supply chain and compete better against discounters such as Wal-Mart in the United States and Aldi in Germany.[19] ECR included quick response models, continuous replenishment, cross-docking, electronic data interchange (EDI), and vendor managed inventory systems.

Kurt Salmon, a retail-consulting firm, was commissioned to document the potential savings. It found that ECR could reduce costs in the supermarket distribution chain by 11 percent, which translated into $30 billion in the United States and $50 billion in Europe. As a cross-functional program, the sources of savings came from better capacity utilization in production, reduced promotion expenses and fewer new product failures in marketing, lower administration costs in purchasing, increased utilization of warehouses and trucks for the logistics systems, less clerical and accounting staff in administration, and higher sales per square foot at the store level. It was anticipated that 54 percent of the benefits would flow to manufacturers while 46 percent of the savings would go to retailers. Not surprisingly, manufacturers and retailers shared great enthusiasm for ECR.

Despite its widespread adoption, ECR has disillusioned CEOs of suppliers. The CEO of one of the largest packaged goods companies remarked, "If there was a dollar to be made from ECR, I haven't seen it."[20] My study of the suppliers of Sainsbury's, one of the United Kingdom's two largest retailers, revealed that with greater levels of ECR implementation in their relationships with Sainsbury's, suppliers achieved higher levels of profitability, turnover, and growth.[21] However, they also reported feeling less equitably treated. These findings explain the prevailing perception of supplier CEOs: that they do not benefit from ECR. Objectively, suppliers do obtain a payback from ECR, but these benefits are perceived to be relatively small compared to what the retailer is perceived to be receiving. Consequently, suppliers feel that that they do not profit from ECR. Yet despite the current disenchantment, suppliers should adopt ECR while accepting the reality that their shares of the returns will be small compared to global retailers.

Customer-Centric Global Account Management

Whereas some companies are moving fast on global account management, most manufacturers have been reactive rather than proactive. What prevents them from reorganizing for global customers is a myriad of internal constraints. Historically, the power in decentralized companies such as Unilever and Nestlé has resided with country managers. In more centralized companies like P&G, most of the power rests with business unit managers (usually organized around product divisions).

Customer-centric global account management requires a single strategic interface for each global customer, which is supported and reported to by business units and country organizations. Delivering an integrated solution requires a greater understanding of the individual retailer worldwide and greater coordination among the supplier's sales and supply chain operations around the world.

Marketing plans and supply chains must become customer-centric instead of country-centric. Implementation involves shifting responsibilities and thereby changing power balances. It necessitates resolving conflicts between what is best for the global customer and what is best for the supplier's local country organization.[22] The ensuing power struggles over who owns the account, how to assess performance, and appropriate incentive systems may seem wasteful but they are real. Companies must move fast, cede control to the center, and resolve their internal problems. To deliver on global retailers' demands for efficiency and lower prices, manufacturers must restructure to decrease potential losses through complexity of organization, work processes, and information.

The transformation challenges discussed within the context of the grocery retailing industry are also being confronted by other industries serving global accounts. Global account management is prevalent in many industries including advertising, airline, audit services, automotive components, hotel, insurance, petroleum, software services, and telecommunications. Examples include:

- IBM firing over forty different advertising agencies worldwide and consolidating the group's entire $400 to $500 million account with Ogilvy & Mather.[23]
- Gates, a leader in belts, supplying General Motors plants worldwide with automotive equipment.
- Deloitte, Touche, and Tohmatsu auditing the accounts of several multinational companies.

Serving global customers is especially problematic when local offices of global account suppliers are independent (for example, audit, advertising, or consulting firms). The transformation required in multinational companies—into an organizational form and process whereby one person or team coordinates the worldwide activities serving a multinational customer—is a Herculean task.

In most companies, half-hearted steps to establish global account management alongside country and product organizations are not delivering the required integration. The situation will only worsen, especially if retailers set up global supplier teams to mirror the supplier's global customer teams. For manufacturers to respond to the challenge of global retailers, changes are required at several levels including strategy, organization structure, information systems, and human resource management.

Strategic Transformation

Nothing is as useful as a well-developed, well-articulated strategy for global accounts. It guides key account managers and customer development team leaders when they are face-to-face with global retailers and under tremendous pressure to cede to everything the retailer demands. A clear strategy gives them the confidence to say to important global accounts, "No, we don't do that," with the knowledge that they have top management support and are following the corporate mandate.

Developing the strategic vision and thrust for the global accounts—perhaps ten customers, accounting for 25 to 50 percent of the firm's total business—must be the responsibility of the CEO and top management. The stakes are too high for the CEO not to be actively involved in this process. Figure 5-2 shows one

FIGURE 5-2

Manufacturer's Global Retailer Portfolio

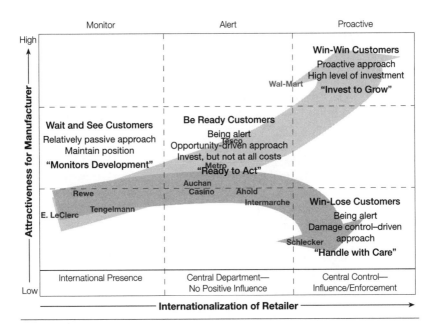

manufacturer's attempt to understand its top twelve global retail accounts on the two dimensions of attractiveness of retailer for the manufacturer (for example, growth, attitude toward the manufacturer), and how coordinated the retailer is with respect to its international operations. Two managers on customer business development teams at one manufacturer noted the benefits of a well-articulated strategy:

> *Those that get that [strategy] right upfront and do the hard work to get it right tend to be almost always more successful than those that don't.*

> *I believe the single most important thing to do in team effectiveness is to get very clear directions. I don't think you can get clear on roles, clear on your structure or get clear on your relationships if you are not clear on the direction.*[24]

Common Policy.   What is needed is a common policy on how to deal with global accounts.[25] Is the company going to be proactive or reactive to their demands? Perhaps the appropriate stance toward global retail accounts depends on the position of the manufacturer.[26] Manufacturers with strong brands and geographies should aspire to category captain positions through partnerships with global retailers. Those manufacturers with strong brands but weak geographical coverage may wish to use global retailers to expand into markets where they are currently underrepresented. Perhaps companies with weak brands but strong geographical coverage will turn into private label suppliers to global retailers, while those with weak positions may have no choice but to exit the category or customer segment.

Brand Portfolio Rationalization.   Some strategic imperatives result from global consolidation and fewer accounts. Global retailers push global brands and use private labels to displace weaker local brands. Consequently, as discussed in chapter 6, manufacturers must take a long, hard look at brand rationalization. The logic for continued support of weak or local brands is becoming harder to defend. It only pushes the relationship between the supplier and the retailer into the "shelf-space bidder" and "assortment filler" boxes of figure 5-1. Consequently, P&G has eliminated many "also-ran" brands including Aleve pain-killer, Lestoil household cleaner, and Lava soap.

SKU Rationalization.   Global retailers deploy sophisticated category management systems that spew detailed results on which SKUs are performing. Suppliers cannot push weaker SKUs onto retailers and should delete those SKUs that are sub-par. Almost every major branded manufacturer has embarked on an SKU rationalization program over the past five years. For example, P&G has reduced its number of SKUs by 25 percent. Even the product line of a leading brand such as Head & Shoulders shampoo has gone from thirty-one to fifteen SKUs.

Transparent Pricing Strategy.   Most retailers now recognize that the demand for uniform global pricing is mostly a negotiating strategy since there are few uniform global products (except Gillette razors or Marlboro cigarettes, for example). Furthermore, comparing net prices across countries is difficult. Typically, the list price in each country is subject to

- quantity discounts (based on volume purchased),
- logistics discounts (based on whether the retailer orders truckloads, pallets, or cases),
- various behavioral discounts (for example, retailer's use of EDI, cash payment, or continuous replenishment),
- marketing allowances (for approved promotions and joint, or "cooperative," marketing activities), and
- performance-based incentives (for example, retailers achieving certain share for manufacturer in the category).

Global retailers have legitimate concerns about the transparency of manufacturer global prices and the standardization of terms and conditions. While prices may differ across countries, manufacturers could harmonize their pricing structures. Discounters like Aldi and Wal-Mart have performed well because they prefer a simpler low net price—no discounts. This preference allows manufacturers to simplify their systems, use a single IT platform, and standardize invoicing, thereby cutting considerable costs that add little value for the end user.

Procter & Gamble has adopted more straightforward, logical, and relatively transparent pricing policies. It withholds actual prices across customers but shares the logic of its pricing structure so that it will not find itself in a situation where it cannot justify its prices across different retail customers or countries.

Globally Competitive Supply Chains.   Finally, as global retailers push for global pricing, manufacturers will need to restructure their operations into globally competitive cross-border supply chains. Many "national" factories and warehouses, especially in Europe, will lose their rationale for existence.[27] Again, these tough decisions affect multiple stakeholders and require top management to champion the process.

Organizational Transformation

Companies tend to choose one of three organizational orientations to global accounts.[28] First, some companies give primacy to the country organization. For example, Coca-Cola started and subsequently disbanded its European account management because the independent bottlers in individual countries operate autonomously. Second, and probably most pervasive, is a balanced approach where the local account manager reports to both the local country manager and the global account manager. A third, more recent structure, in cases where the company organizes around powerful global customers, assigns power to global account managers, not to local sales.

To present a single face to the global customer despite multiple points of contact, regardless of orientation, most firms are establishing global customer development teams, a P&G innova-

FIGURE 5-3

The Structure of P&G's Global Customer Development Teams

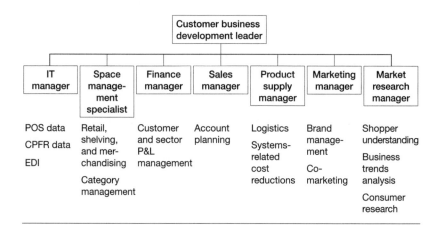

tion illustrated in figure 5-3. These global customer teams run parallel to global business units and country organizations, yielding an intricate matrix organization.[29]

Global Business Units.   Procter & Gamble split its global business unit (GBU) organization along the major lines of business such as food and beverages, fabric and home care, health and beauty, and family care. Each GBU must articulate its strategy and ensure adequate development of the brands and products in its portfolio by driving product innovation and supporting global brands. Managers develop business unit plans and have worldwide responsibility for achieving the sales and profit objectives at this megacategory level.

Country Organizations.   The traditional regional and country organizations are accountable for the country-level revenues and profits. They must understand the local consumers in their area, manage the local stakeholders, and serve local retailers. However, they must also translate the global business unit and global customer plans into local programs that will satisfy retailers and consumers, grow sales, and reduce costs. In addition, they provide input on local conditions for GBU strategies and plans. Recently, P&G began consolidating its country organizations into market development organizations for greater efficiency. Thus, Austria, Switzerland, and Germany are grouped, while the Benelux market organization covers Belgium, Netherlands, and Luxembourg.

Customer Business Development Teams. Finally, dedicated global customer business development teams coalesce to manage the relationship with each global retailer. With representatives across functions, business units, and countries, these teams must understand the global retail customer's strategy, develop the joint P&G/customer business plan, and coordinate with the GBUs and the country organizations to deliver on the agreed joint customer plan. As figure 5-4 indicates, the overall team-based organization can grow complicated quickly.

Joint Planning Processes. Planning processes in most multinational organizations still follow the traditional Army approach. The top of the organization develops strategies on brands and products, plans promotions, and presents those plans to retailers who can "take it or leave it." With increasing retail consolidation, this top-down planning process obviously fails. Instead, manufacturers must engage retail customers in the planning process and strategy conversations, primarily to understand the goals of each other's strategy and create a mutually agreeable joint strategy.

The planning process with a major global customer may look like figure 5-5. The global customer team must identify the three to four critical actions or initiatives that will drive business at a particular retailer, then explain these initiatives to the country organizations so that their local organizations will deliver on them.

To manage the interfaces among the customer development teams, business unit organizations, and country organizations, the manufacturer must identify and assign responsibility for all vendor activities around the global account. It must also specify which actions will be globally coordinated, partially globally

FIGURE 5-4

The Organizational Structure for Global Account Management

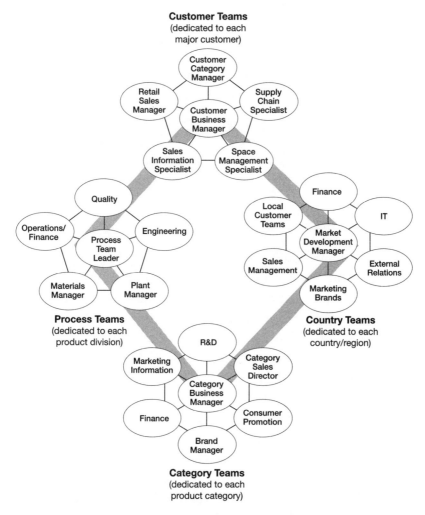

Source: Adapted from Michael George, Anthony Freeling, and David Court, "Reinventing the Marketing Organization," *McKinsey Quarterly* 4 (1994): 43–62.

coordinated, performed locally with some global coordination, or left exclusively to local organizations.[30]

Manufacturers who effectively manage global retailers do a lot of homework before their joint strategy meetings with retailers. One consumer packaged-goods company holds a two-day

FIGURE 5-5

Joint Planning Process with Global Retailers

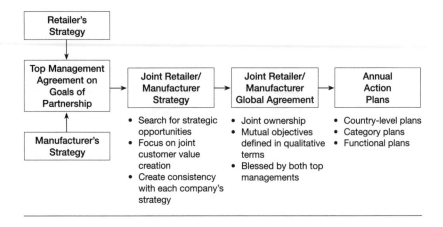

internal customer assessment workshop to prepare. For their Carrefour account, the workshop kicks off with thirty-three country presentations on what the company has achieved with the retailer over the past year, potential opportunities, and problems encountered. Then attendees conduct a SWOT analysis for Carrefour before engaging in an emotional discussion of what the company's overall strategy regarding Carrefour should be over the next three years. The outcomes of this meeting are projected profit and loss statements for Carrefour at the global, country, and brand level. Thus, the global account manager can meet Carrefour armed with an internal agreement on the objectives by country and by brand.

The most effective win-win partnerships stem from mutually agreed-upon performance objectives that bind both parties. Both parties must explicitly agree on a joint scorecard that identifies the key performance indicators. For example, the manufacturer may care about penetration, average ticket, frequency of purchase, sales growth, and margin growth, while the retailer may watch out for stocks, inventory turns, margins, complete orders, sales, and shelf space management.

Usually, both parties commit to quantitative and qualitative goals. Quantitative goals typically focus on increasing the sales of all the manufacturer's brands in their respective categories. Qualitative goals may include an international promotion, such as an in-store display, of a few brands across all countries. In return, the manufacturer may promise certain margins and support. Then, depending on the magnitude of the business, the manufacturer and retailer usually meet once a month or once a quarter to share data and monitor progress on these performance indicators.

Information Systems Transformation

In one of my earliest encounters with global retailing, I witnessed the CEO of a major multinational manufacturing company go crazy because his people could not tell him, with any degree of accuracy, how much profit they generated globally on sales to a global retailer who had just requested a single global price. According to one study, only 11 percent of manufacturers can assess the true cost of serving international retailers, despite rather sophisticated, expensive information systems.[31] Most companies that measure global account profitability use standard cost allocations rather than activity-based costing, and so they cannot generate a reasonably accurate profit and loss account for a global customer.

Since then, I have interacted with a major worldwide supplier to Carrefour. The global account manager had to negotiate a worldwide deal with Carrefour but could not determine his company's worldwide sales to Carrefour. The manufacturer's systems yielded numbers by country and by product line, but not by customer across product lines and countries. He could have compiled the revenue numbers manually but in a couple of African countries the manufacturer sold to Carrefour through agents who would not share sales data by customer with the global account manager. So he relied on Carrefour for data on the manufacturer's worldwide sales to the retailer. How can one negotiate if one does not have basic reliable information? It is like flying a plane without an altimeter.

Even at a sophisticated firm like P&G, the information system can provide aggregate volume data for a customer but one must manually calculate worldwide sales by customer in dollars—and only at list prices. To obtain the worldwide net sales in dollars for a customer would necessitate a rather painstaking manual compilation. Some companies like Hewlett-Packard, however, are investing in systems that can generate profit and loss statements for each global customer.[32]

The inability of marketers to provide financial information on marketing initiatives continually frustrates CEOs. Only 22 percent of companies in a survey monitored the effectiveness of trade promotion spending at the event level.[33] As joint planning with retailers increases, information about the profitability of events is critical in establishing account-specific objectives. Information systems that support global account management should monitor worldwide sales to the retailer, calculate the global profitability of the account, provide internal forums for global account managers to share learning, and help monitor and implement specific reward and evaluation systems.

Human Resource Transformation

Four human resource issues are related to how customer business development teams dedicated to global accounts function: coordination, co-location, composition, and compensation.

Coordination.   The coordination demands on the supplier's global customer team are extremely onerous. Companies must synchronize the various functions, business units, and country organizations through common goals, information, and compensation—and that's on top of harmonizing their marketing, sales, and service organizations to present an integrated face to local customers. Managers must not only reallocate resources across countries, product lines, and types of promotions, but also learn to collaborate internally.

Co-location.   Companies often debate where to locate the global customer development team. The 150-person P&G team for Wal-Mart is located in Bentonville, Arkansas, the home of Wal-Mart. Among the advantages of such proximity to the customer's global headquarters is the access to real human beings who can form individual relationships that roll up into a stronger partnership between the supplier and customer. One customer business development manager remarked, "Some of our teams are co-located, and some aren't. The ones that are co-located tend to do much better [in] adversarial kinds of situations because they can communicate. When everything you touch turns to gold, you can be almost anywhere. . . . But when things . . . get a little rockier, co-location matters."[34]

Co-located supplier teams can also focus on the customer at hand, not on other accounts and company politics. Overwhelmingly, formal and informal conversations within co-located teams are usually about the customer. Co-location fosters esprit de corps, and teams tend to develop a culture that is neither the supplier's nor the customer's. However, sometimes teams living near customers "go native" to the detriment of the supplier's corporate objectives.

Composition.   The composition of global account management teams is an important issue that managers often overlook. Who should lead the team? Who should participate? What skills matter? Most companies have excellent models for allocating resources to investment opportunities, but are still learning how to allocate people to teams. Currently, companies tend to select the leader from the same country as the retailer's headquarters. For example, the leader of a team working with Carrefour would be French and have considerable experience with the retailer. However, firms are evolving on this issue. At one consumer packaged goods company, the Ahold team leader was changed from a Dutchman to an American because most of Ahold's sales currently come from the United States.

However, many suppliers mistake customer business development teams for "sales teams" and therefore fail to incorporate logistics, marketing, finance, and other functions, as well as representatives from different countries and business units into customer business development teams.[35] Sometimes companies under-resource such teams without realizing that worldwide sales to a global customer may exceed those generated by many country subsidiaries.[36] For example, P&G operates in 140 countries with 300 brands. However, its six top customers, Wal-Mart and Costco (United States), Carrefour (France), Ahold (the Netherlands), Tesco (United Kingdom), and METRO Group (Germany), currently account for more than 30 percent of P&G's sales. Its largest fifty customers account for 55 percent, and it expects that its top ten accounts will deliver 50 percent of P&G's sales within five to ten years.

Compensation.   Most companies still link customer team compensation to revenue and volume, because they can not calculate account profitability and do not care about the profitability of their customers.[37] Increasingly, global retailers are asking their suppliers to take some responsibility for the retailer's margins and profitability on the supplier's products. One customer business development manager observed, "It's important to recognize our accountability to customer's measures. For years we used to say, 'margins are not our problems, they are your problems.' . . . Now we are saying, 'we are accountable for that.'"[38]

The best way to ensure accountability is to link part of the team's compensation to retailer profitability on the supplier's products. In addition, suppliers are linking the team's compensation to customer service and account profitability.

Since customer business development teams exist alongside more hierarchical country and business unit organizations, team members need specific career and development tracks, clear reporting relationships, and agreement on compensation.[39] For example, the local manager managing the Wal-Mart relationship for P&G in Germany reports to P&G's global account manager for Wal-Mart as well as the local P&G country manager. If the person does not report to the global account manager, then the company might as well not have a customer business development team. On the other hand, failing to integrate the local organizations within the global teams can lead to overall failure. So should P&G attribute sales to Wal-Mart in Germany to Germany or to the global account manager for Wal-Mart? Most companies resolve this through double counting where both managers get credit.

In non-retail contexts such as advertising or audit services, conflicts arise over compensating independent local offices for their work on global accounts. What is fair when wages vary tremendously around the world? Justifying the payment of diverse rates for the same work, for the same account, may turn into a political and cultural minefield. Companies differ in their approach: Grey Advertising sets interoffice billing rates annually, and British Telecom negotiates all local compensation before signing a global client. Other companies eliminate interoffice billing and distribute the revenues based on the percentage of each office's work.

Companies that fail to resolve this—or any of the remaining Cs—risk alienating their most valuable long-term customers. For example, a few years ago, Citibank discovered that its country managers refused to serve multinational corporations adequately.[40] Citibank's country organizations made relatively low margins from working on multinational accounts and country managers were evaluated on their country's profitability. However, multinational companies represented Citibank's best opportunity for growth by selling them high-margin global services. To solve the problem, CEO John Reed took profit responsibility away from country managers and instead rewarded them for services provided to multinational clients.

Conclusion

As distribution channels consolidate worldwide, the pressure on upstream suppliers will only increase. Their survival will likely depend on their ability to work with powerful global members of the distribution channels. Clearly, the best approach is to develop

Global Account
Management Checklist

- **Customers:** *Have we identified our most valuable clients on a worldwide basis?*

- **Strategy:** *Do we have a clear strategy for global accounts?*

- **Structure:** *Does our structure promote cross-border, cross-division collaboration with global customers?*

- **Relationship:** *Are there single points of contact for global customers?*

- **Culture:** *Do we accept global account managers as advocates for global customers?*

- **Incentive systems:** *Do our compensation and incentive systems align with serving global clients?*

- **Talent:** *Do we have enough people who can serve on global account teams?*

in-demand brands that distributors simply must stock and support. However, even suppliers of such strong brands must continually innovate and diligently manage their distribution channels. Suppliers in trusted reseller relationships will increase the potential for creating value for the end user by reducing superfluous processes.

Suppliers cannot adopt a one-size-fits-all approach with distribution channels. Some retailers will work together in partnerships, while others prefer adversarial relationships. Firms must simultaneously optimize the power and trust games with different retailers. Similarly, suppliers will have both global accounts and traditional accounts, but those that develop real competence in

- **Process:** *Have we synchronized our processes with those of global customers?*

- **Competence:** *Can all of our country organizations perform at global service levels?*

- **Supply chain:** *Have we optimized our supply chain for global efficiency?*

- **Marketing:** *Have we successfully implemented brand and SKU rationalization initiatives?*

- **Pricing:** *Have we harmonized prices/pricing structures?*

- **Accounting systems:** *Do our customer-level worldwide profit-and-loss statements go beyond standard cost allocations?*

- **IT systems:** *Do our IT systems generate the needed data on global customers?*

- **Knowledge management:** *Are we effectively utilizing global customer data to develop new products and improve weak positions in existing products?*

Adapted from Christopher Senn, "Are You Ready for Global Account Management," Velocity, no. 2 (2001): 26–28.

global account management will observe reductions in cost of sales, revenue growth, higher cross-selling of products from weaker divisions, greater sales force efficiency, easier launch of new products, and increased responsiveness to customer-specific needs at the account level.

Managers who answer "no" to any of the questions in the "Global Account Management Checklist" need their CEO's support to effect the necessary changes. Consider Electrolux, a company that has assembled a vast brand portfolio through acquisitions over the years. Suspicious business unit managers are hampering efforts to coordinate across different units to serve global customers such as hotel chains or Shell Oil.[41] Similarly, the more entrepreneurial ABB struggled to serve global clients until Goran Lindahl became CEO and underscored the importance of global account management.

Over time, global customers will start to account for a majority of the supplier's sales with their own global customer development teams. As companies organize around customers, they will consolidate sales and marketing functions, eliminate national offices, and cut back or downgrade central marketing departments. These customers' teams will increasingly perform more of the marketing activities, and their leaders will likely report to the CEO, or a Chief Customer Officer, who reports directly to the CEO. Anyone still called the Director of Marketing or the Director of Sales will probably report to the Chief Customer Officer.

The ultimate Chief Customer Officer is the CEO, who will serve as ambassador to the large global accounts and intervene on issues that the team leaders cannot resolve.

SIX

From Brand Acquisitions to Brand Rationalization

Don't advertise the brand, live it.

IN THE KNOWLEDGE AGE, CEOs realize that the value of their firms is determined less and less by the tangible assets they own, such as factories or inventories, and increasingly by intangible assets such as competences, customer base, distribution networks, employees, and brands. Of all the intangible assets owned by a company, brands are perhaps the most prized. This has led to a dramatic change in how CEOs view their companies, their sources of competitive advantage, and their notion of the firms' strategic assets. In 2000, Niall FitzGerald, cochairman of Unilever, declared: "We're not a manufacturing company anymore. We're a brand marketing group that happens to make some of its products."[1] This from a company that until the mid-1970s derived more than half its profits from its African operations, which included retailing, shipping lines, and trading, as well as plantations producing bulk vegetable oils for margarine and washing powder!

Branding should be the differentiating mechanism, separating the company's products and services from those of its competitors. If done correctly, it allows the seller to escape the commodity magnet, where price and product features are the primary differentiators. A strong brand helps generate greater sales and price premiums. Brand equity should be a rich reservoir of goodwill for the company, making it easier to attract customers, dealers, employees, and investors. As custodians of the brand value, nothing should be as sacred, as precious, to marketers as the brands they manage.

Buying a brand and its market share is often much cheaper and faster than building it. Companies such as Akzo Nobel, Cisco, L'Oreal, and Nestlé have been consolidating their positions by acquiring smaller players. In addition, there have been many megamergers between large companies within the same industry, such as Citigroup-Travelers, DaimlerChrysler, Exxon-Mobil, or Hewlett-Packard and Compaq. As a result of these brand mergers and acquisitions, many companies find themselves with large brand portfolios. In 1998 in Europe alone, Akzo Nobel sold paint under thirty-seven different brand names including Astral, Berger, Casco, Crown, Marshall, Nordsjö, Sadolin, and Sikkens.[2]

Assessing their brand portfolios, top managers worry that many of their brands are serving only small niche segments with few customers, thereby generating insignificant revenues or profits. Consider the following:

- Of its 250 brands, P&G's top ten brands, including Pampers, Tide, and Bounty, account for half of its sales, more than half of its profits, and almost two-thirds of its growth over the past decade.[3]

- The bottom 1,200 brands in Unilever's 1,600-brand portfolio accounted for only 8 percent of the company's total sales in 1999.[4]

- The vast majority of Nestlé's profits come from a tiny percentage of more than 8,000 brands worldwide.

In the face of such large brand portfolios, companies are now killing off famous names rather than acquiring and extending brands, as was the rage over the last two decades. Many famous brands are dead or dying. GTE and Bell Atlantic are now Verizon; General Motors has finally retired Oldsmobile; Merrill Lynch has dropped the Mercury brand; and Citibank—now Citi—has deleted Schroders and Solomon. In the consumer packaged goods industry, historical brands such as La Rouche-aux-Fées yogurt in France, Treets candy in the United Kingdom, and White Cloud toilet paper in the United States have received their pink slips. Such firms as Akzo Nobel, Diageo, Electrolux, P&G, and Unilever have rationalized or are actively rationalizing their brand portfolios. And more companies keep jumping on this bandwagon. For example, Shiseido recently announced plans to cut its brands from 140 to 35 by 2005. The dilemma for companies is to prune their brand portfolios without losing the customers and sales revenue associated with the brands that are to be deleted.

Brand Proliferation Is Costly

Finer market segmentation clearly warrants some brand proliferation. However, mergers and acquisitions, as well as uninhibited brand propagation aimed at alleged market and growth opportunities, account for a fair share of the mushrooming. To justify its existence, each brand in the portfolio must link to a specific target segment and have a unique positioning. The cost of maintaining each individual brand in the portfolio must be less than the revenues that it generates through greater segmentation. The ten questions presented in the following box help managers to determine whether their company has too many brands.

Managing mammoth multibrand portfolios, especially within the same product category, presents the following major problems.

Does Your Company Have Too Many Brands?

1. Are more than 50 percent of our brands not featured amongst the top three brands in terms of market share?

2. Are there brands for which we are unable to match competitors on marketing and advertising expenditures because we lack adequate scale?

3. Are we losing money on our smaller brands?

4. Do we have different brands in different countries for essentially the same product?

5. Are there brands in our portfolio that display a high degree of overlap on target segment, product lines, price bands, or distribution channels?

6. Does the analysis from image tracking surveys, closest competitor studies, and consumer brand switching matrices

1. Insufficient Differentiation

The greater the number of brands within a particular category, the more challenging for the firm to position each one uniquely. Only so many distinctive combinations of benefits and attributes will attract substantial numbers of customers. How well has, say, General Motors differentiated the product lines and brand images of its car brands: Buick, Cadillac, Chevrolet, Pontiac, Oldsmobile, Opel, Saab, and Saturn?

Not surprisingly, the larger the number of brands in the company's portfolio, the greater the overlap of brands on target segments, positioning, price, distribution channels, and product demonstrate that customers see our brands as directly competing with each other?

7. Are retailers only agreeing to stock a subset of our total relevant brand portfolio?

8. Are there brands in our portfolio where an increase in marketing and advertising expenditures in support of one of the brands decreases the sales of another brand in the portfolio?

9. Do we spend an inordinate amount of time discussing resource allocation decisions across brands?

10. Do our brand managers see each other as competitors?

Score 1 point for each question answered with a "yes."

0–2:   Minimal brand rationalization opportunity.

3–6:   Considerable brand rationalization opportunity.

7–10:   Brand rationalization should be an immediate priority. Alert top management.

lines. The overlapping results in cannibalization of sales and duplication of effort. If managed poorly, many of the brands in the portfolio may end up competing with each other rather than with competitors' brands.

2. Inefficiency

Invariably, a larger brand portfolio means lower sales volumes for the individual brands as the total market divides among them. Without scale economies in product development, supply chain, and marketing, firms cannot support each brand at competitive levels. For example, developing a new model in the automotive industry takes almost a billion dollars in development costs and production investments. Without adequate resources to refresh each brand's product line, companies such as General Motors and Volkswagen share product platforms across brands. While this practice increases efficiency, it lowers perceived product variety. According to critics, Volkswagen's sharing of product platforms across brands (for example, the chassis shared between the Volkswagen Beetle and the Audi TT) has diluted the more prestigious brand and reduced differentiation.

Similarly, companies must spend a minimum amount annually on marketing and advertising each brand to attract customer attention, and this amount has been rapidly rising over the years. For example, in 1995, three television advertisements could reach 80 percent of women in the United States; today a company must buy ninety-seven spots to reach the same audience.[5] Thus, small brands sweat to remain competitive. As Unilever's FitzGerald observed, "You need to get through the clutter of communication with consumers and if you spread your budget over all your brands, it doesn't get through. We will have to swing our resources behind a smaller number to achieve higher growth rates for them."[6] Managers often allocate the multibrand firm's brand budget suboptimally, thereby reducing the corporate return on brand investments.

3. Lower Market Power

The rise of powerful mass merchants such as B&Q, Barnes & Noble, Best Buy, Carrefour, Home Depot, and Wal-Mart has triggered brand consolidation perhaps more than anything else. The retailers' tremendous negotiating power, especially against weaker brands, forces manufacturers to critically evaluate their brand portfolios.

Large retailers have also developed top-quality store brands that currently account for one in five units sold in U.S. stores and about twice that in Europe. Retailers have used these store brands to play manufacturers off each other. Many retailers will carry only the top two or three manufacturer brands in a category plus their own private label. Weaker manufacturer brands either lose their shelf space to store brands or else pay dearly to retain it. Hans Straberg, CEO of Electrolux, stated, "Our aim is to become a reliable and trusted partner with our customers and retailers. That means we need a few strong brands. We can't support too many."[7]

4. Management Complexity

Finally, brand proliferation pressures management to coordinate the complicated and larger portfolios of products, package designs, R&D projects, marketing plans, and distributor relationships. Marginal brands end up consuming a disproportionate

TABLE 6-1

The Forces Behind Brand Consolidation

	Past	Future
Corporate	Acquisitions and mergers	Search for synergy
	Search for top-line growth	Search for *profitable* top-line growth
	International expansion	Global strategy
	Brand-management structures	Category-management structures
	Power of country managers	Corporate HQ resistance
Competition	Copycat strategies	Need for differentiation
	Worldwide deregulation and mushrooming media outlets	Emergence of global media giants
Channel/ Consumer	New distribution channels	Consolidating distribution channels
	Demand for exclusive products and shelf space productivity	Demand for category management
	Desire to avoid channel conflict	Growth of private labels
	Multiple consumer segments	Cross-national segmentation
	Local marketing	Emergence of global consumers
	⬇	⬇
	Growing Brand Portfolios	**Shrinking Brand Portfolios**

amount of a company's time and resources, and exacerbate tensions between the narrowly focused brand and country managers. In annual marketing strategy and budget meetings, top managers find themselves focusing internally on resource allocation across the different brands, rather than externally on battling competitors and serving customers.

CEOs are distressed to discover that their most valuable asset, the burgeoning brand portfolio, is devouring company profitability and hampering growth. Moreover, the surge in global media, global segments, and international distributors all reduce the logic behind many brands that were unique to single countries (see table 6-1). CEOs see the wisdom in fewer, larger, and more global brands and realize that brand rationalization provides a critical path to higher profitability and growth.

The Challenge of Brand Rationalization

Deleting brands is easy, but retaining their sales and customers is not. Therein lies the managerial dilemma: How can brand portfolios be pruned without losing the customers and sales revenue of the doomed brands?

Overwhelmingly, firms lose market share, sales volume, and customers to their competitors during brand portfolio rationalization. To stem such losses, managers often try to merge two brands instead of deleting one. Still, studies indicate that only one in eight attempts to consolidate two brands ever delivers the original market shares of the two brands. Consider the following failures:

- Kal Kan and Crave, two of the three leading brands in the U.S. cat food business in the 1980s, merged in 1988 to create a new brand called Whiskas.[8] Five years later, Whiskas had still failed to reach the combined market share of Kal Kan and Crave. To salvage sales, Kal Kan Foods, Inc., finally reintroduced the Kal Kan name on the Whiskas packaging but with limited success.

- In 1987, Mars, Inc., merged the brand Treets, a European candy quite unlike M&Ms, into the M&Ms brand without warning customers.[9] M&Ms suddenly came in two packages, containing very different products, neither of which enticed British and German palates. Sales dropped 20 percent in the first year. In 1991, Mars reintroduced Treets in Germany, as M&M's Treets Selection.

- In 1996, Rite Aid Pharmacies acquired the 1,000 Thrifty/PayLess drugstores, a western U.S. regional chain, and converted them all to Rite Aids. To raise local awareness about the new brand, Rite Aid invested several million dollars in advertising the rebranded chain. However, Rite Aid executives underestimated the value of Thrifty/PayLess's walk-in business, attracted by a product mix that included "award winning" ice cream, beach balls, cosmetics, and magazines. Rite Aid struggled to recapture former Thrifty/PayLess customers who did not equate pharmacies with such impulse buys. Immediately after the rebranding, the acquired stores' sales started declining 10 percent monthly. In 2000, Rite Aid hired two former Thrifty/PayLess executives to manage its western region.

- In 1999, Hilton International acquired four-star U.K.-based Stakis (fifty-four hotels and twenty-two casinos) for £1.5 billion and then killed the Stakis brand. The overnight name change confused and disappointed Hilton International guests, who found that some of the newly acquired hotels did not meet their expectations of the Hilton brand. Despite claims of spending £100 million to upgrade standards to unify its hotels under the Hilton brand, sales fell 6.6 percent in 2000. So, in 2001, when Hilton acquired Scandic's 154 hotels in the Nordic region, it wisely retained the Scandic brand and rebranded only twenty of the properties under the Hilton name.

Brand rationalization hurts. Remember that even weak, money-losing brands have devoted channel members, customers, and prospects—not to mention brand and country managers—who will vigorously defend them. A proposed brand deletion could endanger a distributor's or employee's livelihood, if not a lifetime of commitment to the brand. What will that family-owned Oldsmobile dealership do if General Motors does not offer a replacement brand from its portfolio?

Brand rationalization is neither straightforward nor well understood. No one can easily determine which brands to retain, merge, sell, or delete altogether in a portfolio, and no marketing textbook covers the decision-making process. Without clear methodology and an actively engaged CEO, strategy sessions will likely suffer from politics and turf wars. Antony Burgmans, co-chair of Unilever N.V., observed in a meeting with top executives, "Focusing the brand portfolio is the single biggest issue facing Unilever today. This is not something we can delegate to others. It is too important. We have to do it ourselves—quickly."[10]

The Brand Rationalization Process

Based on the experiences of several successful firms, a shrewd brand rationalization process has four essential steps: (1) Conduct a brand portfolio audit; (2) determine the optimal brand portfolio; (3) select appropriate brand deletion strategies; and (4) develop a growth strategy for the survivors. Managers who plunge directly into brand rationalization (steps 2 and 3) without preparing the organization (step 1) or outlining a growth strategy (step 4) *will* fail.

Conduct a Brand Portfolio Audit

To succeed, a brand rationalization program must win the support of front-line managers. Managers, especially of the brands targeted for deletion, often fear brand rationalization because they fear losing their independence and drowning in the larger company. This anxiety leads them to overstate the down-side of eliminating the brand. To enable an unbiased decision, the

brand rationalization program should first conduct a brand portfolio audit.

The brand portfolio audit objectively exposes managers to the
corporate perspective on the portfolio. The audit raises issues con-
cerning positioning overlap, synergies, and benchmarking, which
help country and brand managers see the big picture. Without
such an audit, these managers could make a case to justify the
existence of every brand. But the goal is to *optimize the portfolio*,
rather than *optimizing each brand in the portfolio*. Table 6-2 provides a template for a brand portfolio audit. Initially, groups of
managers complete the audit independently, and then pool their

TABLE 6-2

Brand Portfolio Audit

Brand	Global Market Share	Regional Presence					
		North America	Latin America	Asia Pacific	Japan	Western Europe	...
A	15%	S / fun					
B	7%	W / value					
C	3%						
D	1%						
E	*						
F	*						
•							
•							
•							
•							

* Less than 1%.

Top half of the box: Market position
  D = Dominant (#1 in the region)
  S = Strong (#2 or #3 in the region)
  W = Weak (#4 or less in the region)
  NP = Not present in the region

Bottom half of the box: Brand positioning
  Quality; value; upscale; fun;
  adventurous; premium; safe; reliable;
  trustworthy; aggressive; cheap; etc.

data. The audit identifies the brands and their global market share. Geographic or other segment markets fall along the columns. For each brand in each market, managers enter two pieces of information: (1) the market position—characterized as "dominant," "strong," "weak," or "not present in the region"—to denote brand strength in the specific market, and (2) a single-word description of the brand positioning to indicate the brand's value proposition. Examples of frequently used words appear in the exhibit, but participants are usually quite creative when completing this column.

Managers can add columns that track the percentage of corporate profits that each brand generates and whether the brand is a cash generator, cash neutral, or a cash guzzler if data are available prior to the exercise. Without hard data, however, these additional two columns can spark long internal debates that detract from the process. Better to use best guesses and verify data later. Remember, brand deletion is an art, not a science.

Obtaining detailed brand-level profitability numbers requires complex allocations of fixed and shared costs, and thus the validity of the resulting data is uncertain. The current profitability of a brand is not the ultimate indicator of which to delete. More important, the brand rationalization decision is strategic: Managers must consider what *could* occur, not what is *actually occurring*. They must imagine the profit and loss for the firm and each surviving brand *after* the purge of marginal brands and the adjustment of the marketing mix for survivors.

Frequently, the results of the data pooling surprises managers: Very few of the company's brands in any category enjoy global market shares greater than 1 percent. Group discussion generally moves through various reasons for sparing pet brands to more balanced observations that many brands in the corporate portfolio

- have small market shares,
- suffer from poor or negative profitability,
- consume rather than contribute to cash flow,
- lack support from important channel members,

- exhaust disproportionate amounts of managerial resources, and

- add little strategic value to the firm.

The audit makes the need for brand portfolio rationalization apparent, impersonal, and broad-based. Top management can use it to outline the remaining three steps of the rationalization program.

Determine the Optimal Brand Portfolio

Companies utilize two complementary processes—the overall corporate portfolio approach and the needs-based segmentation approach—to determine the optimal portfolio.

The results of the brand portfolio analysis feed directly into the overall corporate portfolio approach, a relatively top-down process that sets the overall objectives and direction for the rationalization program. It broadly attacks the company's brand portfolio using a few simple figures such as minimum sales, market share position, growth rate, and geographical reach. The outcomes of this process usually address the following critical questions:

- *How many brands should we retain and how many should we delete?*   For example, the top managers of one company decided that they would delete all brands that were neither number one or two in terms of market share. Unilever determined that it would scrap the bottom 1,200 of its 1,600 brands—accounting for only 8 percent of the company's sales within five years.

- *What is the role of our corporate brand?*   For example, Electrolux decided to develop its corporate name into the master brand—the brand that would ultimately account for 70 percent of the group's revenues.

- *Which brands are core to our company?*   For example, P&G's "core" brands are the twelve that each generate more than a billion dollars annually in sales.

- *Does our portfolio contain any potentially global brands?* Unilever, for instance, designated forty brands as core global brands.

- *Should our company exit any category wherein all our brands are poorly positioned?*

Answers to these questions should help articulate a vision of where, in terms of geographies and businesses, the company wishes to compete.

The needs-based segmentation approach examines the number and types of needs-based segments that exist within each individual category in which the firm competes. The results of this analysis complement the overall objectives and direction of the brand rationalization program identified by the corporate portfolio approach. Since a company must position every brand against a unique segment of consumers, this bottom-up process helps managers to determine the optimal brand portfolio in terms of individual categories and implementation.

Consider these questions:

How many distinct brands can we support in a category?

Which segments should the company cover with its brands?

Which brand should we match against which segment?

Which brands should we merge?

Since one could begin with needs-based segmentation to determine the number of brands to retain and the number to delete, this approach works well for companies where managers want to rationalize a group of brands that compete in the same category. It also helps companies that compete in many categories to select which brands should remain in particular categories where they have too many brands. For example, P&G rationalized its laundry detergents portfolio and consequently decided to merge Solo with Bold.

On the other hand, if companies with complex brand portfolios—that is, hundreds of brands across multiple categories—

tried to rationalize their entire brand portfolio at once, then the data gathering and objective setting of the bottom-up approach would take too long. Better to start with the corporate portfolio-based approach to determine the overall objectives and direction and then move to the needs-based segmentation approach.

Select Appropriate Brand Deletion Strategies

Four possible scenarios exist for the doomed brands: sell, milk, delist, or merge. Companies should *sell* non-core brands that will not likely become competitors but could offer value to others. For example, in 1999, Diageo sold Cinzano vermouth and Metaxa brandy to concentrate on nine core brands that yielded 70 percent of its profits.[11]

Companies should *milk for profits* those brands that have some customer franchise but are neither core to the firm's direction nor valuable to others. Milking entails stopping all but the absolute minimal marketing support, thereby increasing profits in the short run (by cutting costs) as sales slowly decline. When they finally die, the company delists them.

Companies can safely *delist*, or eliminate, minor brands with poor sales that grapple futilely for shelf space. To migrate loyal customers, a company can issue them coupons or samples for the most adjacent surviving brand in the portfolio.

Finally, companies can *merge* two brands into one if the lesser brand is still maintaining significant sales in a core category. Merging, sometimes referred to as brand transfer or brand migration, reduces the number of brands without losing sales because marketing migrates the associated customers to the surviving brand.

Depending on competitive and corporate pressures, companies choose between adopting a "quick change" versus a "gradual brand transfer" strategy. A quick change with a new brand name works when managers want to break cleanly from the past, as was the case for Sandoz and Ciba-Geigy, now called Novartis. After a painful merger, a completely new name can signify egalitarianism, resilience, and fresh opportunity. It can also convey to customers the availability of new capabilities.

Instead of developing a new name, the merged companies can quickly drop one brand, as the two Swiss banks UBS and SBS did in becoming UBS. This move works when global competition requires speed and control over customers for easy migration or when one brand is significantly stronger than the other and can extend its equity while internally signaling the direction of the new enterprise.

If both brand names have strong brand franchises, then one can adopt a gradual brand migration strategy by subbranding or dual branding during the transition before eventually dropping the weaker name. For instance, Dulux Valentine dropped Valentine, and Philips Whirlpool dropped Philips. Gradual brand migration works when markets are stable or customer loyalty to the brands is strong, as long as companies have mapped a careful migration path from the doomed brands to the survivors.

Consider Vodafone, a company formed through acquisition of equity stakes in disparately named mobile operators in various countries. In 2000, it launched a global brand migration plan to switch its constituent operating companies to its master brand by early 2002. It managed the migration in two steps. First, the individual country brands converted to dual branding, such as D2 Vodafone in Germany, Omnitel Vodafone in Italy, Click Vodafone in Egypt, and Europolitan Vodafone in Sweden, to raise brand awareness for Vodafone through the name recognition of the local brands. Next, over two years, it phased out the local prefixes in advertising campaigns and sponsorship programs. Brand tracking studies helped marketers to time the switch from the dual brand to the Vodafone master brand, country by country, when Vodafone recognition reached a certain height. For example, Portugal-based Telecel Vodafone converted to Vodafone three months ahead of schedule because of its successful dual branding program. By adopting a single brand, Vodafone's European subsidiaries obtained cost synergies on brand advertising, media buying, global product/service branding, and advertising, while making it easier to increase customers' usage of Vodafone products and roaming services.

Develop a Growth Strategy for the Surviving Brands

Brand deletions are risky. Without a strategy to grow the remaining brands, all the firm ends up with is a cost reduction program and a smaller top line because of the sales lost from the deleted brands. As part of the process, managers must identify opportunities to build fewer, stronger brands though enhancements and investments.

Brand enhancement involves migrating useful characteristics from the deleted brands to the remaining ones. This can be done in several ways: (1) The deleted brand may have one or two unique or attractive products that could do well under a surviving brand's product line. (2) Some attribute of the deleted brand could resurface in a surviving brand to augment the latter's value proposition. (3) Surviving brands may lack presence where a deleted brand was sold. Replacing the defunct brand with a survivor in that locality will expand its geographical footprint.

Brand investment purposefully redirects the resources freed from the discontinued lines to the surviving brands. By merging brands, companies can generate substantial savings through greater economies of scale in supply chain, sales, and marketing. A more streamlined product line and better inventory optimization may reduce cost of goods sold, and combining the brands' respective sales forces and customer service teams may cut sales and administration expenses. Finally, focused marketing and advertising can generate greater bang for the buck. For example, by concentrating on the fourteen of the three-hundred-odd brands that account for more than half of P&G's sales, A. G. Lafley, the current CEO, increased turnover in ten, including Crest toothpaste, which grew by more than 30 percent.

Bottom-Up Segmentation-Based Approach at Electrolux

Electrolux, based in Sweden, is one of the world's leading consumer durable products companies. Its products include white goods, such as refrigerators, cookers, washing machines, vacuum cleaners, and outdoor equipment like mowers, trimmers, and chain saws. Over the past twenty-five years, the company has made between three and four hundred acquisitions, resulting in a very large brand portfolio.

Under CEO Michael Treschow, the company cut costs with modest success through plant rationalization and a reduction in the number of product platforms. In 1998, Electrolux examined its portfolio of over seventy brands. It discovered that, in almost every country, one of its brands was among the top three, but it was never the same brand across borders. Not surprisingly, the company's fragmented marketing efforts could not achieve economies of global scale or scope.

The brand portfolio's complexity raised a fundamental question about Electrolux itself: Was it a manufacturing company that should just let retailers and others build brands, or was it a branding company? Ultimately, the firm's board of directors favored the latter, and the firm launched a brand rationalization project to create fewer but stronger brands.

The name of the company, Electrolux, would become the master brand. By phasing out weak local brands and having Electrolux endorse strong local brands, executives resolved to generate two-thirds of the company's sales from its master brand by 2007. Within this overall rationalization program, Electrolux's effort in one category—the professional food service equipment business—richly illustrates the bottom-up segmentation-based approach.

In 1996, Electrolux had a 4.2 billion Swedish Kroner (SEK) business selling food service equipment across Europe to professional kitchens in hospitals, restaurants, airports, and cafeterias.[12] The European food service equipment market was highly fragmented, with fifteen to twenty-five competitors per country, and little overlap among the players across countries.

Over the years, Electrolux bought several small individual companies, each of which had a brand and a factory. By 1996, more than fifteen different Electrolux brands (including Molteni in France, Senking in Germany, CryptoPeerless in the United Kingdom, and Nordton in Italy) clamored for Europe's food service equipment business. Only one brand, Zanussi, had a pan-European profile. Given so many local brands, Electrolux ran a decentralized business. The small size and weak coverage of the fifteen individual brands meant that Electrolux was losing money overall with operating losses of 1.3 percent in its food service equipment business in 1996. An Electrolux survey demonstrated that leading brands generate higher price premiums. Hence, brand rationalization in food service equipment became central to restoring profitability and sustaining the company's overall strategic direction: Reduce the number of brands and strengthen the remaining few.

In order to eliminate brands, Electrolux had to decide how many brands it should have in food service equipment. It conducted a major cross-national, needs-based segmentation study to inform this decision. Similar to many other professional markets, the food service equipment industry segmented the market into "low," "medium," and "high" according to price and product specifications. Brands tended to target one of these segments by claiming to be good, better, or best. Electrolux positioned its brands across these three price bands and segmented further by customer profile, such as hospital, canteen, bar, school, convenience store, restaurant, and hotel.

This study pinpointed two problems with the conventional industry approach to segmentation:

1. Customer type did not really predict customer needs. For example, restaurants varied significantly in terms of needs; lumping all restaurants within one segment made little sense. No institution was "average."

2. Each customer sought the best solution for that customer's needs. Why should customers want a good or a better brand rather than the best for their purposes?

Electrolux realized that developing the best solution for each customer required starting from customer needs. The pan-European needs-based segmentation study revealed four distinct segments across countries. Furthermore, each of the four segments had different customer types, product specifications, pricing indexes, distribution needs, and contexts in which customers used the equipment.

The "performance specialization" segment, comprising firms such as airlines, five-star hotels, and hospitals, produced large volumes of meals under circumstances that involved complicated logistics. Customers needed high performance, integrated systems, and a price index of 100 compared to the other segments.

The "basic solution, fast return on investment" segment, consisting of firms such as pubs and convenience stores, used catering as an auxiliary activity geared to generating fast ROI through basic menus. Customers sought conformity with legal and sanitary regulation and very low prices (price index of 25).

The "gastronomy partnership" segment, comprised of firms such as staff canteens, family restaurants, and elderly homes, produced fewer than two hundred meals daily in a normal environment and had low technical competence. Customers required modular solutions, close supplier relationships, and proven technology at reasonable prices (price index of 50–75).

The "prestige gourmet" segment, consisting of gourmet restaurants, independent or within five-star hotels, with celebrity chefs who produced signature dishes. Customers wanted to create a prestigious kitchen—with a very reliable stove—as a status symbol (price index of 200–300).

Electrolux decided that, in the short run, it would forgo the second segment because of the prevailing low prices, fragmented customer base, and lack of an appropriate product range. Instead, it would target the other three segments with unique brands that focused on fulfilling the particular segment's needs. Since it needed only three brands, Electrolux chose the brands Electrolux, Zanussi, and Molteni to serve the performance specialists, gastronomic partners, and prestige gourmets, respectively. Managers arrived at these three brands based on scale and proximity to the desired positioning of the respective target segment.

After the segmentation and deletion, division managers decided that each of three brands should invest in building a brand image appropriate to the target segment. Electrolux used a five-layer brand pyramid to examine each brand's personality, values, rewards, functional benefits, and features.

Thanks to its brand rationalization program, Electrolux now has three pan-European brands smartly positioned as the best for each needs-based segment. Two of the remaining twelve brands, Juno and Therma, had pockets of strength and were temporarily converted into subbrands of Electrolux, while the other ten brands were eliminated.

Three robust pan-European brands instead of fifteen local brands enabled Electrolux to centralize brand management. For consumers to perceive each brand as the best solution for their target segments, Electrolux developed a number of international marketing and communication tools including new advertising concepts, Internet and extranet sites dedicated to the brands, customized commercial documentation, newsletters, road shows, and exhibition and showroom concepts. Most local brands could not have developed these tools due to the costs and competence requirements.

Since managers understood the needs-based segments explicitly, they could develop fewer but more appropriate products for customers. Twice a year, about twenty of the one hundred designers and engineers from the European product development centers work three days alongside restaurant staff in hospitals, hotels, and office canteens.[13] This on-site research unearths useful insights, such as simpler ways to clean the equipment. The needs-based segmentation has also helped the division to redefine itself from an engineering company to an "orchestrator of gastronomic events." In fact, Electrolux insists that all divisions use a needs-based segmentation approach to new product development.

The resulting economies of scale and scope have turned the fortunes of the professional food service equipment business at Electrolux. Its operating income has increased by almost 10 percent, from negative 1.3 percent in 1996 to positive 8.1 percent in 2001—an increase in the bottom line of 390 million SEK.

Electrolux has largely managed to retain sales at 4.2 billion SEK between 1996 and 2001 despite deleting twelve brands. Its next challenge involves increasing revenues by investing substantially in marketing these three brands and targeting the initially ignored fourth segment with a new brand, Dito.

Top-Down Portfolio-Based Approach at Unilever

In 1999, Unilever, the Anglo Dutch consumer products giant, suffered its third straight year of declining revenues. After a 6 percent increase in 1996, revenues had declined by 11, 9, and 0.2 percent respectively in 1997, 1998, and 1999 to a worldwide total of £27 billion. In the 1990s, the underlying annual sales growth of 3 to 4 percent was below the firm's aspiration of 5 to 6 percent. Operating margins at 11 percent, while healthy, were still unacceptable to management. The pending acquisition of U.S.-based Bestfoods in 2000 would bring additional brands such as Hellmann's and Knorr.

On examining its worldwide portfolio of 1,600 brands, the top management discovered that the 400 core brands generated 75 percent of the firm's revenues; the other 1,200 brands contributed only 8 percent. Managers agreed to pursue radical steps.

Unilever embarked on a five-year program, "Path to Growth," that would stress the 400 core brands and, more dramatically, dispose of, delete, or consolidate the remaining 1,200 marginal ones. This strategy had two objectives: (1) increase annual sales growth to the 5 to 6 percent range and operating margins to 16 percent plus by the end of 2004, and (2) generate earnings per share growth over the period of the plan in the low double digits.

First, Unilever developed a process for identifying the 400 core brands. It set the following three selection criteria:

1. *Brand scale:* The brand must have adequate scale and margins to justify further investment in communication, innovation, and technology at competitive levels.

2. *Brand power:* The brand must have the potential to be number one or two in its market and be a must-carry brand to drive retailers' store traffic.

3. *Brand growth potential:* The brand must have the potential for sustainable growth based on current consumer appeal and ability to meet future needs. Unilever favored brands that tapped into global consumer trends (for example, health and convenience) and could potentially stretch across categories. For example, it repositioned Bertolli from Italian olive oil to Mediterranean-inspired food.

Managers established an iterative process whereby each regional brand team proposed candidates for inclusion in the core list, then negotiated with the corporate center. Through this process, the core 400 brands were identified. Since different brand names in different geographies sometimes had similar positioning and innovation, these 400 actually occupied only 200 distinct brand positions. In other words, Unilever had only 200 core brands, 40 of which were global—such as Dove, Flora, Knorr, Lipton, Lux, and Magnum. Another 160 brands, such as PG Tips and Marmite, became "local jewels," strong in a particular region or country.

Brand rationalization efforts succeed only when companies grow the top and bottom line by focusing intensely on the remaining brands. On its "Path to Growth," Unilever had to invest disproportionately in the core brands on four fronts—advertising and promotion, innovation, marketing competence, and management time—financed through two sources. First, it reallocated resources from the 1,200 non-core brands to the 400 core brands. For example, Unilever reassigned innovators and brand marketers once responsible for non-core brands to the core brands, and redirected more than 500 million euros of annual advertising and promotion money to the core brands. Second, Unilever attacked costs. Brand rationalization sparked a restructuring plan that entailed closure of 130 of its 380 factories worldwide; 113 have already been shuttered. Unilever also set out to reduce the 330,000-person global workforce by 10 percent in five years. When combined with the additional savings from consolidated purchasing power and shared services, annual savings through procurement (1.6 billion euros) as well as supply chain restructuring and simplification (1.5 billion euros) yielded approximately three billion euros.

Unilever directed some savings toward improving the bottom line to meet the operating margin target. However, Unilever decided to increase the marketing and promotion expenses from 13 to 15 percent of sales—more than a billion euros a year of additional marketing support—during the five-year period. Combined with the 500 million euros redirected from non-core brand marketing, the core 400 would get more than 1.5 billion euros of additional annual investment by 2004. Given the high levels of marketing support that most brands receive in the consumer packaged goods industry, managers determined that only such a substantial shift in resources would discernibly affect the marketplace.

For each of its core brands, Unilever systematically searched for, and continues to seek, unexploited growth opportunities. It begins by reviewing current positioning as well as related competitive intelligence and consumer insights. It seeks avenues for growth by asking how the brand can:

- reach new customers,
- launch new products and services,
- develop new delivery systems,

- penetrate new geographical markets, and
- generate new industry concepts.

As figure 6-1 illustrates, identifying growth entails a significant switch from a category to a brand mind-set. Knorr can springboard across categories from its dry soup brand heritage.

In some cases, such as with Dove, managers conducted brand growth sessions and dubbed the results "three horizons of growth":

- *Extend and defend core business*—to achieve within the next two years (for example, moving Dove into eighty-four countries)
- *Build emerging business*—to occur in the two- to three-year time horizon (for example, launching Dove deodorants)

FIGURE 6-1

Leveraging Knorr

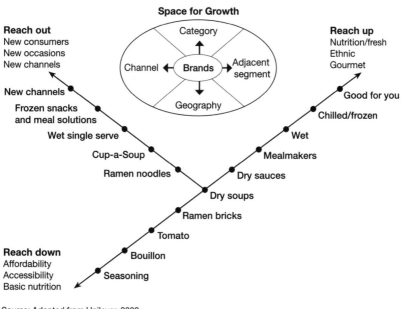

Source: Adapted from Unilever, 2000.

- *Create options for the future*—usually to accomplish in the three- to five-year time horizon by setting up a new team and developing competences currently lacking at Unilever (for example, the creation of Dove spa)

Each of the 1,200 non-core brands, designated the "tail," were sentenced to one of the following four strategic fates:

1. *Sell the brand.*   Unilever put up for sale those brands in categories outside its core. In 2000, it sold the Elizabeth Arden cosmetics and fragrance business to Miami-based FFI Fragrances; in 2002, it sold Mazola corn oil and eighteen related brands to ACH Food Companies, Inc., a subsidiary of Associated British Foods plc. By 2003, Unilever had divested eighty-seven businesses for 6.3 billion euros.

2. *Milk the brand.*   Unilever allowed non-core brands with sufficient brand equity to linger so that it could "milk" them by sacrificing sales growth for greater profits. These brands received in-store marketing only, no advertising, and its marketers were reassigned to the core brands.

3. *Delist the brand.*   Managers eliminated small brands such as Rosella Ketchup in Australia and Dimension Shampoo in Brazil while reallocating their shelf space to more profitable brands in the portfolio. Category managers helped to develop a program to migrate their customers to similar brands in the Unilever portfolio so that Unilever would retain its overall market share in the category.

4. *Migrate the brand.*   The attributes of non-core brands that could enrich a core brand were carefully migrated to the target core brand. As Antony Burgmans reminded Unilever, "You are not migrating brands, but migrating consumers." Besides communicating the change to consumers, marketers developed a promotional plan encour-

aging a trial of the updated brand—an expensive strategy, deployed discriminately.

For example, Unilever positioned Surf, a core-brand laundry detergent with a 6 percent U.K. market share, as "good-hearted, down-to-earth, cuddly, affectionate, and quirky." Unilever's U.K. brand portfolio also included Radion, a non-core brand with a 2 percent share slated for elimination. However, research indicated that consumers clung to Radion's "sun fresh" highly fragrant scent. So Unilever deleted Radion and migrated its scent to Surf by launching a new and improved Surf "with Sun Fresh." This improved brand exceeded the 8 percent combined share of old Surf and Radion within six months.

Now, three years down its five-year "Path to Growth," Unilever has met its operating margins and earnings per share growth targets. Although the sales growth is not yet in the 5 to 6 percent target range for 2004, the overall revenue for 2002 increased by 4.2 percent while the core brands grew 5.4 percent. So Unilever is making progress.[14]

The portfolio has already shrunk to 750 brands. The leading 400 that accounted for 75 percent of sales in 1999 now occupy 200 brand positions and account for 90 percent of sales toward the objective of 95 percent by the end of 2004. Of these, the 40 global core brands alone account for 64 percent of total sales.

Conclusion

With growing retailer power and more global customers, companies cannot sustain weaker brands and must embark on brand rationalization. Since deleting brands usually lowers the firm's revenues in the immediate short run, brand rationalization is a top management concern. Few divisional, country, or brand managers will risk shrinking the firm. Senior executives must approve

Brand Rationalization Checklist

Brand Portfolio Audit

- *Does our brand portfolio hinder us from obtaining adequate scale and scope in our marketing efforts?*

- *Which brands are contributing to our profits?*

- *Which brands have scale?*

- *Which brands are well positioned from consumer and competitive perspectives?*

- *Which brands have multinational footprints?*

- *What needs-based segments exist in each category?*

- *How have we positioned these brands against these needs-based segments?*

- *Which are our core brands and our non-core brands?*

- *How much sales revenue would we risk by deleting the non-core brands?*

- *After brand deletion, will we grow faster, innovate more, and be more profitable?*

Brand Rationalization Program

- *Which non-core brands could we comfortably sell to others?*

- *Which non-core brands deprive core brands of valuable shelf space? Should we delist them?*

- *How can we migrate the customers of delisted brands to core brands?*

- *Which non-core brands have attributes that would add value to the core brands?*

- *How can we migrate these attributes to the core brands?*

- *Which of our non-core brands could we milk for profits?*

- *How can we move our remaining core brands to better positions against customers and competitors?*

- *Where can we grow each of our core brands in terms of new customers, geographies, delivery systems, products and services, and concepts?*

- *Have we explicitly specified financial targets and timelines for the brand rationalization program?*

- *What is the role for the corporate brand?*

Implementation Issues

- *In what time frame will we rationalize brands?*

- *Do we need a quick change or a gradual brand migration?*

- *Do we have top management's commitment for that time period?*

- *Should we adopt a flagship brand or a hierarchical brand approach?*

- *How will we reallocate resources from non-core brands to core brands?*

- *How will our product platforms interact with the brands?*

- *What product roles does each brand need?*

- *How will we realign local and global responsibilities for the brands?*

- *Where can we test the viability of our brand rationalization strategy?*

- *How will we articulate our program and strategy to important stakeholders such as media, analysts, investors, and employees?*

the financial objectives of the brand rationalization and the time-frame by which managers should achieve them. This program is geared to deliver long-term benefits, not an immediate earnings-per-share increase.

Major brand consolidation programs, involving large numbers of brands or multiple categories, may take up to five years. Generally, the profit payoff comes early as unproductive marketing expenditures, inventories, and complexities are rapidly reduced. However, recouping the revenues and market share losses associated with the deleted brands takes time. Top management must be realistic and give managers adequate time to implement the program and demonstrate results (see "Brand Rationalization Checklist").

Brand rationalization is profitable. It can catalyze broad-based restructuring that ruthlessly removes marketing support for marginal brands, rationalizes the supply chain, purges unprofitable products, and reduces organizational complexity and redundancy.

Imagine a brand portfolio where every brand is smartly positioned with a unique role to play. Only then will disproportionate investments of resources, talent, and innovation in the surviving brands deliver top-line growth.

SEVEN

From Market-Driven to Market-Driving

Incrementalism is innovation's worst enemy.

CEOS DEMAND, EXHORT, AND BEG their organizations to innovate. In particular, CEOs stress the value of radical or discontinuous innovation because it helps a company outpace its competition and thus deliver sustained growth. Yet innovation often inches along rather than leaps forward in established firms. Why? Because companies revere the market-driven process that currently dominates business.

Current practice intimates that careful market research of the customers' needs and creative development of differentiated products or services for a well-defined segment will lead to success. Various strong companies such as Nestlé, P&G, and Unilever effectively employ this market-driven approach. However, successful pioneers like Amazon, The Body Shop, CNN, IKEA, Starbucks, and Swatch have created new markets and revolutionized existing industries through radical business innovation. In essence, they have driven the market; they are market-driving.

Consider Aravind Eye Hospital of Southern India.[1] In 1976, a fifty-eight-year-old retired eye surgeon, Dr. G. Venkataswamy, devised a plan to serve the 20 million residents of India who were blind from cataracts. Venkataswamy envisioned marketing cataract surgery, a relatively straightforward operation, like McDonald's hamburgers. Hospitals in India typically fell into one of two categories—private, state-of-the-art hospitals that served the small, wealthy segment of the population or charitable, out-moded, overcrowded hospitals that served the poor, vast majority. Moreover, a large number of the poor, who reside in the country-side, could not access these urban hospitals.

To realize his vision of eyesight for the blind regardless of their ability to pay, Venkataswamy founded hospitals in southern India that serve both the rich, who pay for the modern cataract surgery, and the poor, who receive almost identical service for free. The sales, advertising, and promotion of Aravind Eye Hospital focus on attracting free rather than paying patients. For example, the sales force has annual targets for the number of free patients admitted; weekly "sales meetings" monitor individual perform-ance toward these targets. Aravind's sophisticated salespeople scour the Indian countryside looking for poor patients within their assigned territories and then transport them to the hospital at no cost.

By focusing on eye care and routinizing procedures, Aravind's surgeons are so productive that this nonprofit organization has a gross margin of 50 percent despite the fact that more than 65 per-cent of the patients served do not pay. Unlike most nonprofit organizations in the developing world, it does not depend on donations and attempts to maximize the number of free patients served (see figure 7-1). In 2002, Aravind Eye Hospital served 1.4 million patients and performed 200,000 eye surgeries.

Aravind Eye Hospital's market-driving approach resembles those of Amazon, The Body Shop, Club Med, Dell, Hennes and Mauritz, IKEA, Sony, Swatch, Tetra Pak, Virgin, and Wal-Mart. These market-driving firms did not use traditional market research to devise their status quo–busting strategies. Market research seldom leads to such breakthrough innovations.[2] As

FIGURE 7-1

Growth of Aravind Eye Hospital

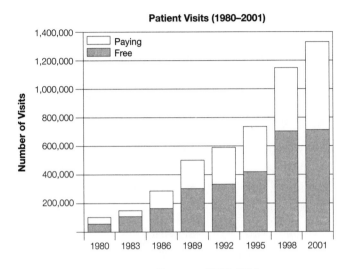

Patient Visits (1980–2001)

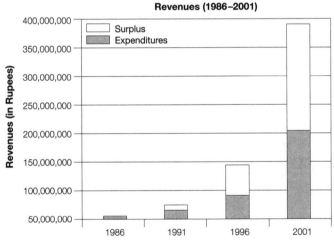

Revenues (1986–2001)

Henry Ford observed, "If I'd listened to customers, I'd have given them a faster horse."

The inspiration for the radical business ideas of market-driving firms came from visionaries such as Venkataswamy, Anita Roddick of The Body Shop, and Richard Branson of Virgin, who saw the world differently and whose vision addressed deep-seated, latent, or emerging customer needs. Rather than focusing on obtaining market share in existing markets, these market drivers created new markets or redefined the category in such a fundamental way that competitors were rendered obsolete (for example, none of the top ten discounters of 1962, the year Wal-Mart was born, are in business today).[3] Ultimately, these firms revolutionized their industries by "driving" their markets, rules and all.

These firms are market drivers for three reasons:

1. They trigger industry breakpoints, or what Andy Grove of Intel calls "strategic inflexion points," which change the fundamentals of the industry through radical business innovation.

2. Visionary rather than traditional market research inspires their radical business concept.

3. Rather than learn from existing customers, they often teach potential customers to consume their drastically different value proposition.

The Market-Driving Firm

The success of market-driving firms stands on radical innovation in two dimensions—a discontinuous leap in the value proposition and the rapid configuration of a unique value network (see figure 7-2). Value proposition, as defined in chapter 2, refers to the combination of benefits and price offered to customers.

Market Driving IKEA Style

Ingvar Kamprad opened his furniture retailer IKEA in the 1950s; it now employs 70,000 people, operates in thirty countries, and generates a turnover of 11 billion euros. Rather than target middle-aged people in city centers as traditional full-service

FIGURE 7-2

Types of Strategic Innovation

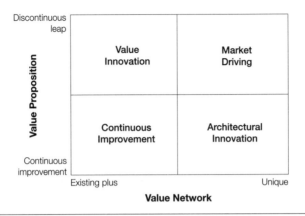

high-end furniture stores did, IKEA focused on young people and young families. To these customers, IKEA offered clean Scandinavian design and image, tremendous assortment, immediate delivery, a pleasant shopping atmosphere, and low prices in exchange for self-service, self-assembly, and self-transportation of purchases. As figure 7-3 indicates, rather than straddle the existing industry iso-value line, market-driving firms such as IKEA deliver a discontinuous leap in customer value.

The transformation in customer value may involve either breakthrough technology or breakthrough marketing. The success of companies such as IKEA is less about new technology than about aggressively exploiting existing technology to serve the customer in an unconventional manner. The key to the success of market-driving firms is that they create and deliver a leap in benefits, while reducing the sacrifices and compromises that customers make to receive those benefits.[4] They create a product or service experience that vastly exceeds customer expectations and existing alternatives, thereby elevating the industry landscape.

Value network refers to the configuration of activities required to create, produce, and deliver the value proposition to the

FIGURE 7-3

IKEA's Leap in Customer Value

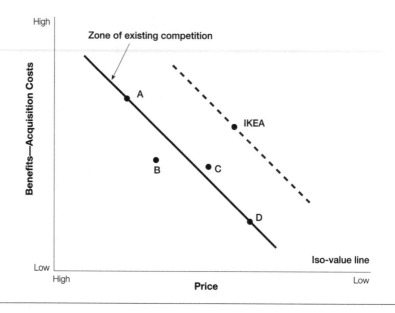

customer. IKEA could not deliver discontinuous value by simply improving upon the business model of traditional furniture stores beleaguered by expensive independent designers, high work-in-progress inventory, labor-intensive handicraft manufacturing, transportation and inventory of finished goods, fragmented marketing, costly retail locations, elaborate displays, and expensive delivery to the consumer. IKEA had to reconfigure the model radically. CEO Anders Dahlvig observes, "Most others were copying what everyone else was doing and tried to do it a little better here and there. We did it totally different."[5]

As table 7-1 reveals, IKEA's unique value network uses cost-conscious in-house design, interchangeable parts, high volume component manufacturing, parts inventory (rather than more expensive finished product inventory), extensive computerization of logistics, its natural Scandinavian image, relatively inexpensive peripheral locations, and simple display facilities, leaving final transportation and assembly to the consumer.[6] To copy IKEA's

TABLE 7-1

IKEA's Unique Value Network

	Design	Parts	Assembly	Logistics	Marketing	Service
Traditional Furniture Stores	• Independent designers • Sophisticated, complex designs	• High work-in-progress inventory • Handicraft, custom manufacturing	• Labor intensive • Built to order	• Transport costly, bulky finished product	• Fragmented • Expensive, main street display	• Full-service • Small-lot delivery to customers
IKEA	• In-house designers • Simple design to cost	• Modular, interchangeable parts • Mass production • New cheaper raw materials	• By customer	• Computerized • Transport modular product	• Leverage Scandinavian image • Cheap, out-of-town display	• Self-service • Customer transports home

Source: Adapted from Xavier Gilbert, "Achieving Exceptional Competitiveness" (presentation at IMO, Lausanne, Switzerland, 1997).

value proposition profitably, firms in the traditional channel would need to dismantle the existing value network while migrating to an IKEA-type network.

Because the value proposition is visible in the marketplace while the value network is harder to discern, competitors often miss the importance of the latter. Without a unique value network, existing players can fairly rapidly copy any advantage gained from a discontinuous leap in the value proposition. Therefore, market-driving firms that change the rules of the game are those that innovate on both dimensions of figure 7-2. The unique value network creates a more sustainable advantage. Would-be competitors need time to acquire the competencies as well as assemble the intraorganizational and interorganizational players necessary for replicating that unique value architecture.

Four Orientations to the Marketplace

In addition to market-driving, there are three other corporate orientations toward the marketplace: sales-driven, market-driven, and customer-driven.

A *sales-driven* organization views marketing as a tool to sell whatever it produces. In such companies (often public utilities, monopolies, and some large manufacturers), marketing and selling are interchangeable.

Market-driven companies develop appropriate products and the desired image for their target segments based on market research. Most successful consumer packaged goods companies such as L'Oreal fall in this category.

Customer-driven companies target "segments of one" and conduct "relationship marketing" to deliver customized value configurations. The Swiss private banking industry, which serves high-net-worth individuals, typifies such customer-driven firms.

Table 7-2 summarizes the key distinctions among these four orientations. All four categories represent ideals, however; no large organization adopts a single orientation through all business units.

TABLE 7-2

Four Orientations to the Marketplace

	Sales-Driven	Market-Driven	Customer-Driven	Market-Driving
Marketing Strategy	Mass marketing (How to sell?)	Differentiated marketing (What image to build?)	Relationship marketing (Who to serve?)	Revolutionary marketing (How to change the rules of the game?)
Segmentation Strategy	Undifferentiated	Market segments	Segments of one	Destroy industry segmentation
Market Research				
"Focus"	Market testing (How to sell it?)	Market sensing (What does the market want?)	Customer sensing (What does this customer want?)	Forward sensing (How can the marketplace evolve?)
"Listen to"	R&D	Voice of the market	Voice of the customer	Seeing differently
Price Management	Cost plus	Perceived value	Bundling/ unbundling	New price points
Sales Management	Sell products	Sell image	Sell solutions	Customer education
Channel Management	Product/ channel fit	Product/ market fit	Multiplex systems	Channel reconfiguration
Brand Management	Product superiority	Broadcast for brand equity	Dialogue for corporate equity	Exploit "buzz network"
Customer Service	Expense	Tactical weapon	Strategic weapon	Overwhelm expectations
Product Development	New products	Incremental innovation	Integrating product/ service platforms	Radical innovation

How Market-Driving Firms Seize Advantage

Based on an in-depth study of twenty-five market-driving firms, this chapter concentrates not only on how market-driving firms compete, but also on the transformational marketing strategies that undergird these companies.[7] The following sections detail how market-driving companies differ from more traditional companies on the various dimensions of marketing strategy.

Lead by Vision Rather Than by Market Research

Consumers and organizational buyers (such as purchasing agents) are excellent at motivating and evaluating incremental innovation. However, customers cannot usually visualize the revolutionary products, concepts, or technologies themselves. Swatch offers an excellent case study. The Swatch models that received the highest intention-to-purchase rating in consumer research looked like traditional watches, but they ultimately generated very few sales. The more radically different Swatch models that rated the least likely to sell were subsequently the bestsellers. Had Swatch followed its market research, it would have missed a runaway success. Similarly, customers did not clamor for Starbucks coffee, CNN, or overnight small package delivery prior to their introduction.

Market-driving firms instead coalesce around visionaries who see opportunity where others do not—an opportunity to fill latent, unmet needs or to offer an unprecedented level of customer value. In market-driving firms, generation and development of "the idea" is a combination of serendipity, inexperience, and persistence. For example, Starbucks was founded in 1983 after Howard Schultz, charmed by the Italian coffee culture of Verona and Milan, promised to bring it to the United States.

Frequently, the visionaries' relative inexperience with the industry meant they had not yet been inoculated with that industry's received wisdom. Nike's Bill Bowerman was a college track coach, Club Med's Gerard Blitz was a diamond cutter, and Ingvar Kamprad of IKEA began his entrepreneurial career selling fish. Often, these visionaries persisted in the face of many failures and rejections to realize their dream. For example, Fred Smith of FedEx developed the guaranteed overnight delivery idea in a business school term paper as a junior at Yale. He received a C for the paper because the instructor was not convinced of its practicality.[8]

Some market-driving firms spent years muddling through refining their vision before perfecting their strategies. Sam Walton's initial attempts at opening stores were underwhelming. David Glass, who later became CEO of Wal-Mart but was at that time employed by a competing store, reportedly opined after checking out the first Wal-Mart Discount City Store, "Those guys will never make it." Sam Walton continued to tinker with the formula until he got it right. Few of these visionaries expected that their business idea would achieve the level of success that was ultimately attained. As Hasso Plattner, the cofounder of SAP, observed: "When people ask how we planned all this, we answer 'We didn't. It just happened.'"[9]

Because they are changing the rules of the game and facing many obstacles on the way to success, market-driving companies recruit and select people who subscribe to the values of the organization. There is often an attempt to attract those with little experience in the industry, individuals who have not been infused with the industry's conventional wisdom about why the market-driving idea is doomed to fail. Such employees are motivated strongly by their belief that they are on a mission, not simply by money. A compelling vision enthusiastically articulated by a charismatic leader turns these employees into crusaders.

- Sam Walton wanted to "give the world an opportunity to see what it's like to save and have a better lifestyle, a better life for all." This mission, paired with the belief that Wal-Mart stores would "lower the cost of living for everyone, not just America," energized his employees.

- Ninety percent of The Body Shop franchisees are women who have no formal business training but are instead chosen on the basis of personality tests, home visits, and attitudes toward the environment and people. They are motivated by founder Anita Roddick's idea that they can make a difference in people's lives and in the world through The Body Shop.

- In the early days at FedEx, there were couriers who pawned their watches to pay for gasoline.

Such historic, sometimes mythic, stories become part of the organizational culture of most market-driving firms.

Redraw Industry Segmentation

By attracting their customers from a variety of previously defined market segments, a new market coalesces around the market-driving firm's product-service offering and marketing strategy. This creates havoc in the industry by destroying the industry segmentation that existed prior to the market driver's entry and replacing it with a new set of segments reflecting the new, altered landscape.

- Aravind Eye Hospital did not accept the normal segmentation between rich and poor patients.

- Southwest Airlines destroyed the segmentation between ground transportation and airlines, attracting many who would not otherwise have flown at all.

- Swatch, with its cheap and fashionable watches, bridged the chasm between the segments for cheap, utilitarian watches and expensive, fashionable ones.

- Wal-Mart demonstrated that small rural towns could support huge discount stores, which previously had been located only in large urban areas.

- While existing software vendors concentrated on developing different software packages for different departments (for example, manufacturing, sales, human resources), SAP destroyed these distinctions by developing enterprise software that could integrate and run the entire business.

Create New Price Points for Value

To deliver a leap in customer value, market-driving firms establish new industry price points for the quality or service levels they deliver. Swatch, Aravind Eye Hospital, Southwest Airlines, and Charles Schwab all set prices much lower than those previously available for similar products. This puts existing competitors under tremendous pressure. The competitors must make dramatic changes in operations and product lines to survive, but they cannot swiftly meet the challenge because they cannot quickly and successfully reproduce the innovative value network that enables the lower price point. Continental learned this the hard way when it tried to compete against Southwest Airlines with "Continental Lite."

- When Southwest Airlines enters a new city, it prices against ground transportation, not just against existing air service, so that its prices fall at least 60 percent below competitive airfares. For example, early in its history, Southwest charged $15 for a trip from Dallas to San Antonio when Braniff, the next most inexpensive competitor, was charging $62. A shareholder asked the CEO, "Could you not raise the price two or three dollars?" The response: "We are not competing against other airlines but ground transportation."

- Swatch adopted a simple introductory pricing strategy— $40 in United States, 50 CHF in Switzerland, 60 DM in Germany, and 7,000 yen in Japan—and held those prices for the first ten years despite high demand.

Whereas the trend is toward higher performance at lower price points, there are market-driving firms who have established elevated price points that are higher than typical in an industry. CNN, Starbucks, and FedEx set prices considerably above what customers had been paying. Inducing the buyer to pay these higher prices requires that these market-driving firms have a value proposition that is substantially more compelling than the available alternatives.

Educate Customers for Sales Growth

Given the radical new concept, the sales task for market-driving firms is not to sell but rather to educate the customer on the

existence of, and how to consume, their radical value propositions (see figure 7-4).

- Aravind Eye Hospital must continuously educate its "free"
  patients, who are predominantly illiterate, that their vision
  can in fact be restored and that the necessary surgery is
  available to them free of charge.

- IKEA had to teach consumers the benefits of transporting
  furniture components home for self-assembly instead of
  buying it preassembled and delivered. When IKEA entered
  Switzerland, they ran advertisements that joked about the
  Swiss unwillingness to transport and assemble furniture,
  even for lower prices. The advertisements poked fun at the
  self-delivery and self-assembly aspects, saying "That is a
  stupid thing" and "You can't do that to the Swiss."

Reconfigure Channels

In almost every market-driving firm, channel reconfiguration
initiated the architectural innovation that yielded a unique business system. Consider the following:

- FedEx transports packages using its own planes via a "hub
  and spokes" air freight system rather than "point-to-point"
  commercial flights used by competitors such as Emery.
  FedEx is twice as likely as Emery to deliver on time.

- Benetton subcontracts simple, nonessential tasks and
  performs only crucial quality-maintenance tasks such as
  dyeing. By knitting products before rather than after dyeing, Benetton can respond faster to sales data on color
  preferences than its competitors.

- Wal-Mart insists that P&G and other suppliers rationalize
  product lines, adopt everyday low prices, eliminate whole-
  salers, present one invoice per company, and establish
  electronic links with Wal-Mart stores, all to eliminate
  considerable costs in the network.

FIGURE 7-4

easyCar's Welcome

Welcome – Bienvenue – Bienvenido

Our Goal   At easyCar we aim to offer you outstanding value for money. To us value for money means a reliable service at low price. We achieve this by simplifying the product we offer, and passing on the benefits to you in the form of lower prices.

How Do We Do This?

- easyCar provides every customer with fully comprehensive insurance that guarantees no damage charges.
- Our bring the car back clean policy allows us to significantly reduce the number of staff employed at each site. This enables us to reduce the cost of car rental. Customers who do not wish to bring the car back clean can return the car dirty and easyCar will provide this service for a charge of £10 (€16).
- easyCar operates an empty to empty fuel policy. By not providing a refueling service we are able to further reduce the number of staff required at each site.
- Through the use of yield management we ensure everyone pays a fair price for each day of their rental. The earlier you book, the less you pay. See *our prices* for details.
- easyCar ensures that over 90% of our cars are on rent at any time to our customers. easyCar pays for the vehicle whether it is on rent or in the car park. High utilisation means that the average price paid is significantly reduced for all of our customers.
- By separating the cost of *preparing* the car from renting the car, we ensure that those renting for a longer period of time do not subsidise those renting for a shorter period of time.
- By not giving refunds for cancellations, we are able to offer low prices. If you are not prepared to take the risk of a potential cancellation, you should consider booking with one of our competitors.
- By setting a *free mileage allowance*, we ensure that those people who wish to travel higher distances meet the cost of doing so.
- By offering one type of *car* at each of our locations, we avoid the expense of maintaining a range of cars that people only occasionally need.
- Bookings can be made via our Web site or call center, therefore avoiding paying commission to middlemen such as travel agents.
- By assessing the *risk profile* of each driver, we ensure that customers only pay the insurance cost for the risk they represent.
- By displaying our name on our cars we increase our marketing exposure allowing us to reduce the amount we spend on advertising.
- By refusing to offer delivery, collection or one-way rentals, we avoid the hidden costs associated with providing these expensive services.
- By operating a premium rate telephone *help line*, the cost of providing telephone-based support is borne only by those that have a need for it.

Thank you for visiting us. We hope you enjoy using our site and our service.

Source: easyCar

Exploit the "Buzz Network" for Brand Attachment

Market-driving firms often rely more on the "buzz network" to convey their message. Since these firms offer a leap in customer value, many customers will notify others of their "amazing new find." Reporters in trade publications and the popular press want to be the first to cover the radical new innovation. Early adopters and opinion leaders generate the excitement and brand cachet that market-driving firms strive to maintain. Consequently, market drivers spend less money on traditional advertising; the advertising-to-sales ratio pales compared to that of their established competitors.

- Southwest Airlines boasts, "We have a lot of ambassadors out there, our Customers." Every year representatives from dozens of cities beg Southwest to launch services in their area.

- A 1958 thirteen-page *Life* magazine photo spread on Club Med drew many more customers than capacity. In 1962, twelve years after the first village was built, it turned away more than a 100,000 applicants as it could only accommodate 70,000 members.

- Nike did not run a single national television advertisement until it reached $1 billion in sales. It used "word-of-foot advertising" by getting the best athletes to wear its products.

- Virgin's Richard Branson generates constant free press through his hot air balloon expeditions, highly public media wars against the established players (such as having all planes painted with a banner against the proposed BA-AA merger), and appearing publicly in "drag."

Overwhelm Customer Expectations

Market-driving firms surpass customer expectations by delivering service at levels far above what consumers expect for the market driver's price.

- The poor patients of Aravind Eye Hospital never expected to regain their sight, since surgery was out of their geographical, economic, and psychological grasp.

- Since other discounters lower customer expectations by providing poor service, Wal-Mart seems to provide great value. Whenever it rains in Houston, an umbrella-wielding service rep walks customers to their cars at Wal-Mart's discount store and Sam's Club, a warehouse club that operates on slim 10 percent gross margins. No wonder a typical Wal-Mart customer visits Wal-Mart thirty-two times a year compared to a Kmart customer who shops only fifteen times per year there.

- Twelve times between 1987 and 1993, low-priced Southwest won the unofficial "triple crown" of commercial aviation—fewest customer complaints, fewest delays, and fewest mishandled bags—an unprecedented feat. CEO Herb Kelleher observed, "It's easy to offer great service at a high cost. It's easy to offer lousy service at low cost. What's tough is offering great service at low cost, and that is what our goal is."[10]

Barriers to Market Driving in Incumbent Firms

Large incumbents typically launch incremental innovations rather than radical ones. Since the success of market-driving firms depends on radical innovation in value and network, market drivers are typically newcomers whose founders grew frustrated by their staid employers:

- Ben Franklin franchise headquarters rejected the "big stores in small towns" idea of Sam Walton, one of Ben Franklin's franchisees.

- Many major shoe manufacturers rejected the athletic shoe concept—a shoe with lighter soles and better support, traction, and stability that would be comfortable for athletes—that Nike eventually implemented.

- Ex-IBM employees formed SAP after IBM Germany refused their request to develop enterprise software for ICI.

Why do successful incumbents flounder in combining radical innovation in value proposition and value network? Primarily because their well-established new business development processes cannot accommodate the following four features of market-driving ideas.

Market-Driving Ideas Overturn Industry Assumptions

Market-driving ideas are maverick and serendipitous in nature. Nobody can predict where such an idea will originate or who will generate it. Since most companies organize for efficiency, they react negatively to surprises.[11] Furthermore, individuals often feel pressure to hide market-driving ideas since they rebel against the prevailing industry and incumbent wisdom. The vast industry experience of established firms therefore becomes a barrier to driving markets. People cannot easily unlearn conventional wisdom, however irrelevant.[12] Current market leaders often discard maverick ideas that clash with prevailing industry intelligence. An obsession with history—or even the present—can prevent a firm from shaping its future.

Consider Linotype-Hell, a German company that invented Linotype printing presses in 1886. The "hot-type" Linotype system was widely used for printing books, magazines, and newspapers until the 1970s. Although the company had dominated every advance in publishing technology, the digital age of software- and scanner-based printing blindsided it. As Linotype managers clung to their "hot-type" mind-set, the company's stock fell from a record high of 970 DM in May 1990 to 56 DM in July 1996. In 1997, Heidelberger Druckmaschinen, AG, acquired Linotype-Hell.

Market-Driving Ideas Are Risky

Market-driving ideas involve high risk. For every successful radical innovation in value proposition and value network, probably hundreds fail. An entrepreneur chasing a market-driving dream has delimited downside financial risk as he generally invests enormous effort but limited capital. However, if the idea succeeds, then he has unlimited upside potential to make a vast personal fortune. In most organizations, the originator of a successful market-driving idea may receive a nice bonus or promotion (limited upside potential), but a public failure may destroy his or her career (substantial downside potential). When the high failure rate of radical innovation is combined with the risk/reward ratio in most large organizations, pursuing market-driving ideas is irrational for employees.

Market-Driving Ideas Consistently Lose to Incremental Innovation

The new business development process in most firms tends to disfavor, and therefore squelch, innovative breakthroughs that might create new markets. When competing for attention, resources, and approval, incrementally innovative projects tend to edge out more radical ones. In most established firms, the new product development and new business development processes favor the triable, reversible, divisible, tangible, and familiar. Projects must clearly benefit current customers, move in the organization's direction, and correspond with R&D investments, corporate image management, sales training, and distribution—all of which rarely typify radically innovative offerings.

Established firms select new business development opportunities based on technological feasibility and potential market size. However, in the early developmental stages, no one can definitely know which technology will succeed, with what capabilities, for which markets. The technological and operational problems seem insurmountable, often with no obvious market. Expected applications dissolve and unforeseen opportunities emerge while the firm experiments.

For example, Nutrasweet's two initial applications—replacing saccharin and artificially sweetening breakfast cereals—fizzled because saccharin users actually preferred saccharin's aftertaste and Nutrasweetened breakfast cereal hit technical and regulatory obstacles. Instead, Nutrasweet found a sizzling market in dissatisfied sugar users.[13]

Market-Driving Ideas Cannibalize Existing Business

Finally, established firms often perceive that they have too much invested in the status quo to risk destroying the existing industry and market. The greater the threat of cannibalization, the more intense is the resistance to market-driving ideas.

- IBM focused too long on mainframes because PCs required a different distribution system, had lower margins, and lacked after-sales service opportunities.

- General Motors and Ford responded to the popularity of minivans too slowly because minivans jeopardized their station wagon market.

- Bausch & Lomb ignored the more comfortable disposable soft lens market because of its robust permanent soft lens and solution businesses.

The Market-Driving Transformation Process

Although new entrepreneurial firms can single-mindedly pursue a make-or-break market-driving project, most established firms have too many obligations to chase only radical market-driving ventures. They cannot pursue radical business innovation without improving the existing business and devoting much of their efforts to market-driven activities, such as incremental innovation and traditional market research. Nevertheless, top management must find room and resources for radical innovation or the market leader risks being leap-frogged and deposed by upstart market drivers.

Firms need to be ambidextrous, capable of simultaneously managing incremental as well as radical innovation.[14] However, this is difficult to do since radical and incremental innovation are different animals requiring their own supporting cultures (see table 7-3). As Bernard Charles, president of Dassault Systemes, argues:

TABLE 7-3

Incremental Versus Radical Innovation

	Incremental	Radical
Uncertainty	Low	High
Focus	Cost or feature improvements in existing products	Development of new products/ services and functionalities
Business Model	Known—detailed plan can be developed	Uncertain—plan evolves as learn by doing
Value Network	Utilizes existing industry value network— competence enhancing	Requires new value network— competence destroying
Project Evolution	Linear and continuous	Sporadic and discontinuous
Process	Formal, phase-gate model to allow high control	Informal, flexible model to allow serendipity
Resources	Standard resource allocation process	Creative acquisition of resources
Project Speed	Being first is important	Important to time when market is "ready"
Customer Interaction	Test with, and learn from, key customers	Speculate with fringe customers

Source: Adapted from http://www.1000ventures.com/business_guide.

Company cultures that are more risk averse ultimately drive innovation through a practice of continuous improvement and steady progress, and as a consequence are more consistent in meeting their goals. Cultures that are less risk averse tend to target major gains in a single, bold step. They do not always succeed, but when they do, the impact is significant.[15]

Managers in established firms must choose projects to balance incremental and radical innovation in the companies' portfolios so that both promising incremental projects and radical projects obtain time, money, and resources. An established firm that wishes to engage in market-driving faces two challenges: it must have the vision and environment to generate breakthrough ideas and it must have the capital, fortitude, and risk tolerance to persevere and give the radical idea a fair chance to succeed.

The first challenge involves developing the ability to "see differently." Since radical concepts often spring from a single person's imagination, the firm must create an environment where individual creativity flourishes. Without the ability to see differently, the firm cannot change the rules of the game. The second challenge is to successfully market the unique concept, which requires a team effort. Without the ability to implement a market-driving concept, the firm will join the ranks of companies that failed to capitalize on their inventions, such as Xerox with personal computers and EMI with scanner technology.

Unlike incremental innovation, where innovating is an ongoing process, the development of market-driving ideas is more project-based. Perhaps what Somerset Maugham observed about writing novels applies here: "There are three rules for writing a novel. Unfortunately no one knows what they are." Yet certain practices can help established firms increase their probability of driving market innovations. As Viacom's chairman and CEO Sumner Redstone pointed out, "Size is not a barrier to creativity; it's bad management."[16] Firms aspiring to market-driving innovations should adopt the following processes and practices.

Develop Processes to Identify
Hidden Entrepreneurs

In any large company, many employees have radical business ideas. Top management must formalize processes to encourage out-of-the-box thinking and discover these hidden entrepreneurs within the firm. For example, in 1992, NEC invited its employees to submit proposals for their own start-up companies to give new business ideas space to develop outside the corporate bureaucracy.[17] Entitled "Venture Promotion and Entrepreneur Search Program," it generated 146 proposals.

Shirota, a fifty-six-year-old career NEC employee, submitted one of the selected proposals. His business idea was to develop and market a software program that would provide a high-tech design tool for Japan's kimono makers. By scanning the customer's photograph into a computer and then graphically superimposing kimonos, the customers can "try on" different kimonos without actually changing outfits. The company, Kainoatec, was launched in 1995 with NEC providing 54 percent of the 13 million yen start-up capital and with Shirota and a colleague, Koterazawa, each chipping in 3 million yen. Since its launch, Kainoatec has developed similar software for the eyeglass industry so that customers can try on spectacles without having to remove their own eyeglasses. The venture generated profits of nearly 5 million yen in its first year and has increased sales and profits every year since then.

The in-house entrepreneur program has become an annual event at NEC. More than six hundred new business ideas have been generated. To maximize the number of proposals, the annual invitation is widely publicized to all employees of NEC and its subsidiaries. Furthermore, initial proposals are limited to presenting only an overview of the new business concept. Later, as proposals move through various selection steps, projected sales, profits, and investment information are gathered through detailed business plans. As Shirota, now president of Kainoatec, observes, the program helps discover hidden entrepreneurs among the Japanese salarymen who are waiting for someone to tap them on the shoulder and give them a chance.

Allow Space for Serendipity

Serendipity has played a role in the development of many radical new ideas. To allow for serendipity, 3M researchers are encouraged to spend up to 15 percent of their time on a research project of their choice. This ensures that problem-driven research does not preclude all curiosity-driven research. 3M's famous Post-it notes were invented when an associate was attempting to develop a better bookmark for his hymn book. Similarly, one of Searle's research scientists discovered the artificial sweetener Nutrasweet while looking for a possible treatment for ulcers. As Schumpeter observed: "History is a record of 'effects,' the vast majority of which nobody intended to create." Unfortunately, reengineering efforts in most firms have eliminated much of the slack within which serendipity thrives.

Select and Match Employees for Creativity

To generate new ideas, Nissan Design International deliberately promotes "creative abrasion" by hiring a diverse group of people and putting them to work in contrasting pairs (for example, balancing nerds with hippies). Employees are encouraged to display color charts of their "personalysis" to help managers do the mixing.

In an industry known for both creativity and massive excess, Alain Levy, chairman and CEO of EMI, has similarly found success by matching skills and attitude using a two-headed structure which he refers to as "my creative head and his No." For example, Matt Serletic sniffs out new talent as head of Virgin Music, and Roy Lott keeps Serletic financially in check.[18]

For implementation of creative ideas, Henry Ford looked toward inexperienced employees: "It is not easy to get away from tradition. That is why all our new operations are always directed by men who have no previous knowledge of the subject and therefore have not had the chance to get on really familiar terms with the impossible."[19] In many market leaders, however, rounds of testing and interviews do more to reinforce conformity than to assemble a collection of individuals with diverse capabilities and perspectives. Creativity demands team diversity on function, age, gender, education, culture, mind-set, and life experiences.

Offer Multiple Channels for New Idea Approval

Even firms with a history of prior market-driving activity find it difficult to keep the fires of iconoclastic creativity stoked. Today's successful market driver must beware of ossifying into the cautious, market-driven behemoth of tomorrow. In any large firm many frustrated potential entrepreneurs can be found who have ideas as yet unveiled. In most organizations, approval of a new business idea requires several "yes" votes up the hierarchy while a single "no" can kill it; and a market-driving idea will almost certainly get a "no" somewhere in the process.

To surface promising new initiatives, 3M has numerous channels that employees can use to secure approval and support for a project if their immediate superior rejects it. Providing alternative routes to authorization alters the dynamic to one where a project garnering a single "yes" and several "no's" can still proceed.

Establish Competitive Teams and "Skunk Works"

Early in development, no one can unconditionally forecast the winning technology or final market. Assuming that the marketplace will select the winner, Motorola encourages its wireless divisions to compete against each other. IBM had about half a dozen parallel development teams for the PC. When focusing on a new technology, Sharp often maintains small R&D projects on alternative technologies.

In an established firm, a radical new concept will typically either fall outside the current business definition and target markets of the firm (for example, Nutrasweet for Searle) or threaten to destroy the firm's existing business (for example, IBM's PC). In addition, market-driving projects, by definition, require a unique business system and therefore lack synergy with the firm's existing value network. When people pursue market-driving ideas within the existing structure, other priorities often hinder a speedy fruition.

To overcome organizational resistance and inertia, firms can set up "skunk works," physically and organizationally independent, self-contained entities with dedicated members. Skunk works harness and concentrate the entrepreneurial zeal and urgency of members, and protect the fledgling project from bureaucrats who would otherwise kill it.

Apple, 3M, IBM, Raychem, DuPont, Ericsson, General Electric, Xerox, and AT&T all use skunk works in order to nurture the soul of a small, entrepreneurial outfit within their large corporations. Some companies have recently soured on skunk works, mostly likely because they used skunk works inappropriately, for incremental innovation and adjacencies. Skunk works work best for unleashing "killer apps," not "feature creeps."

Cannibalize Your Own Products

Established market leaders rarely pursue projects that might undermine their core business. For example, Kodak's desire to ensure that its new digital business does not encroach on its traditional film business has slowed its progress in digital imaging. But as Pablo Picasso once observed, "Every act of creation is first of all an act of destruction."

Market-driving explicitly encourages cannibalization, based on the belief that since some firm will cannibalize a company's core business, it might as well do it itself. When Sony introduces a major new product, three teams are created: the first team tinkers with minor improvements, the second seeks major improvements, while the third explores ways to make that new product obsolete. At Hewlett-Packard, which fosters competition among its divisions, products less than two years old account for 60 percent of orders.

Market-driving retailers such as Starbucks and Sam's Clubs of the United States, Sweden's Hennes and Mauritz, and Italy's Benetton strategically cannibalize their own stores to some extent by building new outlets close to existing, successful locations, thereby leaving few vacant spaces for competitors to exploit. They believe in keeping the cannibals in the family.

Encourage Experimentation and Tolerate Mistakes

Developing an experimenting organization that seeks creative solutions requires a tolerance for mistakes. Firms must probe and learn in the marketplace, improving with each successive generation. The first Wal-Mart store was horrible but Sam Walton improved the format over time by trying different ideas and watching customer reactions. Similarly, Nike's original shoe wasn't very good but the company kept learning and improving the technology. As Ingvar Kamprad of IKEA observed, "Only while sleeping one makes no mistakes. The fear of making mistakes is the root of bureaucracy and the enemy of all evolution."[20]

In the United States, the focus on daily stock price, quarterly results, and Wall Street analysts tends to severely punish missteps. This is another hurdle that large, publicly traded market leaders must manage to effectively cultivate market-driving activity. The company must carve out a sheltered area where the risk-taking associated with experimenting can be tolerated and where there is room for the inevitable failures that will ensue. These potential failures are the price the firm must pay to cultivate market driving. As Thomas Edison was quoted as saying, "I have not failed, I have simply found 10,000 ways that do not work."

There must, however, be some rules regarding failures. David Pottruck, CEO and president of Charles Schwab, articulated the following three rules: (1) Don't put the company at risk. By limiting the enormity of possible failure, one ensures that employees bet the horse, not the farm. (2) Take reasonable precautions against failure. (3) Learn something from it.[21] As Philips' CEO, Gerard Kleisterlee, observed, "a learning culture means allowing mistakes to be made but making sure they are not repeated."[22]

Putting It All Together: Sony's Market-Driving Culture

Over time, even successful market-driving firms change, as they should, into market-driven firms. The history of innovation consists of patterns in which bursts of breakthrough innovation that reshape an industry are interspersed by flows of less dramatic incremental improvements and refinements. Once the radical innovation phase is over, incremental innovation to improve the existing offering and business system becomes the primary challenge.

Furthermore, competitors ultimately emerge with competitive, or even superior, value propositions and business systems modeled after the "new" market leader. At this stage, market-driving firms like Tetra Pak must search for their next market-driving innovation. However, as the successful market driver transforms into an established market leader, it faces all the same obstacles to motivating market-driving strategies that the former market leaders faced. As Picasso noted: "Success is dangerous. One begins to copy oneself. It is more dangerous than copying others. It leads to sterility."

With age and size, firms tend to become increasingly bureaucratized, routinized, and risk averse. To date, very few firms—except perhaps Sony—have consistently launched a series of successful market-driving ideas.[23] Sony has been a powerhouse in developing and launching innovative products that have created new markets and businesses, such as the transistor radio, Walkman, 3.5-inch diskette, and audio compact disc. "New products create new markets" is a guiding credo at Sony. Sony claims that their strongest assets are employees who combine dreams of creating new products or markets with the passion and enthusiasm to execute them.

Sony practices several principles that large, established companies should adopt to become more market-driving. Sony leaves room for experimentation, tolerates mistakes, cannibalizes its own, encourages competitive teams, and offers multiple channels for approval of new ideas. It also nurtures and rewards individual creativity, as illustrated by the following story.

In 1980, three teams in two departments were working in parallel to develop a $10\times$ improvement to the conventional 5.25-inch "floppy" diskette. Initially, each team was a single individual with a distinct vision of the product concept. The first individual envisioned it as a more compact floppy, the second individual visualized it as a 3.5-inch plastic-encased disk, and the third individual, who was in a different department, was working on a 2-inch diskette with high rotation speed. At this stage, it was unclear whether any of these would deliver a product that could be marketed successfully.

After three months, the first team had encountered several technical problems while the second team, led by twenty-eight-year-old Kamoto, had developed a promising prototype (an early version of the 3.5-inch plastic-encased diskette that is the world standard today). Since they belonged to the same department, the first team was disbanded with the former members redirected to other projects, including a few who were assigned to the second team. The head of the department asked the former leader of the first team to author and present a paper on the 3.5-inch diskette at an upcoming Japanese technical conference. It was explained to Kamoto that while all the internal recognition at Sony for the invention of the 3.5-inch diskette would go to Kamoto, it was important to keep the former leader of the first team motivated.

The 3.5-inch diskette, unveiled at the Chicago industry show in 1981, piqued Apple's interest. In 1983, Steve Jobs, the founder of Apple Computer, adopted the new diskette for the Macintosh, but demanded assurances that the product would be substantially improved within one year. The enhanced system would be double-sided rather than single-sided, incorporate an automatic inject and eject system, and still reduce power consumption, height of the disk drive, and price by 50 percent. Despite these improvements, the product was still ignored by most of the larger IBM-compatible world, and was adopted by only two major customers, Apple and Hewlett-Packard. In 1987, Kamoto was transferred to sales and marketing despite having no experience in these functions. It was thought that only he, having invented the 3.5-inch diskette, had the passion to make it a worldwide standard. It replaced the 5.25-inch floppy diskette as the standard format for storing data by personal computer users.

In 1991, Sony put Kamoto in charge of improving its languishing personal computer internal hard drive business, hoping that he would do for hard drives what he had done for the 3.5-inch diskette. Unfortunately, despite his best efforts, the venture was an expensive failure and Kamoto was asked to close down the operation. Given this highly visible failure, Kamoto thought his career at Sony was effectively over. Sony, however, recognized that he was motivated by his enthusiasm to contribute to the company and accepted the failure as a learning experience. Following the hard drive fiasco, Sony gave Kamoto the responsibility for managing another data storage device, the magnetic tape drive. Under his charge, Sony's worldwide market share for magnetic tape drives increased from 3 to 25 percent over three years.

While Kamoto and the 3.5-inch diskette were moving from one success to another, the leader of the third team, Ken Kutaragi, was struggling. His design for the 2-inch diskette was completed in 1982, the year after the 3.5-inch diskette. Kutaragi's diskette delivered excellent performance, but its architecture required significant changes in the associated hardware. As a result, Sony was the only company to adopt it for their laptop, "Produce." Unfortunately, the laptop did not succeed and Kutaragi had to search for other applications for the 2-inch diskette.

The diskette found its next home in Sony's new still camera, "Mavica," which also failed, despite high expectations. Kutaragi, doggedly persisting in the face of continuing failure, then approached Nintendo in the hope of persuading them to use the 2-inch diskette with their video game software. When Nintendo signed a contract with Sony for the 2-inch diskette, Kutaragi thought he had finally found the killer application for his invention. But three years later, Nintendo canceled the contract without ever using the product.

A disappointed Kutaragi approached Sony's leadership with a proposal to develop their own line of video games using CD-ROMs. Kutaragi convinced Sony that his three years of discussion with Nintendo had given him a deep understanding of the video-game business and insights into Nintendo's strengths and weaknesses. With assistance from Sony's business strategy group, PlayStation video games were developed and launched in 1994 as a competitor to Nintendo. Since its launch, Sony has sold more than 90 million PlayStations and controls 70 percent of the global video-game market of $10 to 15 billion.[24] The game unit that Sony first deemed tangential to its operations now generates a third of the company's profits and embodies Sony's vision of integrating games and consumer electronics.

Conclusion

This book began with Peter Drucker's observation, "The business enterprise has two and only two basic functions: Marketing and innovation. Marketing and innovation produce results; all the rest are costs." Yet large business enterprises in particular struggle with both marketing and innovation.

Marketing must become more innovative—but it must do so in a way that will help the organization to make discontinuous leaps. It must provide more business model and business concept innovation by finding underserved markets, developing radically new value propositions, and creating new delivery mechanisms. Marketing cannot rely solely on R&D for new product development. The following box provides a market-driving checklist.

Market-Driving Checklist

Market-Driving Mind-Set

- *Does our top management continuously reinforce the need for market-driving ideas?*
- *Do we actively seek to cannibalize our own products?*
- *Is the pursuit of competing emerging technologies permitted?*
- *Are new ideas routinely imported from the outside?*
- *Are time and resources allocated for curiosity-driven explorations?*

Market-Driving Culture

- *Do we tolerate failures when people are attempting something really new?*
- *Are processes in place to capture learning from failures?*
- *Are people encouraged to share their failures publicly?*
- *Do we constrain innovation through too much respect for hierarchy?*
- *Are organizational rules and norms enforced too rigidly?*
- *Do we tolerate mavericks and allow space for champions to flourish?*

In addition, innovation must be linked more tightly to marketing. History is replete with innovative new products and business ideas that have failed to succeed because of poor marketing. In incremental innovation, marketing's role is clear: provide customer feedback and market research as well as manage the market launch process. For radical innovation and market-driving ideas, the role of marketing is more obtuse and often contrary to deep-seated marketing beliefs. The challenge in these cases is to

Market-Driving People

- *Do we hire people who will increase the genetic pool of our company?*
- *Do we mix people on teams to generate creative abrasion?*
- *Are novices included on important projects to question assumptions?*
- *Do we think our people are entrepreneurial?*
- *Are exceptional innovation achievements and efforts recognized and rewarded?*

Market-Driving Processes

- *Do we allow for long payback horizons for innovation projects?*
- *Do we accept alternative routes to obtain funding and approval for market-driving ideas?*
- *Do we have processes that move ideas from the bottom to the top without obstruction?*
- *Do we run competitions to generate radical new concepts?*
- *Do we ensure that radical ideas do not lose resources to incremental ideas?*

---

find a segment of the market for whom the radical value proposition is attractive. This initial "innovator" segment is then used as the beachhead from which to improve the firm's attack on the more mainstream markets.

From the CEO's perspective, lack of time, resources, or money are poor excuses for a failure to be innovative in large companies. As Scott McNealy, Sun Microsystem's cofounder, noted, "there's never been a successful well-funded startup. If you have too much money, you're not going to find a new and different and more efficient and effective way. You're just going to try and overpower the current players with the same strategy. You can't win a sailboat race if you're behind by tacking behind the boat in front of you."[25]

The CEO's mandate is clear. As Francisco Gonzalez, technophile chairman of Spain's Banco Bilbao Vizcaya Argentaria SA, puts it, "We've got one clear premise: we want entrepreneurs more than administrators."[26] But hiring entrepreneurs is easier than giving them the space to be creative. For example, while most media companies struggle to manage the interface between creative thinking and the corporate profit center, HBO prides itself on having an edgy creative outfit within a vast corporation. It does it by creating a small boutique-like identity and granting creative independence within a tightly controlled operation. As an HBO creative noted, "It's an amazing place to work. Once they have hired the right people, they give you the liberty to do what you want." The result, directors and writers coming knocking at their door rather than the other way round, as at most media companies.[27]

Perhaps there is no better way to end this chapter than to note that at market-driving firms, the sense of radical innovation starts at the top. Sony's President, Kunitake Ando, declares, "Sony's mission is to make our own products obsolete. Otherwise somebody else will do it."[28] With this attitude, everyone in the company, including marketers, must always be aware that a customer is someone who has not yet found a better alternative.

EIGHT

From Strategic Business Unit Marketing to Corporate Marketing

Marketing is strategy.

IN GENERAL, THE LITERATURE on marketing strategy focuses on business units and ignores the role of marketing at the corporate level. This has probably reinforced the traditional belief that all marketing is local—a belief that has resulted in the placement of the marketing function in SBUs or in country organizations, rather than at headquarters. Relatively few companies have a chief marketing officer (CMO) alongside a chief financial officer (CFO) or a chief operating officer (COO) to influence the CEO and corporate strategy.

While most of the marketing functions and almost all marketing activities in an organization have historically fallen to the divisional and country organization levels, more firms are enhancing the role of marketing at the corporate level. The CMO position is emerging in companies as diverse as Coca-Cola, Nokia, KPN Qwest, Pizza Hut, and Reuters. However, many CEOs and companies still hesitate to appoint CMOs or build a large corporate marketing function because they do not know whether marketing can add any significant value from the corporate center. The more diversified the individual businesses, the more decentralized the organization; the larger the number of brands in the portfolio, the more challenging to conceptualize the benefits of corporate marketing.

The Role of the Corporate Center

If marketing is to break out of the shackles of the conventional business unit boundaries and play an important role at the corporate strategy level, then corporate marketing must help the CEO address the following three questions about corporate strategy:[1]

1. *Portfolio choices*:   What business should we be in? Companies generally choose their portfolio of businesses by arraying individual business units on matrices such as the Boston Consulting Group matrix or General Electric matrix. Regardless of the two-dimensional portfolio model, one dimension reflects market attractiveness while the other indicates the company's competitive strength.

   Companies differ on how they use such matrices. Some diversified companies seek a "balanced" portfolio of cash cows, rising stars, question marks, and so on. Others have specific rules, like General Electric's condition that each business be first or second in market share; otherwise, the manager must "fix it, close it, or sell it!"

2. *Portfolio relationships:*   What value should our businesses add to each other? Which relationships among the businesses actually create synergies that benefit an individual unit as part of the whole?

   Disney searches for synergies within its portfolio of movies, music, theme parks, merchandising, videos, software, retail, and television business. Companies constantly seek economies of scale by sharing operating resources such as procurement, manufacturing, and advertising.

3. *Parenting skills*:   What value does the corporate center add? The so-called parenting advantage is when the parent company adds such value to its portfolio businesses that any individual business unit is worth more as part of this particular parent than as part of another parent or as a freestanding unit. Parenting advantage exists if the parent has unique capabilities, resources, skills, expertise, or access to important stakeholders that can help the individual business units.[2]

For example, in the heavily regulated Indian market between 1960 and 1990, when operations required a license from the government, highly diversified conglomerates emerged due to the parenting advantage of access to key bureaucrats. After market deregulation, these conglomerates divested many business units to concentrate on a few core activities.

Corporate marketing can help the CEO address these three corporate strategy challenges. Regarding the appropriate portfolio and portfolio interactions, a strong corporate marketing team brings fresh insights by using a marketing lens to examine the strategic coherence of portfolio choices while searching for synergies between the business units. The outcome of this analysis should be a number of top- and bottom-line initiatives that corporate marketers lead to leverage the corporate portfolio. Regarding the parenting advantage, corporate marketing can champion the development of market-based capabilities that make the individual business units more customer-focused.

The Search for Marketing Synergies

Underlying the portfolio of business units in a global corporation are many complex implicit and explicit marketing choices (see

FIGURE 8-1

The Complex Corporate Marketing Logic

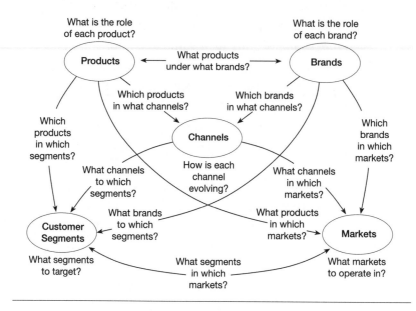

figure 8-1). Each business unit decides what products to sell, under which brand names, targeting which customer segments and markets, and through what channels of distribution. In any large company, the potential number of possible combinations of these five dimensions can overwhelm managers. For example, having 8 product lines, 4 customer segments, 10 brands, 5 distribution channels, and operating in 100 markets or countries leads to 160,000 decision points!

Given the complexity of the problem, each business unit must make these decisions for itself and optimize its own logic without fully considering the impact on the other units. Individual business units and country managers may not see opportunities to leverage other units or may struggle for cooperation. Corporate marketing can add value here by reexamining the company's portfolio of products, brands, channels, customer segments, and markets, and asking questions (per figure 8-1) from the global corporate perspective, not from an individual one.

Consider Sara Lee, a conglomerate with 160 core brands, thousands of product lines, and some 200-odd operating companies, each with its own profit center. No one shared even packaging systems because, as CEO Steven McMillan observed, "the decentralized culture was so ingrained they thought a sister company would overcharge them."[3]

In its search for synergies, corporate marketing must ensure that the company does not sacrifice variety for efficiency. Marketers must balance the desire for cost savings through economies of scale and the potential for increased penetration of customer segments and markets through economies of scope and managed variety.

By adopting the corporate perspective, corporate marketers can view the products, brands, channels, customers, and markets as potential platforms to exploit across individual business units. Corporate marketing can lead the push from the "vertical think" about individual countries and product divisions to "horizontal thinking" around customer needs and segments. Table 8-1 outlines some of the potential sources of marketing synergies, distinguishing primarily top-line initiatives from predominantly bottom-line ones. Corporate marketers should look for synergies from both.

Leverage Product Platforms

Could the firm leverage the products of some business units in the distribution channels, brands, or markets of other business units? For example, Wal-Mart's entry into China familiarized it with potential product suppliers there, and enabled it to set up a Chinese global sourcing center. Products sourced for and tested in the Chinese stores have now migrated to stores outside China: Chinese suppliers now provide approximately $12 billion worth of products annually for Wal-Mart. If, by more efficient sourcing from China, Wal-Mart can reduce its worldwide costs of goods

TABLE 8-1

Leveraging the Corporate Portfolio

	Products	Brands	Channels	Segments	Markets
Top-Line Initiatives	• Modular approach for variety and segmentation	• Brand extensions	• Channel migration	• Customer solutions	• Knowledge transfers
	• Global product concepts for multinational launch	• Redirect resources to fewer core brands	• Multi-channel marketing	• Cross-selling systems	• Emerging market push
		• Corporate branding			• Buzz marketing
Bottom-Line Initiatives	• Consolidate supply sources through ingredient rationalization	• Advertising platforms	• Global account management	• Cost-to-serve analysis	• Regional structures
	• Global R&D centers	• Brand consolidation	• Low cost to serve channels	• Prune losing customers	• Cross-national segmentation
	• Product platforms	• Brand assessment tools			

sold (COGS) by half a percent, that's more than any profits that it could generate in China over the next ten years.

How can a company create the product variety necessary to penetrate multiple segments while keeping product development and manufacturing costs from spiraling? By working off a few standard platforms with strictly defined interfaces, companies such as Toyota, Dell, Sony, and Volkswagen can achieve variety without the deleterious effects on economies of scale. The Toyota Camry, Lexus ES300, Sienna minivan, Toyota Highlander, and the Lexus RX300 SUVs have shared many interchangeable parts and a common platform across generations. The RX300, in particular, demonstrates the success of platform sharing. By sharing platforms, Toyota has used a well-tested, stable, engineered car platform as a starting point for what ultimately ends up as a rather "truck-like" vehicle. The RX300 has a truck or SUV-like appearance and utility while maintaining car-like attributes such as ride comfort and smooth handling.

How can a firm develop and launch products simultaneously across countries rather than introduce them through sequential country-by-country rollout? Setting up cross-national product concept and market launch teams prevents the reinvention of new products for each country, thereby reducing product development costs and increasing speed to breakeven volume.

Exploit Brand Platforms

Would some brands in the corporation add value to other business units? What brand extensions can the company launch? Can it merge brands in different product categories for greater impact and efficiency? Has the company allocated resources across brands most effectively? Can the corporate brand add value by endorsing business unit brands? Chapter 6 on brand rationalization should help corporate marketers answer these questions.

Corporate marketing is also the steward of the corporate brand. It develops, refines, and protects the common brand heritage and strengthens brand equity. At Electrolux, corporate marketing develops standard brand planning processes and templates for all marketing organizations and trains marketers on brand and marketing communications standards. In addition, Electrolux as an endorser brand bestowed the values of international expertise and global technical competence upon the local brands. Corporate marketing sets the guidelines on how individual brands and business units can leverage the corporate brand.

Extend Channel Platforms

Could other business units leverage the strong distribution channel of a particular business unit? Would the company increase its distribution clout by approaching the channels as a company rather than as individual business units? For example, Ford Motors's luxury brands of Volvo, Land Rover, and Jaguar could combine their distribution points and consolidate into larger dealerships rather than individual dealers for each brand.

Chapter 4 on channel migration should help corporate marketers answer questions about moving customers to lower-cost channels and penetrating faster-growing channels. Corporate marketing can help to develop the necessary competence to effectively manage multichannel marketing across business units.

Nurture Customers as Platforms

Could we increase our share of a customer's wallet by cross-selling products or innovating solutions for certain customer segments? Could we add products to the corporation's portfolio? Citibank merged with Travelers to cross-sell banking services, credit cards, and insurance to each customer. Amazon is adding categories rapidly to leverage its customer base of 25 million. By seeking synergy and leverage, corporate marketing can create complex product-service bundles to exploit customer relationships.

Bottom-line initiatives usually involve developing the competence to understand the lifetime value of, and the cost of serving, each customer. Based on this analysis, one can prune unprofitable customers from the portfolio, especially if cross-selling and solution-selling initiatives to such customers fail. Many banks, credit card companies, and telecommunications firms are currently discouraging customers who will never yield a profit.

Develop Markets as Platforms

Corporate marketing can initiate regional consolidation of marketing staff to exploit economies of scale and scope. Instead of segmenting markets at the country level, companies are developing segments on a pan-European basis. For example, across eleven European Union countries, four cross-national segments for yogurts exist to varying degrees in each country.[4] One of these segments, health and innovation, comprised approximately 26 percent of yogurt consumers in Denmark, Germany, and Great Britain, 18 percent in Ireland and Netherlands, about 7.5 percent in Belgium and Greece, and 3 to 5 percent in France, Italy, Portugal, and Spain. As a result, the appropriate yogurts and brand positioning can be developed for each of the four segments rather than for each individual country, which results in faster product development cycles and shared advertising platforms.

Can we transfer the knowledge of markets of one business unit to another business unit not in those markets? For example, B&Q, the do-it-yourself retailer, traditionally operated on one floor with merchandise stacked to the ceiling. In China, relatively shorter customers would not reach up for merchandise and often called for assistance in what was intended to be a self-service format. As a result, B&Q China designed and installed a two-story store, which it imported into B&Q's home market, the United Kingdom, to cope with soaring property prices and tough planning restrictions. The importance of emerging markets as a growth engine for companies merits a closer look.

Emerging Markets as a Growth Platform

Companies can get too comfortable with existing customers and countries and limit growth initiatives to wringing more sales from those segments. Too often, companies and their competitors go to the same well, overlooking underserved opportunities. In order to expand their customer base, companies increasingly will have to consider the mass markets of emerging economies.

Target Growing Masses in Emerging Markets

Companies in the developed world face a fundamental challenge. The slow birth rate in North America, Japan, and Western Europe has resulted in an older population with limited, if any, overall population growth. In particular, in Europe the ratio of actively working people to pensioners will drop from 4 to 1 to 2 to 1 within the next two decades. Certain industries such as health care, elderly homes, and leisure will grow, but others will struggle.

Companies tend to have ambitious growth targets. Aspirations to grow 10 to 15 percent per annum are common, even when the overall industry is growing by 3 to 5 percent. If we combined the five-year projections of the top five or six players within an industry, it would appear as if industry sales were expected to double. Since a firm cannot increase prices forever or sell more shampoo to receding hairlines, it cannot meet these growth projections in the developed markets. Yes, product innovation helps, but sustained product innovation is rare in mature markets with mature products.

To generate growth, companies must focus intently on the emerging markets of Asia, Latin America, and Africa.[5] For example, Ford estimates that the automotive market in developed countries will grow at 1 percent per annum and 7 percent in emerging economies.[6] In 2002, passenger car sales in China rose 55 percent over 2001. In the U.S. and European passenger vehicle markets, cheap financing is fueling price wars to stabilize volume.

The almost 2.5 billion people in the emerging markets of China, India, and Indonesia account for more than 40 percent of the world's population. No wonder Coca-Cola invested $2 billion in these three countries during the 1990s. Over the past five years, Danone, Heinz, and Unilever have spent more than a billion dollars acquiring local companies in Indonesia to position themselves favorably with the mass population there.

Some companies from the developed world trip on the doorstep of emerging markets. In the mid-1980s, Honda led the worldwide market for motor scooters with its superior technology, outstanding quality, and brand appeal.[7] After successfully entering Thailand and Malaysia, Honda turned to India, once again peddling its existing models through outlets in big cities rather than listening to potential customers, most of whom lived in rural India and expected low costs, durability, and reliability. Honda withdrew from India in three years.

The business models of most companies from developed countries force them to target a very small segment of the developing market population—at most, the top 20 percent of the income pyramid. Major multinational corporations are missing opportunities to innovate solutions for the 4 billion of the 6 billion people on this planet who make less than $2,000 per annum.[8]

Keep the Value Proposition Simple, and Keep It Cheap

The typical value proposition of multinational companies in the emerging markets is usually a global product with slight modifications. Thanks to cheap local labor and other input costs, companies can usually offer products made in emerging markets at somewhat lower prices than those in developed markets, though not low enough for mass consumption.

The value networks in which multinationals operate cannot yet deliver value propositions that suit the masses of the developing world. Billions of people with unmet needs—the millions of HIV-AIDS sufferers in Africa, the billions without clean drinking water, electricity, housing, education, or adequate medicines— could be a source of growth and profits for those firms willing to experiment with as-yet-unimagined ways to create customer value.

We need innovative market concepts and business models that target the overlooked bottom 80 percent through attractive and profitable value propositions. The overriding principles in reaching emerging market masses are simplicity and affordability. Keep it simple and keep it cheap. In India, to target villages with a population of 5,000 or less, Max New York Life's typical term policy has a payout of $208 and an annual premium of $2. In Africa, London's Freeplay Energy Group has designed a wind-up radio, charged by cranking a handle, which allows its African customers without electricity or expensive batteries to get vital health and agricultural information. Word has it that a few of these radios surfaced in the United States in 2003 during North America's worst blackout in history.

To realize the poor as an opportunity requires thinking differently about the value proposition. To lower costs and increase the market, companies are shifting from ownership and individual users to low-cost access and communities of users, especially involving high-fixed-cost products infrequently used. If nobody in a village can afford a telephone or personal computer, then maybe the entire village could, by paying per use as Grameen Telecom has demonstrated in Bangladesh.

Reinvent the Three Vs Model for the Masses

Simple and inexpensive value propositions are only possible by reinventing the value networks that underlie the current industry business models at much lower costs. Consider the business model of multinational pharmaceutical firms: It factors in high research and development expenses, massive marketing budgets, and prohibitive prices for patent-protected drugs. How could it possibly work to reach the billions who really need those products? Fortunately, companies have successfully reinvented the industry three Vs to serve the poor profitably.

Grameen Bank in Bangladesh pioneered the microcredit industry that dispenses loans averaging $15 to people who lack collateral, a service that would never be profitable for multinational banks given their cost structure. By removing the need for collateral and creating a banking system based on mutual trust, accountability, participation, and creativity, Grameen Bank has grown to serve 2.3 million borrowers, 98 percent of whom are women with very low default rates. As many as 9,000 microlenders now serve the developing world; some in Bolivia, Mexico, Kyrgyzstan, and Uganda are becoming big and profitable enough to tap into private capital and evolve into banks.[9]

Banco Azteca has similarly targeted a large underserved market in Mexico, the 16 million households that earn between $250 and $1,300 per month—factory workers, taxi drivers, teachers—whose accounts are too small (too uneconomical) for the large established banks.[10] The bank's sister company, Grupo Elektra, is Mexico's largest appliance retailer and has fifty years experience in providing consumer credit to this segment. With a repayment rate of 97 percent, this firm knows the segment and its financial means better than anyone else. Converting the credit departments of its extensive store network into bank branches made perfect strategic sense.

With the motto "a bank that's friendly and treats you well," Azteca welcomes customers that other banks shun. Realizing that most of its customers lack proof of income or proper identification, it invested $20 million in high-tech fingerprint readers. No need for any documentation. The database includes consumer's credit histories and names of neighbors who can help track down delinquent debtors. Credit becomes a matter of community pride.

Nothing inherent, except perhaps their mind-set, prevents multinational companies from serving the poor in emerging markets through three Vs innovation. In fact, they probably have more resources and potential capabilities. For example, Unilever's Indian subsidiary, Hindustan Lever, is one of the best at reaching the masses in developing countries.

Hindustan Lever: An Emerging Market Winner

Hindustan Lever is constantly searching for growth initiatives that can effectively serve the billion-person Indian mass market. Realizing that most Indian consumers were too poor to buy a full-size bottle of shampoo or detergent, besides having no space to store it, Hindustan Lever pioneered the individual-use sachets which sell for about 2 cents each. They are enormously popular.

Initially, Hindustan Lever set up a distribution system that reached only 100,000 of the 638,000 villages in the country. To access the largely untapped rural market, where 70 percent of the population lives, the company initiated Project Shakti ("strength").[11]

Under Project Shakti, Hindustan Lever trains women in small villages, usually with a population under 2,000, in business skills so that the women can launch small owner-operated businesses.

Since the women have little education and no experience in running an independent business, they receive follow-up training, essential to success. Many of these women are offered, and choose, to become rural sellers or distributors of Hindustan Lever products, creating a low-risk, sustainable microenterprise for themselves. By selling Hindustan Lever products in their neighboring four or five villages, they can generate a steady income of approximately 1,000 rupees (around $20) per month, almost doubling their previous household income.

Hindustan Lever has achieved these breakthroughs by developing a cadre of managers who understand the bottom-of-the-pyramid consumer. Each executive recruit must spend eight weeks in the villages of India on a community project to empathize with these consumers. Imagine if every multinational company, pushed by corporate marketing, developed a pool of emerging market experts who really understood the poor as a business opportunity rather than as a problem.

Transfer Best Practices Across Markets

Hindustan Lever has exported some of its successes with low-price, low-cost products, such as iodized salt and Wheel, a laundry detergent. When Unilever launched the detergent brand "Ala" in Brazil, Indian managers provided product development knowledge, low-cost manufacturing solutions, and low-cost advertising techniques such as wall paintings and rural display counters.[12] Ala has become a runaway success in Brazil.

An emerging market mind-set requires one to monitor positive spillover effects when marketing in developed countries. For example, an average NBA basketball game draws a television audience of 1.1 million households. On November 20, 2002, a Houston Rockets game featuring the new Chinese star, Yao Ming, against one of the league's worst teams, the Cleveland Cavaliers, drew 5.5 million live viewers in China and another 11.5 million for the evening replay.[13] That makes Yao Ming more influential than any other basketball player since Michael Jordan. With global media, everyday marketing decisions in the developed countries can influence prospects in emerging markets. Here again, corporate marketing can foster greater horizontal thinking.

Building Customer-Focused Capabilities

Despite public declarations, few companies are truly customer-focused. If you are fielding more customer complaints, seeing declining marketing productivity, or watching new products die on the vine, then your company probably needs to become more customer-focused. Corporate marketing can help build crucial capabilities that increase customer focus throughout the organization.

Responding totally to customers requires both educating the organization on customer-focused behavior and developing a methodology for assessing responsiveness. In organizations, what gets measured, gets done. Figure 8-2 presents a six-step approach to developing and measuring the customer-focused organization using value curves and the star model.[14]

What does "customer-focused" really mean? Does it refer to a mind-set, a culture, activities, or an organization? It refers to all of these. A customer-focused organization has a customer orientation (strategy and culture), a customer-driven configuration (organization and processes), and customer investments (competences and resources).

Customer-Focused Strategy Map

Corporate marketing defines the customer-focused firm as one that, above all, delivers demonstrated customer value in each of its business segments. No one can build a customer-focused organization without clear definitions of the valued customers and the value proposition to deliver. A strong customer culture without a well-articulated strategy is as useful as a car without a steering wheel.

FIGURE 8-2

The Customer-Focused Organization

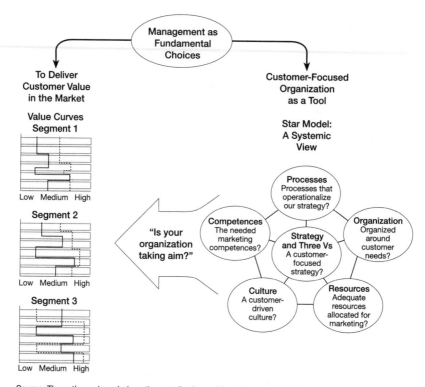

Source: The author acknowledges the contributions of Andy Boynton to this figure.

A Picture Is Worth a Thousand Words.   This oft-heard saying also applies when demonstrating a customer-driven strategy. Drawing a value curve to show how the firm's value proposition differs from the competition's for a target segment (discussed in chapter 2) is the most effective way to depict how the organization creates value for its customers. In figure 8-2, the relevant attributes for the customer appear on the vertical axis of the value curve. The lines exhibit the performance of the focal firm (solid lines) on each attribute versus the competition (dashed lines).

Once everyone understands the value curves, corporate marketing can more easily mobilize the organization to deliver this value to customers. A number of companies have used the star model and figure 8-2 to recognize the levers of customer-focused organizational capabilities.

Strategy Is Asking the Right Questions. Drawing value curves for each segment can help answer the following questions: (1) Have we clearly defined target segments? (2) Do we have differentiated value curves for each target segment? (3) Have we validated the value curves through market research? (4) Have we positioned ourselves in key segments? (5) Have we aligned our value network to deliver our value propositions to the target seg-

FIGURE 8-3

Building the Customer-Focused Organization

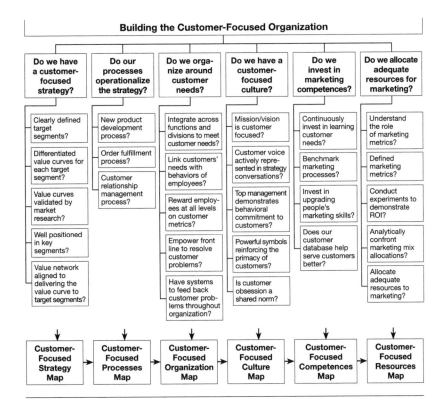

ments? Building a customer-focused organization requires efforts across multiple dimensions. For a poster version of the questions to ask in order to assess the degree to which an organization is customer focused, see figure 8-3.

Customer-Focused Processes Map

Ultimately, customers get a bundle of processes, usually the new product development process, the order fulfillment process, and the customer relationship management process. Managers must align the apparently contradictory logic of these three main processes to deliver the value curves to the valued customers.

New Product Development Process.   The new product development process is a creative activity and may attract employees who eschew financial or customer discipline. The challenge is to strike a balance between the freedom to create and the commitment to deliver customer value. Tight constraints will hinder creativity, and loose ones will result in expensive new products that suffer from "feature creep" (features that nobody wants). For example, Gillette's razor strategy (build a better product and consumers will trade up) did not work for its Duracell batteries because consumers did not want better batteries, just cheaper ones.

Encouraging R&D personnel to spend time with customers, rotating them through marketing and sales, focuses the product development process on the differentiation articulated by the value curves. A Sony engineer may, for example, spend six months selling stereos on the pavement before ever participating in product design.

Order Fulfillment Process.   The goal of the order fulfillment process is to reduce costs through economies of scale. To lower costs, operations typically prefer long production runs and low variety. One industrial company had a fill rate of about 50 percent on distributors' orders, resulting in lost sales, a frustrated sales force, and dissatisfied customers. Investigators found that the factory managers were compensated on plant-level profits, and so the plant always processed the few large long-run standard orders promptly and pushed the short-run orders further out in the production schedule. Clearly, the company had not aligned its order fulfillment process with its strategy. The plant should have processed the orders of more "valued" customers and more urgent orders rather run the process exclusively on cost considerations.

Customer Relationship Management Process. The customer relationship management process focuses on acquiring and retaining customers. Companies typically look for flexibility and economies of scope in this process. A disciplined approach here requires seeking meaningful flexibility by aligning customer acquisition and retention to the value curves that help pinpoint where one should be flexible and for which customers.

By understanding the three Vs, sales can concentrate on the valued customers instead of scattering efforts across all customers. For example, in the customer retention process, an online grocer differentiates among customer A, B, and C based on their value to the firm. If an item, say tomatoes, fails to arrive, then all customers who complain receive immediate credit, but B customers get the tomatoes free with their next order, and A customers get the tomatoes free immediately.

Firms typically assess each of the above three processes on quality, speed, and efficiency. However, the customer-focused firm also assesses how customer-friendly the process is, whether it prioritizes customers according to their value to the firm, and how well it delivers the defined value curve.

Customer-Focused Organization Map

Companies all too frequently make it difficult for the customer to do business with them because of how they are organized. For example, a residential customer wishing to purchase a fixed land line, an ISDN line, and a mobile phone from British Telecom would have to call three different departments. A customer-focused company continuously strives to bring its organizational logic close to the customer's logic so that it is effortless for the customer to interact with the firm.

Organize Around Customers.   Whereas the processes above typically require cross-functional coordination to satisfy customers, most companies still operate in functional silos. Corporate marketing can push to integrate functions and divisions by identifying where internal cross-functional cooperation is critical for customer satisfaction. For example, the supply chain and sales people must coordinate closely to meet promised delivery dates. Marketing and R&D must collaborate to produce a greater number of "hit" new products. Operations and marketing must partner internally to improve the global market launch process.

After defining the functional interfaces, corporate marketing can set up forums for interaction between marketing and the other functions. It should push to establish (1) the rules of engagement among marketers and other internal and external partners, and (2) performance expectations that encourage cooperation with these partners. Ideally, companies should organize around market segments and treat them as individual profit centers, as Capital One does. This arrangement increases the capability to sense and respond to customer opportunities faster.

Specify, Measure, and Reward Customer-Oriented Behaviors. Corporate marketing must articulate the customer-focused financial measurements. While most companies attempt to reward customer-oriented behaviors, successful companies differ in level of detail, extent of participation, and weight placed on such rewards.

For the organization to produce customer-defined quality, it must translate the attributes of the value curves into precise behaviors for the front line and then reinforce these behaviors through rewards. For example, MBNA, the credit card company, has established goals of thirty-minute credit increase approval, twenty-one-second or second-ring telephone pick up, twenty-four-hour replacement of lost or stolen cards, and fourteen-day new account application processing. Each day that the staff exceeds these goals, the company contributes to the employee bonus pool. No wonder MBNA meets or exceeds 98 percent of its goals daily.[15]

Siebel ties 50 percent of management incentive compensation and 25 percent of salesperson compensation to measures of customer satisfaction. Unlike most companies that pay it immediately, Siebel pays the incentive a year after the sales contract is signed, when it can accurately determine customer satisfaction with results.[16]

Harrah's, the casino operator, has a bonus plan that rewards workers with extra cash for improved customer satisfaction scores at the property. In 2002, the employees at one property, despite having record-breaking financial results, received no bonus because their customer satisfaction score was mediocre.[17] What a powerful message to send the entire organization.

Empower Employees to Resolve Customer Problems.   Corporate marketing must empower employees to resolve customer problems and complaints. This freedom improves the speed and often the efficiency of complaint resolution. Marketers should also develop a feedback loop to communicate customer problems throughout the organization as Microsoft does for Windows.

Customer-Focused Culture Map

Building a customer-focused culture takes time. However, the culture that permeates the organization is perhaps the most important differentiator of customer-focused firms. A customer-driven culture starts at the top of the organization.

Create a Customer-Driven Mission.   Has the company stated its mission in terms of what the organization does for customers? For example, Wal-Mart's "lowering the cost of living for the world" is better than "being the best in our industry." Customer-driven companies infuse their strategy conversations with the customer voice through market research, time spent with important customers, and internal conflict resolution based on customer needs and expectations. At some companies, the annual strategy meetings begin with a presentation by an important customer.

Involve General Managers with Customers.   Nothing is more powerful than CEOs regularly calling on customers. Corporate marketing can cultivate a customer-driven culture by creating opportunities for senior managers to grapple with customer-related issues and by challenging senior general managers to devote time to marketing and engaging customers. At MBNA, executives devote four hours a month to answering or listening to customer calls.[18] Corporate marketing can also appoint general managers to serve on marketing oversight or award boards, as the Electrolux Group Brand Award does, not just to improve quality but to recognize superior or innovative employee efforts toward customers.

Manipulate Symbols to Reinforce the Primacy of Customers.   Symbols can be powerful in fostering shared beliefs about the primacy of customers. At MBNA, the pay envelopes of employees remind them that customers are the source of their salaries. At the department store Nordstrom, employees leave the parking spaces closest to the store entrance for customers' cars.

Develop Norms of Customer Obsession.   Whereas a company needs formal rules and procedures for standardizing performance in ordinary situations, standardization does not usually result in outstanding customer service or quality. Why? Because outstanding customer service depends on how a company deals with extraordinary situations that are impossible to anticipate, unique to a particular person, and difficult to solve.[19] Companies need a shared norm of customer obsession, one that emphasizes how the organization exists for, and goes out of its way to help, the customer. Such strong norms increase clarity about priorities and expectations. The CEO and CMO must vocalize, live, and reinforce these norms daily. Jan Carlson, former CEO of SAS, noted, "Our moment of truth is when our customer meets our frontline. A bad moment can depreciate our assets. We have 100 million moments of truth each year at SAS."[20]

Customer-Focused Competences Map

Corporate marketing must take primary responsibility for enhancing the marketing competence of the organization through four different actions: continuously learning about customers; benchmarking marketing; developing marketing talent; and investing in customer-focused systems.

Continuously Learn About Customers.   Marketing departments should invest continuously in learning about customer needs and testing managerial instincts against consumer reality. Too often, consumer research turns into a sterile presentation by an external market research firm delivered through mind-numbing PowerPoint slides. Corporate marketing can develop processes and tools to gather, understand, use, and share consumer insights. At IDEO, the California-based design firm that designed the Apple mouse and the Palm handheld computer, designers personally visit experts and consumers at points of consumption and then share their insights through photographs hung on company walls.

Benchmark Marketing.   Benchmarking can improve the quality of marketing processes. Internal benchmarking across divisions and countries can facilitate the identification of marketing best practices and record practical lessons to improve organizational marketing effectiveness. Some firms build and manage marketing councils to connect their various marketing organizations. To push innovative ideas not performed anywhere in the company, corporate marketing can: (1) identify sources of best practices outside the organization, (2) develop and share external and internal best practice process maps, and (3) create a network that encourages competition for results and resources among the different marketing units within the company.

Develop Marketing Talent.   Corporate marketing leads the development of marketing talent across the organization. This requires a whole host of initiatives, including establishing appropriate recruiting, reward, recognition, and retention systems. Defined career paths for marketing experts that rotate marketers across the organization can be effective in building informal communities across divisions to facilitate transfer of ideas.

Procter & Gamble has developed excellent training programs that create a cadre of marketing experts.[21] Procter & Gamble's marketing training program has incubated many CEOs, such as Jeffrey Immelt of General Electric, Steve Ballmer of Microsoft, Paul Charron of Liz Claiborne, Stephen Case of AOL, Margaret Whitman of eBay, and Scott Cook of Intuit. Each year, about a thousand marketing recruits attend a week-long boot camp, and more than twenty marketing electives are available for more experienced employees. Procter & Gamble has designated 20 employees to serve as deans and 265 employees to serve as teachers. All of its 3,400 marketers around the world receive the same training.

Too often, companies pay lip service to developing customer competence in their employees. As a rule, the CEO should participate in some marketing training each year to set an example for investing in learning. At Harrah's, all employees must undertake a curriculum based on factors that motivate loyalty among Harrah's best customers. Since employees earn much of their compensation through tips, they receive their tipped wages while in training.[22]

Invest in Customer-Focused Systems.   Over the past two decades, companies have invested considerably in technology. Yet many of these investments have not enabled companies to focus more on customers. The CMO and corporate marketing can discuss technology investments in terms of their effect on customer acquisition, satisfaction, and retention. Does the technology create common organizational databases to capture knowledge? Do the information systems allow employees to share customer data freely across the organization? Do the integrated customer databases create complex views of the customer? Do IT processes enable employees to use databases in key marketing activities such as corporate branding and customer relationship management?

Customer-Focused Resources Map

To receive organizational resources, marketers must demonstrate tangible financial outcomes. Bottom-line marketing involves five steps: understand the role of marketing metrics; define marketing metrics; conduct marketing experiments; confront marketing mix allocations; and allocate adequate resources for marketing.

Understand the Role of Marketing Metrics.   When linking marketing to shareholder value and financial performance, one can easily forget to balance indicators of past financial performance (financial metrics) and indicators of potential financial health (marketing metrics). Andy Taylor, chairman and CEO of Enterprise Rent-A-Car, observes, "I went through a period of healthy paranoia in the early 1990s. We were a billion dollar company, growing fast; profitability was good. . . . Background noise . . . suggested our customer service had started to slip. The Enterprise service quality index [ESQI] was a breakthrough for us. Over the years, we have refined it until now we ask customers only two questions: Are you satisfied with our service? Would you come back?"[23]

Completely satisfied customers are three times more likely to return to Enterprise. Each of the 5,000 branches of Enterprise receives regular feedback on ESQI, and no one gets promoted from branches with below-average ESQI scores, no matter how impressive their financial performance. Rising ESQI scores reassure Taylor more than Enterprise's strong cash flow or increased market share. He explains, "ESQI doesn't mean we can ignore other [factors] but it will keep us on track."[24]

Define Marketing Metrics.   Corporate marketing can influence the definition of the relevant marketing metrics at each of the five levels of business and ensure that each division and country tracks, collects, and reports the appropriate metrics using a common methodology so that executives can compare data across the firm (see table 8-2). Managers can slice and dice comparable data in various ways to diagnose the overall performance of the corporation and demonstrate the productivity, or lack thereof, of marketing expenditures. At Grand Vision, the European optical chain, corporate meetings devote a day to discussing marketing metrics after participants present the financial numbers and employee statistics.

Conduct Marketing Experiments to Demonstrate Return on Investment.   Corporate marketing must demonstrate the links between marketing spending, customer satisfaction/retention data, and financial outcomes, such as revenues and profits. By tracking this data over time, the organization can differentiate between marketing investments like brand building and marketing expenditures such as promotions.

TABLE 8-2

Marketing Metrics

Products	Brands	Channels	Customer Segments	Markets
• Relative product quality	• Brand awareness	• Channel penetration	• Customer satisfaction	• Market penetration
• Perceived product quality	• Brand esteem	• Channel trust	• Average transaction size	• Market share
• Percentage of sales from new products	• Brand loyalty	• Channel efficiency	• Customer complaints	• Sales growth
• Product profitability	• Brand profitability	• Market share in each channel	• Customer acquisition costs	• Market profitability
		• Channel profitability	• Customer retention rate	
		• Shelf space	• Customer profitability	

Marketing experiments help the company identify which types of marketing expenditures yield results. For example, to assess the efficacy of sales training, Motorola-Canada selected eighty-four employees with similar sales productivity and trained half of them.[25] The newly trained group increased sales by 17 percent in the first three months after training, whereas the control group's new order volume dropped by 13 percent. Motorola estimates that every dollar spent on training yields $30 over three years.

A company such as Anheuser Busch (AB) constantly experiments to examine effective practices in marketing and advertising. Once it finds a program that works, its discipline and persistence in implementation sets AB apart from competitors. Galeries Lafayette, the French department store chain, calls these two stages experimentation (identifying the most profitable actions) and industrialization (prioritizing and applying the best formulas). Experimenting with its 1.5 million cardholders, the firm has isolated several actions that increase turnover through cross-selling and one-to-one marketing, and has reduced costs by optimizing mass mailings and new channels such as e-mail and short messaging service (SMS).

Confront Marketing Mix Allocations.   Kraft has developed a method that ranks brands by returns on investment for each marketing mix element. For example, it compares the return on investment on advertising across brands and then reallocates advertising dollars from low ROI brands to high ROI brands. By doing so, and repeating the exercise for each of the remaining elements of the marketing mix, Kraft can optimize its marketing expenditures.[26]

Anyone who wants to reallocate major marketing resources should develop and present buy-down, buy-up, and reallocate alternatives (see figure 8-4). Corporate marketing should champion such an analytical approach, forcing the organization to confront questions such as, what would happen if we transferred a portion of the customer acquisition budget to customer retention? For

FIGURE 8-4

Marketing Allocation Alternatives

Source: Adapted from Paul Sharpe and Tom Keelin, "How SmithKline Beecham Makes Better Resource-Allocation Decisions," *Harvard Business Review* (March–April 1998): 92–105.

example, a creative CMO of a tour operator once took half the marketing budget for the year and devoted it to satisfying customers on their holidays and found substantial positive impact on the next year's bookings.

One consumer packaged goods company realized that it was spending $12 annually per U.S. household on mostly mass media advertising with only a scattered shotgun effect. Its research indicated that about 12 million of the 120 million U.S. households accounted for 80 percent of the company's profits, of which 6 million accounted for 50 percent of the profits. Why not reduce the advertising expenditure by $1 per household annually and redirect the savings of $120 million into developing a database of the 6 to 12 million heavy-use households? It could then target these important households with more personalized direct marketing techniques.

Allocate Adequate Resources to Marketing.   Functions and divisions often lobby for the largest possible share of human, financial, and systems resources in any organization. A savvy CEO or CMO can ask important questions to redefine the debates in customer terms: Have you dedicated enough resources to customer acquisition and retention? Will you spend them in the most optimal manner? What benefits will the customer obtain from these expenditures?

The Challenge of Being a Customer-Focused Firm

One should not mistake a customer-focused organization with a powerful corporate marketing function and bloated marketing departments. Some academics and marketers still determine the degree of an organization's customer focus by asking whether executives value, respect, and view marketing as a benefit to the firm relative to other departments.

A powerful marketing group at the corporate level does not necessarily result in a better, more customer-focused organization. Caring about and organizing around customers and overriding company-think with customer-think in designing a firm's operations must transcend any particular function. To promote such an organizational mind-set requires corporate marketing to define what it needs from all the other functions, what it will contribute, and where collaboration is necessary, as shown in table 8-3. A company can never be too customer driven because as soon as it gets close, the customer moves. Targeted segments change, customers' needs evolve, and new competitors, channels, and technologies materialize, all of which necessitate a new customer-driven strategy.

TABLE 8-3

Marketing and Its Functional Interfaces

	What the CMO needs:	What the CMO provides:	Where the CMO collaborates:
CEO	Support to build a customer-focused organization	Leadership in marketing to support the firm's strategy	Defining transformational efforts that can be led by marketing
CFO	Funding for marketing initiatives	Systematic investment in marketing to enhance and accelerate cash flow while reducing risk	Measuring the return on investment of marketing investments and expenditures
COO	Delivery of a consistent customer experience (e.g., no stock-outs, service and product quality)	Lower complexity through brand and SKU rationalization	Determining product platforms and customer experience objectives
HR	Reward and training systems that make all employees customer-oriented	Strong brands that help recruitment of employees	Specifying the recruitment criteria for front-line employees
CIO	Information systems that give an integrated customer picture and are easy to use	Inputs that keep customer databases updated	Developing the needed functionalities with respect to information systems
R&D	New products that provide customer-value and differentiated features; speed to market	Clear inputs on valued customer and desired-value curves	Speculating about products that no customer has asked for but would delight them (market launch process)

Source: Inspired by "Stewarding the Brand for Profitable Growth," Corporate Executive Board, Washington, DC, 2001.

Making Market Transformations Happen

Naturally, we can expect corporate marketing to champion those marketing initiatives that potentially benefit multiple business units or require coordination among them, especially if such initiatives are innovative, long-term, costly, high-risk, or transformational in nature. The seven marketing transformations enumerated in this book all share these attributes. However, given the substantial nature of these initiatives and the potential organizational resistance, marketers need the CEO on board in order to thrive.

Change, even for the better, usually traumatizes organizations. It forces people to think and act differently. More important, the seven major transformations of the CEO's marketing manifesto will likely spark significant shifts in the relative power of individuals and divisions within the organization. Individuals typically adopt four postures to change depending upon how it affects them (positive or negative) and their profile (active or passive).[27]

Given human nature, those for whom the change has a negative impact will either actively resist or undermine it (*resisters*) or adopt a passive wait-and-see attitude (*traditionalists*). Managers must empower the *change agents*—those for whom the potential impact of change is positive and who have the energy to lead it—while energizing the *bystanders* who see the potential good but dither over taking an active role. The question is, should the CEO be the primary change agent for market transformations?

The CEO as Commander, Chairman, Coach, and Catalyst

Instinctively, the CEO may assume ownership of the seven transformations that comprise his marketing manifesto. The CEO as leader lends the change program credibility and high priority. However, top executives should counsel the CEO against directing every transformation initiative. The typical demands on the CEO, especially of a public company, may consume the time and the energy needed to tackle the matter, and the CEO may lack expertise in the subject.

Professor Paul Strebel has mapped the degrees of urgency and resistance in four different transformation processes (see table 8-4). Intriguingly, each change process requires the CEO to assume a specific role in that process. There are two caveats: (1) Since the urgency and resistance to change will differ across companies, managers cannot state categorically that an individual transformation, such as brand rationalization, should follow a particular

TABLE 8-4

Transforming Processes

Strong Resistance	**Task Force Change**	**Top-Down Turnaround**
	CEO Role: Chairman (Intensive solicitation of opinions) **Process:** • Ask *change agents* to staff task forces • Ensure task forces solicit *bystanders'* opinions • Confront *resisters* with choice of buying in • Put *traditionalists* in implementation roles	CEO Role: Commander (Take it or leave it) **Process:** • Ask *change agents* to cascade down • Unequivocal message to *bystanders* • Force *resisters* out by making buy-in immediate • Rapid reorganization for *traditionalists*
	Widespread Participation	**Bottom-Up Initiatives**
Weak Resistance	CEO Role: Coach (Collaborator) **Process:** • Ask *change agents* to facilitate participation • Initiate widespread collaboration with *bystanders* • Crowd out *resisters* with growing support • Involve *traditionalists* in network of linked teams	CEO Role: Catalyst (Provocative) **Process:** • Challenge *change agents* to take initiative • Encourage *bystanders* to imitate • Throw performance challenges to *resisters* • Integrate *traditionalists* into entrepreneurial teams

Low Urgency for Change, Unclear Direction — High Urgency for Change, Clear Direction

Source: Adapted from Paul Strebel, *The Change Pact: Building Commitment to Ongoing Change* (London: FT Prentice Hall, 1998).

change process; and (2) major organizational transformations are messy. Typically, one must apply a different process at each stage of the initiative, as more of an evolution, not a revolution.

Chapter 3 presents the transformation from selling products to innovating solutions at IBM. At the start of the transformation, IBM was losing money and under pressure to divest some of it its divisions; there was great urgency for change. When the incoming CEO, Lou Gerstner, decided to remake IBM into a solution-seller, he faced stiff internal resistance from IBM product and country heads, who had historically enjoyed complete independence. Providing solutions forced them to kowtow to those who actually coordinated and delivered customer solutions and to cooperate in the customer's best interest. Lou Gerstner had to adopt the classic top-down turnaround process with him as commander-in-chief.

The move to global distribution partnerships in FMCG companies described in chapter 5 is usually more gradual. Since retailers are still integrating their own international operations for worldwide purchasing, the urgency for change is less dramatic. Given that global account management would diminish the dominion of country managers, firms must often adopt the task force approach to overcome resistance. Amid this transformation process, some FMCG companies are confronting recalcitrant managers individually and calling on the CEO to coordinate work groups and synthesize dissimilar points of view, so as to keep everyone moving forward.

When resistance is weak or isolated, frontline managers can drive change or use widespread participation methods. Top management cannot readily know who in the organization has valuable market-driving ideas. In chapter 7, NEC and Sony demonstrated that open competitions can surface these ideas and their proponents, while the CEO plays coach and sponsor of the market-driving process.

Finally, as chapter 4 notes, the emergence of the Internet enabled many firms to sell directly to smaller customers. During the dot-com boom, companies rushed impetuously to enter this channel of distribution. At one computer manufacturer, there was little internal resistance to direct online sales, but nobody really knew how to approach this channel. Therefore, in a bottom-up process with CEO as catalyst, executives freed division heads to approach online selling in whichever manner best suited their individual division. Knowing that several divisions wanted to explore the new channel, the CEO challenged them to do so. After one division's modest success, the CEO encouraged other divisions that could potentially benefit from the channel to imitate it.

Regardless of which change process a company adopts and which corresponding role the CEO plays, transformational marketing initiatives absolutely need top management support in order to succeed. Since the initiatives developed in this book traverse different functions and country organizations, they will undoubtedly encounter turf battles that pervade large companies. The CEO is usually the peacemaker in such subversive situations.

Stimulate Great Conversations Around Customers

Besides their role in the transformation process, CEOs should be customer champions at the board level, by stimulating great conversations around customers' needs and behavior. To spare marketing from the daily tactical matters, CEOs should ask the broad questions about how their company creates value for customers; what role their brand plays in their customers' lives now and in the future; and what role advertising will play in the next decade. CEOs should challenge top corporate management to create the time and space for such conversations about customers—and maybe even institute rules, as Lou Gerstner, the former CEO of IBM did, against using overheads and PowerPoint presentations.[28]

CEOs must be role models for rigor and rationality by contrasting widely held assumptions about the customer against the results of marketing experiments. As Socrates observed, we approach wisdom only through rigorous questioning to level false arguments. Rather than making a rash decision, Alfred Sloan of General Motors once suggested to his board: "I propose we give ourselves time to develop disagreement and perhaps gain some understanding of what the decision is all about." CEOs must institutionalize the questioning of assumptions about consumers, channel members, employees, and their respective actions and aspirations. Without such conversations, a company is unlikely to form a shared understanding of the company's mission, strategy, and values.

Leadership is about doing the right thing when nobody is watching. We have witnessed too many CEOs and corporate leaders follow the path of Thrasymachus, a skillful Greek sophist who argued that wise men do as they like without being caught. Rather, they'd do better to follow Plato's argument that, as repositories of collective behaviors, leaders must exercise self-discipline and lead for the broader good. Consumer trust is in the long-term interest of companies and society. The mission of a truly customer-focused firm should be to improve customers' lives, and its values should encompass customer welfare. Only then can customer capitalism rule.

Marketing as a Change Agent

There has probably been no better time than now for the rise of marketing. Today, marketing is in a perfect position to galvanize the organization, as value creation strategies shift from the financial engineering of the past decade to old-fashioned customer value creation.

The challenges to marketing are many, but each unearths new opportunities for seizing organizational leadership. Given increasing price pressures, marketing must spearhead the firm's move from selling products to providing solutions. As distribution channels consolidate, marketers must jump-start the transition to global account management structures. Despite industry commoditization, marketing must adopt a brand rationalization program to concentrate on and differentiate the company's core brands. As channels proliferate, marketing must swiftly exploit new channels of distribution to generate growth. Marketers must resist sterile consumer and market research that results in incremental innovation and instead drive market concept innovation to deliver unimagined consumer experiences.

Marketing must prove that it is willing and ready for its leadership role in transforming the company. It must convince others of its unique capabilities, resources and skills, and its mind-set to lead—and that it has matured as a discipline to become more strategic, cross-functional, and bottom-line oriented.

NOTES

ONE

1. Peter F. Drucker, *The Practice of Management* (New York: Harper Collins, 1954).

2. Michael George, Anthony Freeling, and David Court, "Reinventing the Marketing Organization," *McKinsey Quarterly* 4 (1994): 43–62.

3. John Brady and Ian Davis, "Marketing's Mid-Life Crisis," *The McKinsey Quarterly* 2 (1993): 17–28.

4. John Brady, Carolyn Hunter, and Nirmala Santiapillai, "Marketing in the UK," *McKinsey Quarterly* 2 (2000): 15–17.

5. George et al., "Reinventing the Marketing Organization," 43–62.

6. Jane Simms, "Do We Need More Marketing CEOs?" *Marketing*, 12 April 2001, 24–25.

7. Ibid.

8. Ibid.

9. Tim Ambler, *Marketing and the Bottom Line* (London: FT Prentice Hall, 2003).

10. "Marketers Turn to Metrics to Measure Impact of Their Initiatives," 21 August 2002, <http://searchcio.techtarget.com/originalContent/0,289142,sid19_gci 845685,00.html> (accessed 21 May 2003).

11. Frederick E. Webster, Jr., "The Future Role of Marketing in the Organization," in *Reflections on the Futures of Marketing: Practice and Education*, ed. Donald R. Lehmann and Katherine Jocz (Cambridge: Marketing Science Institute, 1997), 39–66.

12. David Dell, "The CEO Challenge: Top Marketplace and Management Issues—2002," *The Conference Board Research Report* (New York: The Conference Board, 2002).

13. Stephen A. Greyser, "Janus and Marketing: The Past, Present, and Prospective Future of Marketing," in *Reflections on the Futures of Marketing: Practice and Education*, ed. Donald R. Lehmann and Katherine Jocz (Cambridge: Marketing Science Institute, 1997), 3–14.

14. Ibid.

15. Niladri Ganguli, T. V. Kumaresh, and Aurobind Satpathy, "Detroit's New Quality Gap," *McKinsey Quarterly* 1 (2003): 148–151.

16. George S. Day, "Aligning Organization to the Market," in *Reflections on the Futures of Marketing: Practice and Education*, ed. Donald R. Lehmann and Katherine Jocz (Cambridge: Marketing Science Institute, 1997), 67–93.

17. Webster, "The Future Role of Marketing in the Organization," 39–66.

18. George et al., "Reinventing the Marketing Organization."

19. Ibid.

20. S. H. Haeckel, "Preface," in *Reflections on the Futures of Marketing: Practice and Education*, ed. Donald R. Lehmann and Katherine Jocz (Cambridge: Marketing Science Institute, 1997), ix–xvi.

21. Jagdish N. Sheth and Rajendra S. Sisodia, "High Performance Marketing," *Marketing Management* 10, no. 3 (2001): 18–23.

22. Ibid.

23. George et al., "Reinventing the Marketing Organization," 43–62.

24. Ibid.

25. Sheth and Sisodia, "High Performance Marketing," 18–23.

26. Simms, "Do We Need More Marketing CEOs?" 24–25.

27. Franklin D. Raines, speech delivered at the Forrester Research Finance Forum, New York, NY, 12 June 2001 <http://www.fanniemae.com/ir/speeches/2001/0612f.jhtml?s=speeches> (accessed 23 May 2003).

28. "CEOs: Customer Is King," *ZDNet*, 22 November 2002, <http://www.nc-india.com/news/stories/71048.html> (accessed 23 May 2003).

29. For more on this, see Nirmalya Kumar, "The Revolution in Retailing: From Market-driven to Market-driving," *Long Range Planning* 30, no. 6 (December 1997): 830–835.

30. Nirmalya Kumar, "Internet and the Information-Empowered Customer: Will Price Transparency Destroy Your Margins?" *IMD Perspectives for Managers* 70, no. 2 (July 2000).

31. Amy Merrick, "Software May Give Retailers a Leg Up on Markdowns," *Wall Street Journal Europe*, 7 August 2001.

32. Micheline Meynard, "Detroit's Costly Bid for Market Share Fails," *International Herald Tribune*, 25 October 2002, <http://www.iht.com> (accessed 4 February 2003).

33. Ibid.

34. Paul F. Nunes and Brian Johnson, "Stimulating Consumer Demand Through Meaningful Innovation," research report, Accenture Institute for Strategic Change, November 2002.

35. Webster, "The Future Role of Marketing in the Organization," 39–66.

36. Douglas A. Ready and Jay A. Conger, "Why Leadership-Development Efforts Fail," *Sloan Management Review* 44, no. 3 (Spring 2003): 83–88.

37. Lenn Grabiner and Kande Hall, "CEOs and Their Sales and Marketing Organizations: Creating a Winning Team," <http://www.grabinerhall.com> (accessed 2 January 2001).

38. Roger S. Peterson, "A Marketer's Perspective on CEOs," *Sacramento Business Journal*, 4 December 1998, <http://sacramento.bcentral.com/sacramento/stories/1998/12/07/smallb5.html> (accessed 26 January 2003).

39. Michael Shekter, "A Voice in the Wilderness," 28 May 2001, <http://www.workopolis.com/servlet/News/marketingadvisor/20010528/mkt_voice> (accessed 26 January 2003).

40. George et al., "Reinventing the Marketing Organization."

41. Henry Ford, *My Life and Work* (Salem, NH: Ayer Company Publishers, 1987), 67.

42. Ready and Conger, "Why Leadership-Development Efforts Fail."

43. For an excellent discussion on marketing metrics, please see Ambler, *Marketing and the Bottom Line.*

44. Robert E. Riley, "Mandarin Oriental Hotel Group: Delivering the Eastern Promise Worldwide," in *Brand Warriors: Corporate Leaders Share their Winning Strategies*, ed. Fiona Gilmore (London: Harper Collins Business, 1999), 201–202.

45. Drucker, *The Practice of Management.*

46. Theodore Levitt, *The Marketing Imagination* (New York: Free Press, 1983), 5.

47. Philip Kotler, "From Sales Obsession to Marketing Effectiveness," *Harvard Business Review* (November–December 1977): 67–75.

48. Neil Buckley, "Wal-Mart to Offer Discount Financial Services," *Financial Times*, 7 January 2003, 1.

49. See <http://www.jnj.com>.

50. For a good discussion on make-believe metrics for leadership development efforts, see Ready and Conger, "Why Leadership-Development Efforts Fail."

51. Gary Hamel and C. K. Prahalad, "Competing in the New Economy: Managing Out of Bounds," *Strategic Management Journal* 17 (1996): 237–242.

TWO

1. This initial distinction between market and strategic segments was developed in Jacques Horovitz and Nirmalya Kumar, "Getting Close to the Customer," *Financial Times*, 2 February 1996, special insert on "Mastering Management," 2–4.

2. What I call value network has usually in the past been referred to as value chain. I prefer the term value network because firms are increasingly relying on partners to deliver major parts of the value chain. Outsourcing of R&D, manufacturing, and distribution are now common.

3. Horovitz and Kumar, "Getting Close to the Customer."

4. The distinction between customer logic and company logic comes from my IMD colleague, Professor Jacques Horovitz.

5. Alex Taylor III, "Porsche Slices Up Its Buyers," *Fortune*, 16 January 1995, 24.

6. Nilanjana R. Pal and Rajiv Lal, "The New Beetle," Case 9-501-023 (Boston: Harvard Business School, 2000).

7. The Midas example is drawn from Horovitz and Kumar, "Getting Close to the Customer."

8. My conceptualization of the three Vs model is inspired by my IMD colleague Professor Derek Abell, who proposed that companies must define: Who is going to be our customer? What products and services are should we offer the chosen customer? How should we offer these products and services cost efficiently? See Derek Abell, *Defining the Business: The Starting Point of Strategic Planning* (Englewood Cliffs, NJ: Prentice Hall, 1980). The who, what, and how approach has also been adopted and well presented in Constantinos Markides, "Strategic Innovation," *Sloan Management Review* 38, no. 3 (1997): 9–23.

9. Nirmalya Kumar and Brian Rogers, "easyJet: The Web's Favorite Airline," Case IMD-3-0873 (Lausanne: IMD, 2000).

10. Kim W. Chan and Renée Mauborgne, "Value Innovation: The Strategic Logic of High Growth," *Harvard Business Review* (January–February 1997): 102–112.

11. The value curve technique was proposed by Chan and Mauborgne, "Value Innovation."

12. Adapted from Gary Hamel, *Leading the Revolution* (Boston: Harvard Business School Press, 2000).

13. John Brady and Ian Davis, "Marketing's Mid-Life Crisis," *McKinsey Quarterly* 2 (1993): 17–28.

14. Some of the questions of the strategy growth map are influenced by Donald C. Hambrick and James W. Fredrickson, "Are You Sure You Have a Strategy?" *Academy of Management Executive* 15, no. 4 (2001): 48–59.

15. Nirmalya Kumar and Brian Rogers, "easyEverything: The Internet Shop," Case IMD-3-0874 (Lausanne: IMD, 2000).

16. Hamel, *Leading the Revolution.*

17. Ibid.

THREE

1. See <http://www.sun.com> (accessed 1 March 2002).

2. The IBM story is drawn from Nirmalya Kumar, "The Path to Change," *Financial Times*, 6 December 2002, special insert on "Mastering Leadership," 10–11.

3. Amy D. Wohl, "Lou Gerstner Comes to IBM," May 1993 <http://www.wohl.com/g0029.htm> (accessed 31 January 2003).

4. Warren Lewis, <http://www.windowsfs.com/executive_view/winter2002_Warren_Lewis.asp> (accessed 18 March 2002).

5. 3Com Annual Report 2000, <http://www.3com.com/corpinfo/en_US/investor/financials/annua.../create_strategies.htm> (accessed 21 March 2002).

6. Many of the points in this paragraph are from the following excellent article: Eric V. Roegner, Torsten Seifert, and Dennis D. Swinford, "Putting a Price on Solutions," *McKinsey Quarterly* 3 (2001): 94–97.

7. Spencer E. Ante, "The New Blue," *Business Week*, 17 March 2003, 44–50.

8. The Hendrix Voeders story is from Juan Rada and Per V. Jenster, "BP Nutrition/Hendrix Voeders BV: The Consultancy Support System," Case IMD-5-0386 (Lausanne: IMD, 1992).

9. The ICI Explosives story is from Robert S. Collins and Michael L. Gibbs, "ICI-Nobel's Explosives Company," Case IMD-6-0170 (Lausanne: IMD, 2001).

10. The Grainger example utilizes the following sources: Market Facts Inc.; Grainger's Annual Survey: "Trends and Issues in MRO Supply Purchasing and Management: A Survey of MRO Purchasing Decision-Makers," February 2000; James A. Narus and James C. Anderson, "Rethinking Distribution: Adaptive Channels," *Harvard Business Review* (July–August 1996): 112–120; W.W. Grainger, *Grainger Annual Report 2000: Highlights,* "Chairman's Letter," <http://investor.grainger.com/pdf/AR2C7.pdf> (accessed 1 March 2002).

11. William Hall, "Nestlé Pulls IT Centres Together," *Financial Times,* 7 March 2002, 29.

12. Nathaniel W. Foote, Jay R. Galbraith, Quentin Hope, and Danny Miller, "Making Solutions the Answer," *McKinsey Quarterly* 3 (2001):84–93.

13. Robert Sandberg and Andreas Werr, "The Three Challenges of Corporate Consulting," *Sloan Management Review* 3 (Spring 2003): 59–66.

14. David Shook, "IBM: Winning as a Team Player," *Business Week Online,* 6 December 2001, <http://www.businessweek.com> (accessed 30 January 2003).

15. Foote et al., "Making Solutions the Answer."

16. Roegner et al., "Putting a Price on Solutions."

17. Ibid.

18. Edward Luce and Louise Kehoe, "Cisco on the Ropes but Still in with a Strong, Fighting Chance," *Financial Times,* 6 April 2001, 20.

19. Michael Kanellos and John G. Spooner, "IBM's Outsider: A Look Back at Lou," <http://news.com/2100-1001-828905.html> (accessed 1 March 2003).

20. This information is based on a presentation by Professor James Anderson, 2003.

21. Carole Low and Nirmalya Kumar, "Yahoo! From Free to Paid Services," Case IMD-3-0965 (Lausanne: IMD, 2001).

22. Koen Bouckaert, Daniel Deneffe, and Herman Vantrappen, "How Product Companies are Competing through Services," *Prism* 4 (1997): 29–41.

23. Foote et al., "Making Solutions the Answer."

24. Ibid.

25. For customer activity cycle concept, see Sandra Vandermerwe, *The Eleventh Commandment: Transforming to "Own" Customers* (Chichester: John Wiley & Sons, 1996).

26. Frank Cespedes, *Concurrent Marketing: Integrating Product, Sales, and Service* (Boston: Harvard Business School Press, 1995), 17–18.

27. Barry James, "Industry Is Troubled, but Airbus Is Soaring," *International Herald Tribune,* 13 January 2003, 1.

28. C. C. Tung, "Orient Overseas Container Line: Growth Reflecting the Rise of the Asia Pacific Economies," in *Brand Warriors: Corporate Leaders Share Their Winning Strategies,* ed. Fiona Gilmore (London: Harper Collins Business, 1999).

29. Russell Eisenstat, Nathaniel W. Foote, Jay R. Galbraith, and Danny Miller, "Beyond the Business Unit," *McKinsey Quarterly* 1 (2001): 54–63.

30. Foote et al., "Making Solutions the Answer."

31. Eisenstat et al., "Beyond the Business Unit."

32. Ibid.

33. Foote et al., "Making Solutions the Answer."

34. Doug Carr, *IBM Redux: Lou Gerstner and the Business Turnaround of the Decade* (New York: HarperBusiness, 1999).

35. Wohl, "Lou Gerstner Comes to IBM."

36. Ante, "The New Blue."

FOUR

1. Michael O'Leary, "Flying Above the Clouds," *Newsweek*, 23 June 2003, 64.

2. Graham Bowley, "How Low Can You Go?" *Financial Times*, weekend edition, 21–22 June 2003, W2.

3. Parts of this and the next section appeared earlier in Nirmalya Kumar, "Internet Distribution Strategies: Dilemmas for the Incumbent," *Financial Times*, 15 March 1999, special insert on "Mastering Information Management," 6–7.

4. Christopher Parkes, "America's Armchair Film Fans Boost the Box Office," *Financial Times*, 16–17 November 2002, 11.

5. For an excellent description of Dell's experience with retail, see Das Narayandas and V. Kasturi Rangan, "Dell Computer Corporation," Case 9-596-058 (Boston: Harvard Business School, 1996).

6. Ibid., 11.

7. For more details see Nirmalya Kumar and Brian Rogers, "Gramophone Company of India (A): The Digital Distribution Challenge," Case IMD-5-0568 (Lausanne: IMD, 2002).

8. Laura M. Holson and Geraldine Fabrikant, "Sales Plunge as Net Competition Grows," *International Herald Tribune*, 14 January 2003, 1.

9. Benoit Bertrand, "Germans Burn a Hole in Music Sector Pockets," *Financial Times*, 16 July 2002, 8.

10. Jon Pareles, "Bowie's 4th Decade of Ch-ch-ch-changes," *International Herald Tribune*, 11 June 2002, <http://www.iht.com> (accessed 4 February 2003).

11. The idea of distinguishing between the strategic logic and the implementation logic for change came from Professor Derek Abell. I have adapted his questions for strategic logic.

12. Nirmalya Kumar and Carole Low, "Priceline (A)," Case IMD-5-0593 (Lausanne: IMD, 2001).

13. Frank Ahrens, "Sony Uses Games as Launchpad," *International Herald Tribune*, 26 December 2002, <http://www.iht.com> (accessed 4 February 2003).

14. Bob Tedeschi, "An Online Reality Check," *International Herald Tribune*, 9 January 2003, 11.

15. Kalyanam Kirthi and Shelby McIntyre, "Hewlett-Packard Consumer Products Business Organization: Distribution through E*Commerce Channels," Teaching Note (Santa Clara: Leavey School of Business, 1999).

16. For an excellent description of Goodyear's dilemma, see John Quelch and Bruce Isaacson, "Goodyear: The Aquatred Launch," Case 9-594-106 (Boston: Harvard Business School, 1994).

17. Once again, the questions for implementation logic came from Professor Derek Abell, who used them in the context of change management.

18. Donald V. Fites, "Make Your Dealers Your Partners," *Harvard Business Review* (March–April 1996): 84–95.

19. The author's ideas regarding channel conflict have been greatly influenced by his many years of interaction with his dissertation advisor, Professor Louis W. Stern.

20. David B. Godes, "Avon.com (B)," Case 9-503-041 (Boston: Harvard Business School, 2002).

21. Peter F. Drucker, "The Discipline of Innovation," *Harvard Business Review* (August 2002): 95–104.

FIVE

1. Sabine Bonnot, Emma Carr, and Michael J. Reyner, "Fighting Brawn with Brains," *McKinsey Quarterly* 2 (2000): 76–87.

2. Nirmalya Kumar and Brian Rogers, "Wal-Mart: Competing in the Global Marketplace," Case IMD-3-0969 (Lausanne: IMD, 2000).

3. See <http://www.toysrus.com/about> (accessed 30 June 2003); <http://www.hm.com/at_de/hm/facts_history/sh facts.jsp> (accessed 30 June 2003); and <http://www.ikea.com/about_ikea/timeline/splash.asp> (accessed 30 June 2003).

4. See <http://www.blockbuster.com/bb/about/internationalops> (accessed 30 June 2003) and <http://www.starbucks.com/aboutus/international.asp> (accessed 30 June 2003).

5. See <http://www.kingfisher.com/english/index.htm> (accessed 30 June 2003).

6. See <http://www.techdata.com> (accessed 30 June 2003).

7. Nirmalya Kumar, "The Revolution in Retailing: From Market Driven to Market Driving," *Long Range Planning* 30, no. 6 (1997): 830–835.

8. James Kynge, "It's as Much about Buying as Selling," *Financial Times*, special insert on China, 12 December 2002, v.

9. Kumar and Rogers, "Wal-Mart: Competing in the Global Marketplace."

10. This is drawn from Nirmalya Kumar, "The Power of Trust in Manufacturer-Retailer Relationships," *Harvard Business Review* (November–December 1996): 92–105.

11. Anonymous, "Pritchett on Quick Response," *Discount Merchandiser*, April 1992, 64–66.

12. Sam Walton and John Huey, *Sam Walton, Made in America: My Story* (New York: Doubleday & Company, 1992), 186.

13. Large parts of this section are drawn from Kumar, "The Power of Trust in Manufacturer-Retailer Relationships."

14. Nirmalya Kumar, Lisa K. Scheer, and Jan-Benedict Steenkamp, "The Effects of Supplier Fairness on Vulnerable Resellers," *Journal of Marketing Research* 32, no. 1 (1995): 54–65.

15. For an excellent article on the impact of global retailers on manufacturers, see Bonnot et al., "Fighting Brawn with Brains."

16. Jonathan D. Hibbard, Nirmalya Kumar, and Louis W. Stern, "Examining the Impact of Destructive Acts in Marketing Channel Relationships," *Journal of Marketing Research* 38, no. 1 (2001): 45–61.

17. Kumar, "The Power of Trust in Manufacturer-Retailer Relationships."

18. Kumar et al., "The Effects of Supplier Fairness on Vulnerable Resellers."

19. This section borrows heavily from Daniel Corsten and Nirmalya Kumar, "Profits in the Pie of the Beholder," *Harvard Business Review* (May 2003): 22–23.

20. Ibid.

21. Ibid.

22. Julian Birkinshaw, "Global Account Management: New Structures, New Tasks," Financial Times Mastering Management Online Resource, 20 February 2001, <http://www.ftmastering.com/mmo/mmo05_2.htm> (accessed 11 February 2002).

23. George S. Yip and Tammy L. Madsen, "Global Account Management: The New Frontier in Relationship Marketing," *International Marketing Review* 13, no. 3 (1996): 24–43.

24. These quotes are taken with permission from Sundar Bharadwaj and Thomas W. Gruen, "Organizational Structural Approaches to Account Management: Developing a Model of the Effectiveness of Customer Business Development Teams," Presentation to the AMA B2B Faculty Consortium, 3 August 2000.

25. Bonnot et al., "Fighting Brawn with Brains."

26. Ibid.

27. Ibid.

28. Birkinshaw, "Global Account Management."

29. Michael George, Anthony Freeling, and David Court, "Reinventing the Marketing Organization," *McKinsey Quarterly* 4 (1994): 43–62.

30. Julian Birkinshaw, Omar Toulan, and David Arnold, "Global Account Management in Multinational Corporations: Theory and Evidence," *Journal of International Business Studies* 32, no. 2 (2001): 231–248.

31. Bonnot et al., "Fighting Brawn with Brains."

32. Birkinshaw, "Global Account Management."

33. Kari G Alldredge, Tracey R. Griffin, and Lauri K. Kotcher, "May the Sales Force Be with You," *McKinsey Quarterly* 3 (1999): 110–121.

34. Bharadwaj and Gruen, "Organizational Structural Approaches to Account Management."

35. Alldredge et al., "May the Sales Force Be with You."

36. Bharadwaj and Gruen, "Organizational Structural Approaches to Account Management."

37. Alldredge et al., "May the Sales Force Be with You."

38. Bharadwaj and Gruen, "Organizational Structural Approaches to Account Management."

39. Birkinshaw et al., "Global Account Management in Multinational Corporations."

40. Russell Eisenstat, Nathaniel Foote, Jay Galbraith, and Danny Miller, "Beyond the Business Unit," *McKinsey Quarterly* 1 (2001): 54–63.

41. See Birkinshaw, "Global Account Management," for details on Electrolux and ABB.

SIX

1. John Willman, "Slimmer, Leaner, Fitter, Cleaner and Healthier Is the Stated Aim," *Financial Times,* 23 February 2000, 27.

2. Nirmalya Kumar and Brian Rogers, "Akzo Nobel UK: Managing the Brand Portfolio," Case IMD-5-0555 (Lausanne: IMD, 2000).

3. Andrew Edgecliffe-Johnson, "Procter & Gamble Cautious Over Recovery," *Financial Times,* 2 August 2000, 17.

4. John Willman, "Slimmer, Leaner, Fitter, Cleaner and Healthier Is the Stated Aim."

5. Matthew Boyle, "Brand Killers," *Fortune,* 11 August 2003, 51–56.

6. John Willman, "Culling the Brands," *Financial Times,* 29 October 1999, 18.

7. "Electrolux: Brand Challenge," *The Economist,* 6 April 2002, 60.

8. Trond Riiber Knudsen, Lars Finskud, Richard Törnblom, and Egil Hogna, "Brand Consolidation Makes a Lot of Economic Sense," *McKinsey Quarterly* 4 (1997): 189–193.

9. Jean-Noel Kapferer, *Strategic Brand Management* (New York: The Free Press, 1992).

10. Antony Burgmans, letter to author, 13 June 2003.

11. John Willman, "Culling the Brands."

12. 4.2 billion Swedish Kroner at the foreign exchange rate 1996 average was equivalent to about $627 million.

13. Peter Marsh, "Recipe to Keep Cooker Sales on the Boil," *Financial Times,* 10 June 2003, 11.

14. Adam Jones, "Path to Growth Paved with Good Intentions," *Financial Times,* 25 October 2002.

SEVEN

1. V. Kasturi Rangan, "The Aravind Eye Hospital, Madurai, India: In Service for Sight," Case 9-593-098 (Boston: Harvard Business School, 1993) and Nirmalya

Kumar and Brian Rogers, "Aravind Eye Hospital 2000: Still in the Service of Sight," Case IMD-3-0908 (Lausanne: IMD, 2000).

2. Gary S. Lynn, Joseph G. Morone, and Albert S. Paulson, "Marketing and Discontinuous Innovation: The Probe and Learn Process," *California Management Review* 38 (1996): 8–37. These authors also make the point that market research is less useful in generating radical innovation. In a study of "breakthroughs" it was noted that in every case it was the curiosity of the inventor rather than market pull or financial need that was the motivating force behind the breakthrough (P. Ranganath Nayak and John M. Ketteringham, *Breakthroughs* (Oxford: Mercury, 1993).

3. Stephen P. Bradley, Pankaj Ghemawat, and Sharon Foley, "Wal-Mart Stores, Inc.," Case 9-794-024 (Boston: Harvard Business School, 1994).

4. George Stalk, Jr., David K. Pecaut, and Benjamin Burnett, "Breaking Compromises, Breakaway Growth," *Harvard Business Review* (September–October 1996): 131–139.

5. Katarina Kling and Ingela Goteman, "IKEA CEO Anders Dahlvig on International Growth and IKEA's Unique Corporate Culture and Brand Identity," *Academy of Management Executive* 17 (2003): 31–37.

6. I am deeply indebted to Professor Xavier Gilbert for sharing his presentation "Achieving Exceptional Competitiveness," IMD, Lausanne, 1997. His conceptualization of the IKEA business system has been adapted.

7. Nirmalya Kumar, Lisa Scheer, and Philip Kotler, "From Market-driven to Market-driving," *European Management Journal* 18 (2000): 129–142.

8. See Nayak and Ketteringham, *Breakthroughs,* for the Federal Express story.

9. Hasso Plattner, "Accidental Empire," *Computer Business Review*, August 1996, 9–12.

10. James L. Heskett and Roger Hallowell, "Southwest Airlines—1993 (A)," Case 9-694-023 (Boston: Harvard Business School, 1993).

11. Professor Jay Galbraith observed this during a lecture at IMD in 1997.

12. Gary Hamel and C. K. Prahalad, *Competing for the Future* (Boston: Harvard Business School Press, 1994).

13. Lynn et al., "Marketing and Discontinuous Innovation."

14. Michael L. Tushman and Charles A. O'Reilly, "Ambidextrous Organizations," *California Management Review* 38, no. 4 (1996): 8–30.

15. Keith Johnson, "That's a Great Idea: More European Companies See Innovation as Vital to Their Growth," *Wall Street Journal*, 29 November–1 December 2002, R1.

16. "How to Manage a Dream Factory," *The Economist*, 18 January 2003, 67–69.

17. I am grateful to Professor Dominique Turpin for introductions to NEC and Toyota managers.

18. "How to Manage a Dream Factory."

19. Henry Ford, *Today and Tomorrow* (Portland, OR: Productivity Press, 1988).

20. Christopher A. Bartlett and Ashish Nanda, "Ingvar Kamprad and IKEA," Case 9-390-132 (Boston: Harvard Business School, 1990).

21. David S. Pottruck, "Charles Schwab: Maverick Retailer." *Retailing Issues Letter 9* (College Station, TX: Center for Retailing Studies, Texas A&M University, 1997).

22. Johnson, "That's a Great Idea."

23. I thank Professor Bob Collins for introductions to Sony managers.

24. Sony Corporation Annual Report 2002; "PlayStation 2: Killing the Competition," *BusinessWeek Online*, 7 November 2002, <http://www.businessweek.com> (accessed 14 February 2003); John Gaudiosi, "Report: Games Make Record $10.3 B in 2002," *Video Store* 25, no. 6 (2003): 6.

25. Stephen B. Shepard, "A Talk with Scott McNealy," *BusinessWeek*, 1 April 2002, 77.

26. Johnson, "That's a Great Idea."

27. "How to Manage a Dream Factory."

28. Michiyo Nakamoto and Tim Burt, "The Father of PlayStation Envisages the 'Networked Home,'" *Financial Times*, 10 February 2003, 19.

EIGHT

1. I am grateful to my IMD colleague Professor Peter Killing for sharing his presentation "Strategy and the Diamond-E" (2003), which presents these three questions.

2. Andrew Campbell, Michael Goold, and Marcus Alexander, "Corporate Strategy: The Quest for Parenting Advantage," *Harvard Business Review* (March–April 1995): 120–132.

3. "Fashion Victim," *The Economist*, 26 February 2000, 73–74.

4. Frenkel ter Hofstede, Jan-Benedict E.M. Steenkamp, and Michel Wedel, "International Market Segmentation Based on Consumer-Product Relations," *Journal of Marketing Research* 36, no. 1 (February 1999): 1–17.

5. My ideas on emerging markets are much influenced by Professor C. K. Prahalad. See C. K. Prahalad and Allen Hammond, "Serving the World's Poor, Profitably," *Harvard Business Review* (August 2002): 48–57.

6. Aneel Karnani, "Five Ways to Grow the Market and Create Value," *Financial Times*, 22 October 1999, 8.

7. Brent Chrite, "Local Knowledge Will Provide the Key," *Financial Times*, 25 August 2002, 4.

8. Prahalad and Hammond, "Serving the World's Poor, Profitably."

9. Pete Engardio, Declan Walsh, and Manjeet Kripalani, "Global Poverty, Much Remains to Be Done," *BusinessWeek*, 14 October 2002, 54.

10. Geri Smith, "Buy a Toaster, Open a Bank Account," *BusinessWeek*, 13 January 2003, 22.

11. Khozem Merchant, "A Salesforce for Indian Villages," *Financial Times*, May 16, 2003, 11.

12. Manjari Raman, "Prahalad—Market to the Poor," 12 January 2000, <http://www.expressindia.com/fe/daily/20000112/fst12077.html> (accessed 25 February 2003).

13. Philip P. Pan, "Chinese Basketball Star Is Megabucks Big," *International Herald Tribune*, 14 December 2002, 1.

14. The author acknowledges the valuable contribution of his IMD colleague Professor Andy Boynton in helping him conceptualize this exhibit.

15. Marc Rubin, "Creating Customer-Oriented Companies," *Prism* 4 (1997): 5–27.

16. George S. Day, "Creating a Superior Customer-Relating Capability," *Sloan Management Review* 44, no. 3 (Spring 2003): 77–82.

17. Gary Loveman, "Diamonds in the Data Mine," *Harvard Business Review* May 2003, 109–113.

18. Rubin, "Creating Customer-Oriented Companies."

19. Jennifer A. Chatman and Sandra E. Cha, "Culture of Growth," *Financial Times*, 22 November 2002, 2–3.

20. Rubin, "Creating Customer-Oriented Companies."

21. Erika Kinetz, "A Top-Shelf Education: Executives Are One of P&G's Big Products," *International Herald Tribune*, 16–17 November 2002, 12.

22. David O. Becker, "Gambling on Customers," *McKinsey Quarterly* 2 (2003): 46–59.

23. Simon London, "Enterprise Drives Home the Service Ethic," *Financial Times*, 2 June 2003, 8.

24. Ibid.

25. Rubin, "Creating Customer-Oriented Companies."

26. Marketing Leadership Council, "Stewarding the Brand for Profitable Growth," (Washington, DC: Corporate Executive Board, 2001).

27. My ideas on change management are drawn from my IMD colleague Paul Strebel. For more details, please see *The Change Pact: Building Commitment to Ongoing Change* (London: FT Pitman Publishing, 1998).

28. Sumantra Ghoshal and Lynda Gratton, "Getting to Great Talk," 11 October 2002, <economictimes.indiatimes.com> (accessed 25 February 2003).

INDEX

268   Index

Nirmalya Kumar is Professor of Marketing, Director of the Centre for Marketing, and Codirector of the Aditya V. Birla India Centre at London Business School. He has also taught at Harvard Business School, IMD in Switzerland, and Northwestern University's Kellogg Graduate School of Management.

As a coach, consultant, seminar leader, and speaker on marketing, Kumar has worked with almost fifty *Fortune 500* companies in forty different countries. He is an award-winning teacher who has designed and delivered programs for companies as diverse as Akzo Nobel, Bertelsmann, Caterpillar, Dow Chemical, Elkem, and Sara Lee. He serves on the boards of directors of Bata India and Zensar Technologies (an RPG Group Fujitsu-Siemens joint venture).

Kumar is the author of more than eighty articles, cases, teaching notes, and videos. His management practice articles have been published in the *Financial Times* and the *Harvard Business Review*, while academic articles have appeared in the *Academy of Management Journal*, the *Journal of Marketing*, and the *Journal of Marketing Research*.

Kumar has been widely quoted in such periodicals as *Automação Comercial* (Brazil), *Børsen* (Denmark), *BusinessWeek*, *Dawn* (Pakistan), *Economic Times* (India), *Empresso* (Portugal),

Elsevier (Netherlands), *Financial Times* (United Kingdom), *International Herald Tribune* (United States), *Les Echos* (France), *Negocios* (Argentina), *Nikkei Business* (Japan), and the *Wall Street Journal*. He has appeared on CNBC, Channel 2 (Sweden), and Star TV and was the closing speaker at the 2000 Global Marketing Forum cosponsored by CNN, *Fortune*, and *Time*.

Kumar received his Bachelor of Commerce from Calcutta University, his M.B.A. from the University of Illinois at Chicago, and his Ph.D. in marketing from Kellogg Graduate School of Management at Northwestern University, where he won the Marketing Science Institute's Alden G. Clayton Award for his Ph.D. dissertation. Readers may contact him at nkumar@london.edu or <http://www.nirmalyakumar.com>.